ETHICS: A LIBERATIVE APPROACH

ETHICS

A Liberative Approach

Miguel A. De La Torre, Editor

Fortress Press / Minneapolis

ETHICS

A Liberative Approach

Cover image: *Abstract #20*, by Diana Ong © Diana Ong/SuperStock
Cover design: Laurie Ingram
Book design: PerfecType, Nashville, TN

Library of Congress Cataloging-in-Publication Data
De La Torre, Miguel A.
  Ethics : a liberative approach / Miguel A. De La Torre.
    p. cm.
  Includes bibliographical references.
  ISBN 978-0-8006-9787-7 (pbk. : alk. paper) — ISBN 978-1-4514-2622-9 (ebook)
1. Christian ethics. 2. Liberation theology. 3. Marginality, Social. 4. People with social disabilities—Conduct of life. I. Title.
  BJ1151.D4 2013
  24—dc23
                              2012035091

The paper used in this publication meets the minimum requirements of American National Standard for Information Sciences—Permanence of Paper for Printed Library Materials, ANSI Z329.48-1984.

Manufactured in the U.S.A.

18   17   16   15   14   13   1   2   3   4   5   6   7   8   9   10

To:

Our colleagues at the Society of Christian Ethics

CONTENTS

CONTRIBUTORS

Patrick S. Cheng is associate professor of historical and systematic theology at Episcopal Divinity School in Cambridge, Massachusetts. He is the author of *Radical Love: An Introduction to Queer Theology* and *From Sin to Amazing Grace: Discovering the Queer Christ*. Cheng holds a PhD from Union Theological Seminary in New York City, a JD from Harvard Law School, and a BA from Yale College. He is an ordained MCC minister and writes for the *Huffington Post*.

Ezra Chitando (Zimbabwean) serves as theology consultant on HIV and AIDS for the Ecumenical HIV and AIDS Initiative in Africa (EHAIA), a program of the World Council of Churches (WCC). He is also professor of history and phenomenology of religion at the University of Zimbabwe. He has published widely on theology and HIV, and method and theory in the study of religion.

Deborah Beth Creamer is dean for academic affairs and director of library and information services at Iliff School of Theology in Denver, Colorado. She is a founding member and past chair of the Religion and Disability Studies Group of the American Academy of Religion and is the author of *Disability and Christian Theology: Embodied Limits and Constructive Possibilities* (Oxford University Press, 2009).

Alejandro Crosthwaite (Mexican) is associate professor of Catholic social teaching and social,

political and cultural ethics at the Faculty of Social Sciences of the Pontifical University of St. Thomas Aquinas (Angelicum) in Rome, Italy. He is also the director of the Ethical Leadership International Program (http://sites.google.com/site/fassleadership program). He is the author of several lectures and articles on the social and political thought of St. Thomas Aquinas, Latin American and Latino/a social ethics, and media studies.

Keri L. Day is assistant professor of theological and social ethics and director of black church studies at Brite Divinity School in Fort Worth, Texas. She has published several book essays and articles on womanism, theology, and economics. She is the author of *Unfinished Business: Black Women, the Black Church, and the Struggle to Thrive in America*.

Miguel A. De La Torre (Cuban) is a scholar-activist and ordained minister. Since obtaining his doctorate in 1999, he has published over twenty-five books, five of which have won national awards. He presently serves as professor of social ethics and Latino/a studies at Iliff School of Theology in Denver, Colorado. He was elected the 2012 president of the Society of Christian Ethics. Additionally, he is the editor of the *Journal of Race, Ethnicity, and Religion* (www.raceandreligion.com).

Mark Freeland (Sault Ste. Marie Tribe of Chippewa Indians) is an activist and scholar. He is currently ABD in the joint PhD program at the University of Denver and the Iliff School of Theology, where his concentration is in religion and social change. He also serves as the president of the Four Winds American Indian Council, a community center for urban American Indians in Denver, Colorado.

Robyn Henderson-Espinoza (una Tejana y queer-meztiz@) is currently finishing a PhD in philosophical ethics; situating her work in the field of queerethics. Her research interests reside in interrogating the mestizaje body, particularly its materiality. She uses critical spatiality, queer theories, and Gloria Anzaldúa's thought and theories to conceive a more robust notion of bodies, mestizaje, race, and the epistemological importance of the mestiz@'s moral agency.

Keun-joo Christine Pae is assistant professor of ethics/Christian ethics in the Department of Religion, Denison University (Granville, OH). As a Christian feminist ethicist, she teaches and researches social ethics, sexual ethics, feminist interfaith peacemaking, transnationalized militarism, and Asian liberation theologies. She has presented and published numerous articles related to race, gender, militarism, and peacemaking. As a co-convener, she serves the Asian American Ethics Working Group of the Society of Christian Ethics (2011–2013).

Rubén Rosario Rodríguez, a graduate of Princeton Theological Seminary, is associate professor in the Department of Theological Studies at Saint Louis University. His book, *Racism and God-Talk: A Latino/a Perspective* (New York University Press, 2008), won the 2011 Alpha Sigma Nu Book Award for Theology. Dr. Rosario, an ordained Presbyterian minister, is currently working on a second book, which examines martyrdom as a theological and ethical virtue in the context of empire.

Laura Stivers is associate professor of social ethics and director of the graduate humanities program

at Dominican University of California. She is the author of *Disrupting Homelessness: Alternative Christian Approaches*; coauthor of *Christian Ethics: A Case Method Approach*; and coeditor of *Justice in a Global Economy: Strategies for Home, Community, and World*. She was also the 2010 president of the Southeast Commission for the Study of Religion and is a past board member of the *Journal of the Society of Christian Ethics*.

Sharon M. Tan is McVay Associate Professor of Christian Ethics at United Theological Seminary of the Twin Cities, Minnesota, where she also teaches in religious studies and comparative ethics. She was born into a Chinese family in Malaysia, and came to the United States to attend college. Both her JD and her PhD are from Emory University. She identifies as both Asian in America and Asian American.

Michelle Tooley is Eli Lilly Professor of Religion at Berea College. Her field of specialization in the academic world is in the area of religion, social ethics, and public policy, with special attention to peacemaking and economic justice. Her most current research focuses on the role of Christian religious communities in peacemaking. She also researches the interrelationship between Christianity, social ethics, and public policy, particularly women's poverty and welfare reform.

Thelathia "Nikki" Young is visiting assistant professor of women's and gender studies at Bucknell University. She received her PhD in Christian social ethics in 2011 from Emory University's Graduate Division of Religion. For her research in ethics, race, gender, and sexuality, Nikki received doctoral and dissertation fellowships from the Fund for Theological Education and a dissertation scholarship from the Human Rights Campaign. Nikki is currently working on her manuscript, *Imagining New Relationships: Black Queers and Family Values*.

PREFACE

You hold in your hands the first textbook written on the fairly new academic discipline known as liberative ethics. To accomplish this goal, it was written from the perspective of different marginalized communities. This is not to say that this is the first time these perspectives have been voiced or presented in written form. Obviously, those who both originally and through the generations have participated in the practice of liberation theology—congregants, clergy, and scholars—were also engaged in ethical reflection. In true fashion of the liberationist model, this book merely attempts to put into writing what has become normative, over decades, among communities experiencing dispossession and disenfranchisement. Reflection on theological concepts makes no sense if it fails to be contextualized in the everyday lives of the marginalized and seriously considers their hopes and struggles for liberation. Following the lead of those relegated to the underside of history, this book attempts to reflect the praxis—the actions—that the oppressed of the world are employing as they seek their own liberation. What makes this work unique is that until now within the academy, a textbook dedicated solely to liberative ethics from multiple global perspectives, inclusive of US marginalized voices, has not existed.

The text examines how the tenets of liberation theology, originally a Latin American Catholic manifestation, found expression within different disenfranchised faith traditions and how these theologies contributed to the formation of an ethical discourse. Instead of a diverse collection of essays where each contributor approached their task on his or her own terms, the authors made a concerted effort in this volume to create a unified textbook.

Therefore, each contributor to this textbook provides the reader with a basic overview, similar in format to every other chapter. Each chapter specifically explores (1) some of the basic tenets of liberative ethics within a particular group, focusing on its development and history; (2) why a need for liberation from specific structures exists; (3) issues and question with which the group wrestles; (4) some major themes faced by the particular group and the methodologies they employ; (5) leading scholars and figures within the movement; and (6) possible future trends.

I would be remiss if I did not end this short preface without expressing my gratitude to those who made this text possible. First, I wish to publically thank Ross H. Miller, former senior acquisitions editor at Fortress Press, for approaching me with the idea of writing a textbook such as this one. Second, I wish to thank the contributors of this textbook, who willingly wrote their chapters according to my format and cheerfully responded to my critiques, making changes to their chapters in a timely matter. And finally, I want to lift up a couple of the contributors who worked around the clock, stepping in to write an entire chapter when the original writers who were asked were unable to fulfill their commitments.

INTRODUCTION

I BELIEVE BASED ON who I am. In other words, what I (as well as you) hold to be true, right, and ethical has more to do with our social context (our community or social networks) and identity (race, ethnicity, gender, orientation, or physical abilities) than any ideology or doctrine we may claim to hold. Those from dominant cultures usually find that the ethical worldview they advocate, forged within their social context before they were even born, is usually in harmony with maintaining and expanding the power and privileges they hold. In other words, even if an ethics is constructed within the dominant culture that is capable of critiquing and demanding reform of the social structures that privilege their race, ethnicity, gender, orientation, class, and/or ableism, it will seldom call for a dismantling of those very same social structures. As cutting edge as such an ethics might appear to be, it would seldom threaten their privileged place in society.

While the ethical positions held within the dominant culture are neither uniform nor monolithic, certain common denominators nevertheless exist, such as a propensity toward hyperindividualism, a call for law and order, an emphasis on charity, an uncritical acceptance of the market economy, an emphasis on orthodoxy, and a preponderance for deductive ethical reasoning. While such an ethics is congruent with the dominant culture, it is damning for those residing on the margins of society because of how it reinforces the prevailing social structures responsible for causes of disenfranchisement.

How, then, is ethics to be done at the margins? What is the ethical moral reasoning that develops among the dispossessed and disenfranchised, who are both relegated to the margins of the dominant culture and whose disadvantage is more often than not capitalized upon so that the dominant culture can thrive? For some among the marginalized, the answer becomes assimilation. Instead of forging an ethical perspective indigenous to their social location, they assume the ethical "rightness" of the dominant culture, advocating for ethical perspectives that in the long run prove detrimental to their own communities. Not surprisingly, such individuals are usually placed upon pedestals as spokespersons to prove that the dominant social structures are not really racist, sexist, heterosexist, or classist.

What happens, then, when those on the margins refuse to accept the ethical perspectives of the dominant culture? When they insist on constructing a moral reasoning rooted in their social location? Those resisting assimilation often use the term "ethics from the margins," which recognizes the moral perspective of those residing in the United States or under the domain of the US empire. Nevertheless, it is an artificial designation amalgamating "who we are" with "where we live." This term, "ethics from the margins," reflects our proximity to the dominant culture, a term whose very existence is dependent on a dominant culture.

1

Without a center, there can be no periphery. However, when we talk among ourselves, we seldom refer to ourselves as marginalized; for the act of naming ourselves as such simultaneously subordinates us to the power of those who make the naming possible. While marginalization language is necessary for locating our identity, the danger remains that it also constructs us as an object for the dominant culture to possess and shrouds us in the very act of appropriation.

To exist under the influences of the dominant culture while holding on to a different social location creates a hyphenated identity, one that attempts to reconcile two distinct and separate cultures in one being. Thus we live a schizophrenic (Latin for "split mind") existence. All too often our physicality prevents acceptance by the dominant culture, while our interactions with the dominant social structures (specifically within the academy) have made us too "Americanized" to be accepted by our compatriots within our own communities. We who write to raise consciousness live on this hyphen, a seesaw between the marginalized community from which we come and the dominant culture where we are forced to live, belonging to both but not necessarily fully accepted by either. While life on this hyphen causes alienation, it also creates the space to write with authority, due to the double consciousness (à la W. E. B. DuBois) or multiple consciousness of our very being. All the contributors of this book know what it means, out of necessity for survival, to exist in two different cultures, and are cognizant that those from the dominant culture have no need, and seldom the desire, to know or understand what it means to be marginalized. The hyphen as seesaw allows us to move within the different cultures of our existence.

Before continuing, we must pause to complicate this hyphenated existence. It would be simplistic to set up a neat dichotomy between "them," the dominant culture, and "us," the marginalized. The truth of the matter is that multiple marginalities exist. For example, as a Latino, I know

discrimination intimately. I know what it means to be disenfranchised because of my unapologetic Hispanicness. Still, although I may be a man of color—brown to the dominant culture—within my own Latina/o social location I am white due to my light skin pigmentation. A race cross-dresser, if you will. I am constructed as brown within the dominant culture (hence dispossessed) and as white within my Hispanic community (hence privileged). Likewise, as a male, I hold certain privileges women do not hold, even though I still fall short of the glory (sic) of being a white male. The same can be said about my class privilege as a full-tenured professor, my heterosexual orientation, my temporary ableness, or my residency within the heart of the empire. Yes, I am rooted in marginality, while I simultaneously experience some privileges because of my proximity to the so-called white ideal.

The truth is that there really is no us and them. In some ways "us" is "them." Nevertheless, the complexities of how oppressive structures operate do not diminish the need to dismantle those structures, which are designed to privilege the few over the many. The problem is not white heterosexual able-bodied males with class privilege. Any group, given sufficient time, might potentially amass sufficient power to eventually capture the social structures designed to privilege a particular group over other groups. Let us not forget that while Hispanics like me today are marginalized, our conquistador forefathers (seldom foremothers) were the recipients of the wealth, power, and privilege extracted from the then-margins. And who knows, centuries from now, which group will surmount the apex of the existing globalized social structures. For liberation to occur, we must wrestle not against flesh and blood (able heterosexual white males—and more recently women—with economic privilege) but against principalities, against powers, against the rulers of the darkness of this world (social structures that cause oppression). Those of the dominant culture who stand in solidarity with the marginalized consequently soon discover that the very structures designed to privilege them work to their detriment in order to protect the very privilege they wish to now dismantle.

If we want to live within a more just social order, then we need to move toward the ethical perspectives emerging from marginalized communities, communities that know how to survive within the dominant culture. Such a survival ethics would be liberative. It is important to note that we are not calling for a liberationist ethics; but rather, a liberative ethics. What's the difference? While liberationist ethics is a type of liberative ethics, liberative ethics is not necessarily liberationist. Liberation ethics is based on liberation theology (usually rooted in 1960s Latin America), which is characteristically Christian. Liberative ethics, like liberation theology, still emphasizes the preferential option for the oppressed, but in doing so, might—but will not necessarily—center its reasoning on Christian concepts. The focus of liberative ethics moves away from orthodoxy, correct doctrine, toward orthopraxis, the correct actions required to bring about liberation. So while liberationism is Christian, liberative ethics can be Muslim, Hindu, humanist, or Buddhist. I developed this argument in an earlier book, titled *The Hope of Liberation within World Religions* (Baylor University Press, 2008); thus the question of how other faith traditions participate in a liberative theology will remain beyond the scope of this book. The focus of this volume is less on liberative ethics from different world religions than it is on what liberative ethics looks like within different marginalized communities, both globally and locally.

A textbook on liberative ethics must begin with the recognition that one size does not fit all. There is not one liberative ethics upon which everyone agrees; there are multiple manifestations. The reason for this is that *all* ethics is contextual (including the Eurocentric ethics of the dominant culture), rooted in the social location of those seeking faith-based responses to their oppressive situations. Whatever liberation looks like, it can only be determined by the local people living under oppressive structures. How those within the Asian community understand liberative ethics is vastly different from how those in the US disabled community understand it. Even with similar communities, such as African and African American, differences exist. Nonetheless, in the midst of these differences, we can note certain similarities. Whatever this liberative ethics is, different marginalized communities hold certain basic concepts and understandings in common. To these similarities we now turn.

Basic Tenets of Liberative Ethics

There exists no basic checklist of liberative ethics upon which everyone agrees. Some concepts may be dearly held by one disenfranchised group but barely mentioned or noticed in another. Nevertheless, some common denominators undergird liberative ethics as understood within diverse marginalized communities.

Message

Liberative ethics is a spiritual response to unexamined normative and legitimized social structures responsible for privileging a powerful minority at the expense of the disenfranchised majority. It is an ethics deeply concerned with fostering and enriching life, as opposed to the ethics of the dominant culture, which remains complicit with social structures that cause marginalization. The goal of liberation is to break with these death-dealing structures by committing to life (salvation for Christians), a process achieved through consciousness-raising, learning how structures of oppression prevent abundant life. Thus the "evangelical" goal is not to convince nonbelievers to believe doctrinal tenets but convince those society gazes on as nonpersons, thus failing to acknowledge their infinite worth. Liberative ethics does not create, expand, or sustain doctrinal beliefs; rather, it physically (not just intellectually) responds to inhuman conditions, to which the vast majority of humanity is relegated. Liberative ethics is a spiritual call to action whose goal is the rescue and deliverance of all who face sociocultural and economic oppression.

Context

Although the common starting point of theological reflection is the existential experience of the marginalized, the ultimate goal remains liberation from the reality of societal misery. Not all who are disenfranchised have a similar experience; thus all ethical systems are indigenous, unable to be exported into a different social location as if each one were some sort of commodity. As a light-skinned Latino man, I can never speak for black women with any type of authority, even though I may be familiar with womanist thought. To speak for black women, as if I knew what it meant to be a black woman trying to survive within the entrails of the empire, would be highly paternalistic. Consequently, this textbook can only be written as a collection of scholars working from within the context of their own communities. Rejecting the objectification of black women who somehow need me to be their spokesperson and instead recognizing their subjectivity means that the only thing I can ever say with any integrity on the topic is how my own light skin and maleness is privileged by their darker skin and femaleness. The other conversation we can have is how the concurrencies and divergences of our experiences of marginalization operate, a conversation that constitutes the major purpose of this book.

Pastoral

Liberative ethics is oriented toward the future—what can I do, physically and spiritually, to bring about a more justice-based social order that celebrates life? How can the disenfranchised be enabled to discover the path toward their liberation? Most liberative ethicists are more than simply academicians; they are pastoral agents working with and for the disenfranchised. Their concern has less to do with developing a scholarly body of religious thought and more to do with standing in solidarity with faith-based, grassroots movements whose ultimate goal is social justice. Consequently, liberative ethicists are more concerned with engaging in open dialogue with the world rather than preserving the status quo. Far from repeating timeless, ahistorical principles, liberative ethics presents itself as a reflection vigorously involved with the people's daily experience. All chosen praxis (actions) is derived from the perspective of the oppressed. From the underside of power and privilege, praxis is developed from which to address the existing structural injustices. Before we can do theology, we must do liberation while connecting the spiritual with material realities. Hence liberative ethics is praxis oriented, concerned more with orthopraxis (correct actions) than orthodoxy (correct doctrine).

Methodology

Eurocentric theological thought is normatively deductive, moving from theory (or truth) to action (or praxis). First comes some conceptualized universal truth, such as the Bible or church teachings; and based on this truth, an action—as a second step to life—is determined and implemented. Thus orthopraxis flows from orthodoxy. The liberative ethicist turns this methodology on its head by arguing that theology is the second step—orthodoxy instead flows from orthopraxis. A truth beyond the historical experiences and the social location where individuals act as social agents cannot be ascertained, whether said truth exists or not. Only through justice-based praxis, engaged in transforming society, can individuals come closer to understanding the spiritual. From understanding the social location in which the oppressed find themselves, through the praxis of consciousness-raising to understand the causes of oppression, comes a spiritual response. In the doing of liberative acts, theory (theology) is formed as a reflection on praxis. Those engaged in liberative ethics as a spiritual response to material disenfranchisement usually follow a "see-judge-act" paradigm (borrowed from the Young Christian Workers of the 1930s), recognizing that we must first do liberative praxis before we can do liberation theology. Simply stated, believers "see" the oppression that is occurring; through the act of consciousness-raising, they "judge" the causes of oppression; and finally they commit themselves to "act." The praxis implemented is informed by considerations of social analysis, philosophy, and religious beliefs. This action is a reflective praxis rooted in the experience of the oppressed. Such praxis brings us back to "see," that is, evaluating the impact of action.

Seeking the Divine

Liberative ethics begins with the poor, the oppressed, the marginalized, the outcast, and the disenfranchised. To engage in liberative ethics is to do it with and from the perspective of those whom society considers as (no)bodies. Incarnating theological thought among those who are dispossessed roots liberation theology in the material as opposed to simply the metaphysical. Within the Eurocentric context, the primary religious question concerns the existence of God. Among most liberative ethicists, the struggle is not with God's existence per se, but with God's character. Who is this God we profess exists? What is the character of God? As already mentioned, whoever God is, God imparts and sustains life while opposing death. Wherever lives are threatened with poverty and oppression, the divine is present, standing in solidarity with those oppressed. This means that God takes sides over and against the rich and powerful, not because the marginalized are somewhat holier but because they are oppressed. In short, God makes a preferential option for the poor and oppressed, over and against the pharaohs of this world.

Sin

Although sin is by and large a Christian concept, it remains useful for understanding liberative ethics. According to Latin American liberation theologian Leonardo Boff, what social analysis calls "structural poverty," faith calls "structural sin." And what analysis calls the "private accumulation of wealth," faith calls "the sin of selfishness." Suffering exists because of sin, which represents the root of all that is wrong with the world. Sin is responsible for the enslavement of humanity, forcing individuals to act against their best interest. Sin can be the outcome of individuals' choices, or it can be the ramifications of the prevailing social structures. Within liberative ethics, sin is communal. All sins, even those committed by individuals, have communal ramifications. All too often, the salient Eurocentric characteristic of individualism has made sin, and redemption from it, personal. Sin becomes an act of commission or omission, while salvation from sinfulness rests in a *personal* savior. Conversion, however, is never personal. Rather, it must extend to social transformation. The structural nature of sin is mainly missing from Eurocentric religious thought. Oppression and poverty as expressions of sin are mostly caused by societal structures designed to enrich the few at the expense of the many. The ultimate aim of liberative ethics is to go beyond reform, for reform only attempts to make more bearable the sinful societal structures that keep capital in the hands of the few. Liberative ethicists envision a new creation free of injustices, where human dignity and the freedom to seek one's own destiny reign supreme. Liberative ethicists call for social revolution, a radical change of the structures that cause oppression, a move closer to abundant life.

The Church

Christendom has been closely linked to the dominant culture and hence to the political structures designed to protect the interests of the privileged few. By contrast, liberative ethicists focus on human needs rather than ecclesiastical dogma. They believe the church can never be neutral in the face of injustices. When the church stands in solidarity with the marginalized, it ceases being an extension of Christendom and becomes instead the church of the oppressed. God is never found in cathedrals made of crystal, whose ornate steeples serve as monuments to those who reached the pinnacle of wealth on the backs of the poor and disenfranchised. God is only found in the gathering of the "least of these." The church is not only called to signify liberation but also to be an instrument by which liberation is achieved. Although liberative ethicists are usually scholars, many holding privileged PhDs, they attempt to root their academics within the faith community. This understanding of church separates liberative ethicists from most academicians, mainly because they work as "organic intellectuals" à la Antonio Gramsci, connecting the intellectual enterprise, which is informed by the grassroots, with popular movements, where they participate in contributing to its consciousness-raising. Their scholarly contributions also raise the consciousness of those who are unaware of their complicity with oppressive power structures and those who may be aware but nevertheless are committed to working in and with disenfranchised communities during their struggle for salvation/liberation. These liberative ethicists operate as scholar-activists who theorize and theologize for the express purpose of changing oppressive social structures, as opposed to simply better understanding said structures for the sole sake of scholarship.

Text's Thesis

The purpose of the textbook you hold in your hands is to explore how the ethical concepts defined as liberative, which has its roots in a Latin American Catholic liberationist phenomenon, is presently being manifested within the United States across different racial, ethnic, and gender groups. The book's focus will be on elucidating how the powerless and disenfranchised within US marginalized communities employ their religious beliefs to articulate a liberative religious ethical perspective. Our goal is to expose the reader to liberative ethical concepts from the perspective of marginalized communities by surveying different US social contexts presented by leading religious scholars from the communities of faith from which they write. The reader will thus comprehend the diversity existing within the liberative ethical discourse and know which scholars and texts to read in pursuit of more specific and advanced religious concepts.

If liberative ethicists are correct in asserting that a preferential option for the oppressed exists, and that their faith has something important to say about the inhuman conditions they find themselves in, then how their particular social context manifests liberative tenets becomes crucial in understanding different religious perspectives from the underside of the power structures indigenous to these marginalized faith communities. When ethics is explored from the margins of society, specifically those who are normally oppressed due to their race, class, gender, orientation, and ableness, readers who are accustomed to studying ethics from a Eurocentric academic paradigm can be jarred from a normative way of thinking. Reading from the margins of power forces the reader to move beyond a traditional understanding of the faith, an understanding that fuses and confuses how those privileged by the religious tradition present their faith to the Euro-American audience with how the vast majority of believers who exist on the underside of power and privilege interpret the same faith for daily survival. To read from the margins thus provides an approach to dealing with life issues that can be quite liberating.

PART ONE

The Global Context

1

Latin American Liberative Ethics

Alejandro Crosthwaite, OP

BISHOP HÉLDER CÂMARA LOOKS out his window and contemplates his diocese of Recife in northeastern Brazil, which consists of a vast countryside divided into large, rich estates and poor villages. Most of his poor parishioners live in shantytowns. Around midnight, he opens his diary to reflect on the day he spent visiting his people. He recalls a conversation (which he has reproduced in his book *Dom* Hélder Câmara: *Essential Writings*) with one peasant whom he met that day, who in many respects typifies the poor people of his region.

"His name," says Dom Hélder, "is Severino of the Northeast, son of Severino, grandson of Severino." Like his ancestors, Severino does not live; he vegetates. He passes his days not like a shady tree, its roots filled with the sap of life; but like the cactus that survives in arid soil. So far this unemployed farm worker has not rebelled. Raised by illiterate parents and instructed in the faith by the priest in a dusty chapel, Severino learned from them to suffer life under unjust persecutors. Severino's belief supported his resignation to a world in which things could not be otherwise. "Some are born rich and others poor," he says. "Such is the will of God." This conviction stifles any thoughts of liberation. Daily he paces the muddy streets of his *favela*, humbled by unemployment while his family goes hungry. For Severino, hope of a better life lies on the other side of the great divide. Until then, Jesus counsels patience and offers strength to endure.

BOX 1.1

Hélder Câmara

Hélder Câmara (February 7, 1909, Fortaleza, Ceará, northeastern Brazil–August 27, 1999, Recife) was Roman Catholic archbishop of Olinda and Recife, Brazil. He retired as archbishop in 1985, and lived to see many of his reforms rolled back by his successor, Jose Cardoso Sobrinho. He is famous for stating, "When I give food to the poor, they call me a saint. When I ask why the poor have no food, they call me a Communist."

Severino's fatalism comes from many causes: from living in wretched social, economic, political, and cultural conditions; from accepting his lot as powerless before oppressive landowners and government forces; from internalizing "the white man's" or upper-class, racist views and policies; from superstitious religious beliefs; and from the conviction that God wills his suffering and the suffering of those like him. Brazilian liberative pedagogue Paulo Freire, in his classic book *Pedagogy of the Oppressed*, argues that the source of this kind of fatalism stems from centuries of domination. "An oppressed consciousness," he observed, "lacks the capacity to distance itself from reality and thus be critical of it." The poor peasants in Brazil could not objectify facts and problematic situations in their everyday lives to even begin questioning them.

History and Development of Latin American Liberative Ethics

Latin American liberative ethics is a critical reflection on the European/North American ethical tradition in light of the radically different ideals and social, political, cultural, and economic contexts of the oppressed cultures of Latin America. It serves as a tool to unmask ethical theories that justify marginalization and oppression while at the same time guiding and empowering liberative and transformative social practices on the South American continent.

These long-standing ethical traditions that justified violations of human dignity and basic human rights in Central and South America led philosophers, theologians, and pastoral and socially minded agents in Latin America to project new philosophies, theologies, and praxes onto the application of an ethics radically different from traditional ones. According to Aristotle's discussion of the dialectic, "If a conclusion is absurd, something must be wrong with its first principles." In a similar way, liberative ethicists reason that if severe oppression, poverty, and pessimism characterizes so much of Latin American life, then something must be wrong with the infrastructure, as well as with the worldview and ethics that fail to challenge and even perpetuate said infrastructure.

Many consider the critique of the Spanish and Portuguese imperial conquest of the Americas (the beginning of a continent-wide history of domination), the search for a truly Iberian-American identity by the Spanish and mestizos born on the continent, and the philosophical justifications for the wars of independence from the Iberian Peninsula to be the first steps toward a liberative social ethics in the Western Hemisphere. However, Latin American liberative ethics is said to have its explicit origins in the emancipation struggles of the continent from "dependent capitalism" in the aftermath of the Cuban Revolution and the Second Vatican Council. These two historical events exposed several elements of the "theory of dependence" and promoted an anticapitalist understanding of life and of a society based on a communitarian spirit.

Many scholars divide the history of Latin American liberative ethics into four phases. The first phase (1510–1553) begins with the many critiques of the conquest of the Americas by the Iberian powers and the search for a distinct identity by the Iberians born on the continent. The most

BOX 1.2

Paulo Freire

Paulo Freire (September 19, 1921, Recife, Brazil–May 2, 1997, São Paulo, Brazil) was a Brazilian educator and influential theorist of critical pedagogy. His most famous and influential work is *Pedagogy of the Oppressed* (1970).

KEY TERM 1.1

Dependency Theory. An explanation of the economic development of a state in terms of the external political, economic, and social influences on national development policies, dependency theory argues that history shapes economic structure, favoring some countries to the detriment of others and limiting their development possibilities. Dependency theory sees the world economy as comprising two sets of states, those that are dominant and those that are dependent. The dominant states are the advanced industrial nations in the Organization of Economic Co-operation and Development (OECD). The dependent states are those states of Latin America, Asia, and Africa that have low per-capita gross national products (GNPs) and that rely heavily on the export of a single commodity.

renowned of the former was the sixteenth-century Spanish historian, social reformer, and Dominican friar who became the first resident bishop of Chiapas and the first officially appointed "Protector of the Indians," Fray Bartolome de Las Casas, OP. His extensive writings, the most famous being *A Short Account of the Destruction of the Indies* and *History of the West Indies*, chronicle the first decades of colonization of the West Indies. In an attempt to conscientize the Spaniards, he focuses particularly on the atrocities the Spanish colonizers committed against the indigenous peoples. Of the latter, Inca Garcilaso de la Vega and Guamán Poma de Ayala in Peru built interesting bridges between the European worldvision and that of some of the Amerindian civilizations.

The second phase (1750–1830) comprises the philosophical justifications for seeking independence from Spain and Portugal, the first emancipation. The third phase took place during the liberation from dependent capitalism, the second emancipation. This third phase is often divided into three substages: the "constitutional stage" (1969–1973), the "maturation stage" (1973–1976), and the "stage of persecution, debates, and confrontations" (1976–1983). The fourth phase, from 1983 to the present, is that of growth and answers to new questions. For the purposes of this chapter, we will only focus on the third and fourth phases.

The Third Phase: The Constitutional Stage

The Cuban Revolution (1953–1959) and the profound reforms of the Second Vatican Council (1962–1965) within Roman Catholicism generated new paradigms of thought in the numerous Latin American social thinkers during the so-called constitutional stage. This stage produced the way of reflection that has had the most international influence.

KEY TERM 1.2

Second Vatican Council. The twenty-first ecumenical council of the Roman Catholic Church. It opened under Pope John XXIII on October 11, 1962, and closed under Pope Paul VI on November 21, 1965. At least four future pontiffs took part in the council's opening session: Giovanni Battista Cardinal Montini, who succeeded Pope John XXIII as Paul VI; Bishop Albino Luciani, the future Pope John Paul I; Bishop Karol Wojtyła, who became Pope John Paul II; and Father Joseph Ratzinger, present as a theological consultant, who became Pope Benedict XVI. Its *Pastoral Constitution on the Church in the Modern World* (*Gaudium et spes*) has had a profound impact on liberative philosophy and theology.

Fig. 1.1. The start of the Second Vatican Council, 1962.

The Second Vatican Council, convoked by Pope John XXIII (1958–1963) and concluded by Pope Paul VI (1963–1978), provided the foundations for a philosophical social ethics based on the concept of "liberation of the oppressed"—that is, the struggle for the material and educational conditions that would allow for vast sectors of the world population to overcome economic misery.

However, the hostile US reaction to the social changes on the island of Cuba brought about by the revolution of the 1950s exposed several elements of the theory of dependence, whose foundations were established in the 1920s. The theory of dependence sought to break the cycle of "backwardness" in contrast with the industrial development of the first world, while at the same time avoiding the dependency on a single cash crop or product for exportation that fundamentally benefited the economy of the industrialized nations and the local elites.

According to this theory, in order to break the cycle of dependence, it would be necessary for

KEY TERM 1.3

Cuban Revolution. An armed revolt that led to the overthrow of dictator Fulgencio Batista of Cuba on January 1, 1959, by the 26th of July Movement led by Fidel Castro. The term *Cuban Revolution* also refers to the ongoing implementation of social and economic programs by the new government.

each nation to promote financial self-sufficiency, eliminate the high levels of misery, and generate government systems that would not be easily manipulated by the financial interests of large multinational corporations. Also, the "preferential option for the poor," renewed in the Roman Catholic Church, opened spaces for active participation in the struggles to organize and collaborate in movements of cultural, political, economic, and social vindication for marginalized sectors.

Several Roman Catholic theologians, among them the Peruvian Gustavo Gutiérrez and the Brazilians Hélder Câmara and Leonardo Boff, grounded themselves in the initiatives of the Second Vatican Council in order to foster a commitment to social change in Latin America.

Their theoretical and practical work became world-renowned under the name of "liberation theology." Its theoretical foundation is based on the message of the gospel, which gives preferential option to the *anawin* (the oppressed and excluded), denounces injustices, and seeks to create more just social structures. Inspired by the gospel's social message, these thinkers promoted an anticapitalist understanding of life—a society based not on avarice and selfishness but on a communitarian spirit. Its practical application is expressed through basic ecclesial communities in the poorest urban and rural areas, in which

BOX 1.4

Gustavo Gutiérrez

Gustavo Gutiérrez (born June 8, 1928, in Lima) is a Peruvian theologian and Dominican priest regarded as the founder of liberation theology. He holds the John Cardinal O'Hara Professorship of Theology at the University of Notre Dame. Gutiérrez spent much of his life living and working among the poor of Lima. Gutiérrez is of Amerindian heritage, being of mixed Quechua descent, and he is probably the most influential Peruvian scholar of all time. Gutiérrez's groundbreaking work, *A Theology of Liberation: History, Politics, Salvation* (1971), explains his notion of Christian poverty as an act of loving solidarity with the poor as well as a liberative protest against poverty.

solidarity, dignity, liberty of expression, Bible study, and collective mobilization to reclaim the political rights of the marginalized are promoted, fostering the participants' active involvement in the social processes of their own countries.

In the same spirit, but beyond the specifically Christian and theological context, the Brazilian Paulo Freire created a pedagogical theory and praxis of education designed to promote social action and the dynamism of people who have suffered socioeconomic repression for several generations. His *Pedagogy of the Oppressed* (1970) has had considerable influence in international efforts to develop educational models that generate desirable social changes for the majority of the population—such as democratic participation, critical thinking, active production of knowledge—or, in Freire's words, learning practices that help "create a world in which it is easier to love."

BOX 1.3

Leonardo Boff

Leonardo Boff was born December 14, 1938, in Concórdia, Santa Catarina state, Brazil. He is a theologian, philosopher, and writer known for his active support of the rights of the poor and excluded. He currently serves as professor emeritus of ethics, philosophy of religion, and ecology at the Rio de Janeiro State University.

KEY TERM 1.4

Basic Ecclesial Communities (BEC). Began in Brazil in the mid-1960s and then spread throughout Latin America. BECs grew out of efforts of clergy and pastoral agents who helped the people relate their faith to concrete needs. Each community, consisting of fifteen to twenty families, gathered once or twice a week to hear the word of God, to share their common problems, and to work in solidarity toward a solution.

In his liberative pedagogical proposal, Freire considers the practice of liberty and dialogue to be the essence of education and avoids authoritarian models: "No one educates another, no one educates themselves; men and women educate each other, in dialogue with the world." His critical analyses of traditional educational "professor-student" models reproduce the opposition between oppressors and oppressed. In order to break this model, he proposes a dynamic and autonomous model that values the experience and knowledge of each student as well as their social participation, their creative production, and the exercise of an answerable and collective responsibility. In opposition to "banking education," which seems to follow the capitalist model, forcing students to collect data frequently disassociated from their vital experience, Freire proposed a "liberative education" in which problems are presented to the students so that they may solve them in a collective manner under the coordination of their instructors, learning in a practical way the necessity of working as a team, participating and

CASE STUDY 1.1

Base communities arose as a pastoral response on behalf of the Catholic Church. The initial motivation that inspired priests, religious sisters, and pastoral agents was to fulfill their own mission, finding a more effective way for the church to minister to the poor of Latin America. Their objective was not political. Even today, many base communities are essentially pastoral and nonpolitical, at least not in a radical way. However, many base communities were instrumental in preparing the ground for the creation of popular organizations and revolutionary struggle, especially in the extreme difficult circumstances of Central America in the 1970s and 1980s. The social and political impact of base communities is not quantitative but qualitative (since in reality a very small portion of the Latin American Catholic population actively participates in base communities, even less so than Protestants and evangelicals). However, they are key in promoting an initial increase of conscientization, not only of the political, social, economic, and cultural problems facing the oppressed but also an encounter with the gospel that leads to a liberative life-vision and motivation for spiritual, social, and political engagement and liberation.

They also create a sense of community, of mutual support and aid. The participants learn to be subjects and not only objects of their destiny in the experience of popular democracy and direct action that has political and social consequences. The initial stages of conscientization, which people call their "awakening," is the act of questioning the state of things. Base communities use a methodology founded on questions where the people themselves learn some basic categories of analysis. During a weekend meeting, after gathering

CASE STUDY 1.1 (continued)

their ideas about a particular subject like land ownership, the group facilitator may provide statistics to help the people understand their experience in the wider national context. The Scriptures provide an ideal. The people acquire a strong sense that as human beings they are called to be active change agents of their history. Several biblical texts provide images of what liberative human life should look like: a society of brothers and sisters, and life of sharing and equality. If it relates to society as a whole it then becomes a utopian vision. For rural Christians, this utopia provides an out-of-reach ideal or end, which can never be fully realized. However, Latin American Christians find this ideal more comprehensible and energizing than the Marxist phrase: "a classless society."

What makes this ideal more effective is that people have seen its effects, although in a moderate way, in their local base community: the common experience they live in the base communities has destroyed the barriers of mistrust among its members. In many cases, old family or town quarrels have ended. Also, their common projects for the local community are another source of encouragement. Traditionally, the local community leaders have tended to copy oppressive governing models from the dominant society and become themselves little dictators or demagogic populists. In sharing their leadership in the base communities and acting based on community consensus, base communities have given many people a popular form of the democratic process. These experiences have, at the same time, made them more critical of power relations in their societies.

A Brazilian recounts, for example, cases in which the peasants that were members of a base community surrounded and captured the landowner of a large plantation that oppressed them. They took him by force to the military authorities and obtained an agreement from him to respect their human dignity, which they came to recognize through their weekly meetings. During the worst years of the dictatorship in Brazil, base communities provided a small space where the people could reaffirm their dignity and hope. As the military began to soften its iron grasp on Brazilian politics and began to prepare the country for more democratic forms of governance, it was the base communities that had prepared the people to take responsibility of their country's destiny. Some Brazilians thought that the base communities would coerce the rural classes toward a particular political option, for example, voting for the Workers' Party. However, the base communities had educational courses and materials that had as their purpose the development of its members' critical conscience of the political processes and not a "party-centered" ideology. Base communities discussed the criteria to take into account during the elections for a more just- and solidarity-based society. After the elections, research showed that members of base communities voted for opposition parties, but did not vote unanimously for any one particular party. They had made their own free personal choice based on their reflection at the local base communities.

How do base ecclesial communities contribute to the liberation of the oppressed and marginalized? Why do you think these communities do not create in their participants monolithic thinking or only one way of responding to oppressive realities? Do you believe these groups could also transform those who hold power in society?

expressing themselves: "The oppressed only begin to believe in themselves when they discover the source of their domination and join themselves to the struggle organized for their liberation. This discovery cannot be only academic, but must include action; but it cannot limit itself to mere activism, but must include serious reflection."

The Third Phase: The Maturation Stage

During its maturation stage (1973–1976), Latin American liberative ethics oriented itself toward this "serious reflection," which includes praxis in order to overcome the history of domination and social inequality. Its most influential proponent has been the Argentinean Enrique Dussel.

Beginning with an analysis of the history of European invasion and conquest of the Americas, and how it created structures of domination, marginalization, and dependency, Dussel shows how these practices of domination based themselves on a "universalist ethics" of Western Europe. By attributing to itself authority over universal knowledge, European philosophies have defined "human nature" according to the paradigms, behavior patterns, and rationalist orientation of the West, condemning the invaded cultures to conditions of nonbeing, chaos, and irrationality. In this way, Western philosophies have historically legitimatized the domination that oppresses the so-called third world, masking it under the appearance of "promoting civilization."

To respond to these conditions, Dussel proposes an ethics based on dialogue with and listening to the excluded, the "radical Other"—that is to say, the subject that has been converted into an object by Western domination. This reflexive praxis would organize a "liberative analectic" as an alternative to the current "analectic of domination." Dussel's theoretical development is based on a detail criticism of the ontology of Kant, Hegel, Heidegger, and other German, French, and English philosophers. For Dussel, the voice of the oppressed has to pass through the paradox of

BOX 1.5

Enrique Dussel

Enrique Dussel was born on December 24, 1934, in La Paz, Mendoza, Argentina. In 1973, a bomb attack at his house by a paramilitary group forced him into exile in Mexico, where he has lived since 1975. Today he is a Mexican citizen. He is a professor in the Department of Philosophy in the Metropolitan Autonomous University (Spanish: Universidad Autónoma Metropolitana) (UAM), Campus Iztapalapa in Mexico City and also teaches at the National Autonomous University of Mexico (Spanish: Universidad Nacional Autónoma de México) (UNAM). He is the founder with others of the movement referred to as the philosophy of liberation, and his work is concentrated in the field of ethics and political philosophy. Through his critical thinking he proposed a new way (a critical way) to read history, criticizing Eurocentric discourse. Author of more than fifty books, his thought covers many themes, including theology, politics, philosophy, ethics, political philosophy, aesthetics, and ontology. He has been a critic of postmodernity, preferring instead the term *transmodernity*.

speaking with the language of the oppressor in order to question it and overcome it: "In order to discover new categories that can open the possibility of us thinking of ourselves, we need to begin speaking like the Europeans and, from them, prove their limitations."

In addition to his immense philosophical project of liberation, which includes ontology, analytics, pedagogy, and the erotic, Dussel also writes for the common person through conferences with specific examples accessible to those untrained in philosophy. He uses the following liberative pedagogical schemas:

Dominating Dialectic	versus	Liberative Dialectic
conquering attitude	v.	collaborative attitude
divisive attitude	v.	converging attitude
demobilizing attitude	v.	mobilizing attitude
manipulative attitude	v.	organizing attitude
invading attitude	v.	creative attitude

The Third Phase: The Stage of Persecution, Debates, and Confrontation

Liberative philosophy, pedagogy, theology, and ethics constituted a clear initiative to create Latin American thought in search of interpretive social models that generate a more just and creative liberative social ethics. It also represented a radical criticism of Western thought from the margins of Latin America, especially from 1976–1983—the stage of persecution, debates, and confrontation. The foundations of this concept, although taken from other sources, coincide with recent developments of great influence in European and North American thought in the fields of the humanities and cultural studies; for example, in the postcolonial thought of authors such as Edward Said, Homi Bhabha, and Gayatri Spivak, all professors at North American and British universities.

Unfortunately, due to the Marxist and/or Christian language of the Latin American liberative theories, and in part due to the limitations of the diffusion of a bibliography from the third world, postcolonial theorists have mostly ignored the contribution of Latin American thought in the same direction, which was developed before theirs.

KEY TERM 1.5

Postcolonial Theory. A specifically postmodern intellectual discourse that consists of reactions to, and analysis of, the cultural legacy of colonialism. Postcolonialism comprises a set of theories found in philosophy, film, political science, human geography, sociology, and literature.

The Fourth Phase

In dialogue with these theories, during the current fourth stage, of growth and answers to new questions, liberative social ethics is a way to vindicate concepts originally produced in Latin America. Several thinkers have shown the coincidences as well as the differences between Latin American liberative ethics and North American/European postcolonial thought—that is, proposing an alternative way of thinking about sociocultural relations and a philosophical worldview in present-day contexts, namely, the globalization of capitalist markets. The main difference between "northern" and "southern" liberative discourse stems from the context of the reflection: from the periphery or from the center. The Colombians Jesús Martín Barbero and Santiago Castro Gómez, the Argentinians Néstor García Canclini and Walter Mignolo, and the Chilean Nelly Richard, among many others, have written works of philosophical reorganization. Walter Mignolo, for example, proposes the configuration of "post-Western" thought based on the experiences of Euro–North American domination and imperialism, which denounces the conditions of inequality and seeks methods to confront colonialism, which is not only an experience of the past.

Mignolo argues that the so-called modern/colonial world is the product of imperial global designs, be they Christian, imposed by Spain and Portugal, or the "civilizing mission" of both

LIBERATIVE ETHICS IN ACTION 1.1

Liberative Ethics in Action: The Liberative Philosopher—Critical Inquirer "into Things below the Earth and in the Sky."

On October 3, 1975, Enrique Dussel was the target of a bomb attack in his house by an extreme-right corporate union of iron workers ("Comando Rucci"). The following morning, he gave a lecture on Socrates's *Apologia* at the Faculty of Philosophy at the National University of Cuyo commenting on the attempt on his life and the critical-political role of the philosopher in society titled "The Practical-Political Function of Philosophy." Dussel began by describing the note left behind by the terrorists, in which they accused him "of poisoning the minds of the youth"; the same accusation was leveled against Socrates by the Athenians. Meditating on his recent experience and that of Socrates, Dussel probes deeper into the reasons of the accusation. Like Socrates, who is found guilty of criminal meddling, the philosopher is accused of investigating the bottom of things, the foundations of the oppressive and unjust system, and what is worst, teaches others to do so! Referring specifically to the attempt on his life, Dussel states with Socrates that if the powers that be think they can put an end to the criticisms labeled against them by killing the prophetic voices in society, then they are gravely mistaken. The only way to put an end to them is to convert from their unjust and oppressive ways. From all this, Dussel deduces the function of a liberative philosophy: philosophy is to be political without being, essentially, politics in the proper sense of the word. For Dussel, inquiring "into things below the earth and in the sky" means inquiring into the very foundations of our so-called Western and Christian society, and reinterpreting them in a radical and critical way, different from the "official" interpretation, which supports the oppressive, death-dealing status quo that kills a people in the name of the same principles that serve as the foundation for their liberation.

This is the critical-political and liberative function of the philosopher and philosophy: to be the "stinging fly" in a society that "is inclined to be lazy and needs . . . stimulation." The philosopher is appointed to lead the philosophical life, that is, to examine his or her life and that of others, especially that of the oppressed, in order to liberate it. Dussel states that the accusation of not accepting the status quo and the powers that sustain and perpetuate it is the eternal accusation against the philosopher. When asked by a student how to respond to Peronism in his native country of Argentina, Dussel answered: "as a philosopher!" The way of the philosopher is to keep a critical distance from the social reality in question in order to better see and point out its oppressive tendencies: "Philosophy adds critical thinking to the process, although it is not confused with it."

England and France, or the development and modernization projects of the United States in the twentieth century. And it is the market that is now becoming the new global design of the powers that be. Hence, the globalization of culture, understood as the "material aspect in which the history of capitalism and of global designs evolved," has always been there; except that today's modern technology allows it to spread faster and farther than before, but still in one direction, just as in the sixteenth century. For example, the force with which Inca and Aymara culture entered and modified Castilian culture was less significant than the reverse. That is, Castilian knowledge and attitude

CASE STUDY 1.2

The first steps of the Christians for Socialism movement were taken in Chile around the 1970s. However, the movement had its origins many decades before, when Christians and Marxists began to work together for a common cause: the liberation of the oppressed workers. A group of factory workers and Christian faithful discover that the fundamental linchpin of Latin American reality and history was the reality of class struggle. The suffering of the oppressed took on an identifiable face in the political struggle of the working class against a system that supported a wealthy and exploitive oligarchy. The workers found their liberation in socialism understood as the creation of cooperative social relations and self-management, equal power relations, and the reduction of hierarchy in the management of economic and political affairs. In this linchpin, radical politics and Christian radicalism eventually found their common ground.

On September 4, 1970, Salvador Allende obtained a relative majority in Chile. He won over against Jorge Alessandrini, who represented conservative Catholicism and was a ferocious anti-Communist and opposed any kind of social change. He was supported by a large majority of the Catholic hierarchy and by certain sectors of Opus Dei. Allende also won against Radomiro Tomic, who represented progressive Catholicism. The bishops, who generally identified themselves with Christian Democracy, feared Allende's victory, although they also feared a possible victory by the right-wing Alessandrini, ex-president of Chile. Confronted by the fact of Allende's victory, the Catholic bishops maintained a deep silence. To the Right, this silence was interpreted as the church's becoming an accomplice to the victory of Marxism. To the Left, this silence was completely unjustified. In April of 1971, a group of priests and lay faithful decided to break the church's silence and convened a "Conference on Christian Participation in the Construction of Socialism in Chile" to explore ways of collaborating with Allende for the creation of a more just Chilean society. From this meeting arose the so-called Document of the Eighty, from the number of priests who participated in the conference. The Chilean conference of bishops immediately made a public statement against the participants in the conference and published its three-theses proclamation regarding the role of the church in politics: the nonpolitical spiritual mission of the church, the political liberty of Christians, and the importance of church unity. In response, in September of 1971, the Presbyteral Secretariat for Christians for Socialism was created with the mission of establishing a Christian and political presence in popular movements and left-wing parties. Later the Educational Secretariat of Christians for Socialism was established to promote liberative education for all. They did this without creating a parallel group in the church or state. However, three years later, on September 11, 1973, a coup against Allende deposed him from the presidency and opened the way for the thirteen-year right-wing military dictatorship of Augusto Pinochet.

Do you think Christianity and socialism are compatible with each other? Do you think Christians and socialists can work together for a more just society even if they do not agree on fundamental points or self-understanding?

Fig. 1.2. Marchers for Salvador Allende. A crowd of people marching to support the election of Salvador Allende for president in Santiago, Chile, September 5, 1964.

toward life did not change as much as Aymaran and Incan knowledge and attitude toward life.

According to Mignolo, the "modern/colonial world" arose from certain kinds of local histories: *imperial* local histories. Imperial Spain became an instrumental agent that made possible the implementation of Christian designs and then conversion to a global one. Imperial England in complicity with the French Enlightenment displaced (but not replaced) Christian global designs, making room for secular civilizing ones. The imperial United States displaced (but not replaced) the global design of the civilizing mission with a global design of development and modernization. And the market is now becoming the global design of a new form of colonialism, a global coloniality, which is being analyzed as "the network

society" (Castells), "globalcentrism" (Coronil), and "Empire" (Hardt and Negri). Thus the globalization of "culture" was always there, since culture (in whatever technology of the time was available) is the material aspect in which the history of capitalism and of global designs (Christianity, civilizing mission, development and modernization, marketization) evolved.

Technology today allows culture, and financial markets, to move faster. While a globalization of culture may not exist, planetary communication and the coloniality of power nevertheless move faster, and as in the sixteenth century, in one direction. For example, Bolivia's music and restaurants in the United States or Europe are less relevant (aren't they?) than European television and popular music in Bolivia. In La Paz, for example, there is a "German Channel" that provides the state of the weather in Germany and in Europe for the Bolivian audience. I am not aware of a "Bolivian Channel" in Germany that does the same.

It is interesting, then, to conclude this section by observing how Latin American thought achieves its productivity and recognition within contemporary developments thanks to its efforts, not so much in following the precepts inherited from the European conquest and global-vision, but because it critically reflected on that inheritance and united itself with the radical difference of the ideals and production of oppressed cultures before such precepts. Hence, the stereotype that Latin American only produced folklore transforms itself into a valuable instrument to unmask theories of justification of marginalization and to give energy to the mobilizing thought of liberative social practices.

Need for Liberation

Historically, Latin American liberative ethics have their explicit origins in the emancipation struggles of the continent from "dependent capitalism" in the aftermath of the Cuban Revolution and the Second Vatican Council. Dependency theory developed in the late 1950s under the guidance of the director of the United Nations Economic Commission for Latin America, Argentinean Raul Prebisch. Prebisch and his colleagues were troubled by the fact that economic growth in the advanced industrialized countries did not necessarily lead to growth in the poorer countries. Indeed, their studies suggested that economic activity in the richer countries often led to serious economic problems in the poorer countries. Neoclassical theory had not predicted such a possibility but had assumed that economic growth was beneficial to all, even if the benefits were not always equally shared.

Prebisch's initial explanation for the phenomenon was very straightforward: poor countries exported primary commodities to the rich countries that then manufactured products out of those commodities and sold them back to the poorer countries. The "value added" by manufacturing a usable product always cost more than the primary products used to create those products. Therefore, poorer countries would never earn enough from their exports to pay for their imports. Prebisch's solution was similarly straightforward: poorer countries should embark on programs of import substitution so that they need not purchase the manufactured products from the richer countries.

TIMELINE

1492	Christopher Columbus arrives in the Americas
1510–1553	The first phase—critique of the Iberian enterprise and search for an Iberian-American identity
1514	Bartolome de Las Casas begins his struggle on behalf of the Amerindians
1515–1521	Conquest of the Aztec Empire by Hernán Cortés
1529–1533	Conquest of the Inca Empire by Francisco Pizarro
1535	Establishment of the viceroyalty of New Spain (capital, Mexico City)
1542	Establishment of the viceroyalty of Peru (capital, Lima)
1717	Establishment of the viceroyalty of New Granada (capital, Bogota)
1776	Establishment of the viceroyalty of Rio de la Plata (capital, Buenos Aires)
1804–1825	Wars of Independence (the first emancipation)
1825–1900	Consolidation and liberal-conservative conflicts
1898	Spanish-American War (end of the Spanish Empire and beginning of American Interventionism).
1910–1920	Mexican Revolution
1953–1959	Cuban Revolution
1962–1965	Second Vatican Council
1968	Medellin, Colombia, II Conference of the Latin American Catholic Episcopate
1969–1973	Second emancipation: "constitutional stage
1970–1990	Era of military regimes
1973–1976	Second emancipation: maturation stage
1976–1983	Second emancipation: stage of persecution, debates, and confrontations
1979	Puebla, Mexico, III Conference of the Latin American Catholic Episcopate
1980–2008	Washington Consensus (orientation toward neoliberal policies)
1983	Fourth phase begins
1992	Santo Domingo, Dominican Republic, IV Conference of the Latin American Catholic Episcopate
1997	Synod of Catholic Bishops of the Americas
2000s	Turn toward the Left (e.g., Venezuela, Brazil, Bolivia)
2007	Aparecida, Brazil, V Conference of the Latin American Catholic Episcopate

The poorer countries would still sell their primary products on the world market, but their foreign exchange reserves would not be used to purchase their manufactures from abroad.

Dependency theory was viewed as a possible way of explaining the persistent poverty of the poorer countries. The traditional neoclassical approach said virtually nothing on this question except to assert that the poorer countries were late in coming to solid economic practices and that as soon as they learned the techniques of modern economics, then the poverty would begin

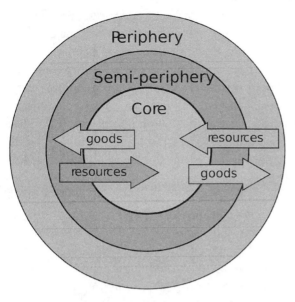

Fig. 1.3. The concept of dependency theory.

of scale used by the richer countries to keep their prices low. The second issue concerned the political will of the poorer countries as to whether a transition to producing primary products was possible or desirable. The final issue revolved around the extent to which the poorer countries actually had control of their primary products, particularly in the area of selling those products abroad. These obstacles to the import substitution policy led others to think a little more creatively and historically about the relationship between rich and poor countries but also, unfortunately, led many to believe that liberative ethics was a methodological and praxeological failure.

The response of liberative ethicists to dependency theory tended to rationalize the control of the state—high protectionist barriers, a closed economy, and a general snobbishness toward the role of the market; and from the end of the 1940s to the 1980s, the state enjoyed absolute control. At the same time, in agreement with the milieu, "national security" became a justification for governments to take over "strategic sectors" of the economy with the presumed objective of satisfying the needs of the country and not those of foreign investors. This led to the creation of government-owned oil companies in several countries, for example. Also, as the phenomenon of globalization was on the rise, some dependency theoreticians and some liberative theoreticians rejected participation in the world market.

Until the 1970s, this focus and praxis seemed to work. However, with the passing of years, the great weakness of the liberative response to dependency theory had to be recognized. The industrial enterprises—private as well as state-owned—that it had encouraged were inefficient due to protectionism, lack of competition, and isolation from innovative technology. In great part, it did not prioritize quality or quality of service. Agriculture suffered substantially. Budget deficits increased by leaps and bounds. With the generalized inflation that hit Latin America in the 1970s, 80s, and 90s,

to subside. However, Marxists and liberative theorists viewed the persistent poverty as a consequence of capitalist exploitation. And a new body of thought, called the "world systems approach," argued that the poverty was a direct consequence of the evolution of the international political economy into a fairly rigid division of labor that favored the rich and penalized the poor.

There are still points of serious disagreements among the various strains of dependency theorists, and it is a mistake to think that there is only one unified theory of dependency. Nonetheless, all dependency theorists attempted to explain the same underlying phenomenon. And most dependency theorists agree, moreover, that international capitalism was the motive force behind dependency relationships.

Although dependency theory proposed an alternative liberative model of economics and economic policy, three issues made this policy difficult to follow and continue to pose questions to Latin American liberative ethicists. The first was that the internal markets of the poorer countries were not large enough to support the economies family savings were wiped out. As a consequence, people could not retire. Inflation grew to incredible heights, pushed by deficits and lax monetary policy. National economies lost the benefits of international commerce and, logically, there was no improvement in social inequality.

Despite these setbacks, Latin American liberative ethics in response to the reality of dependence still has meaning and value in articulating itself in the great process of the second emancipation of Latin America. As a Brazilian liberative ethicist said: "If there was no philosophy of liberation, one would have to invent one" (Dussel, 1994). In the end, the great contribution of Latin American liberative ethics has been to speak to power with a voice born from the experience of misery, poverty, and exploitation, even if its practical solutions, especially in the realm of economics, have not borne the desired fruit.

from one moral order to another. A liberative ethics meditates and explains the meaning of practical goodness at the time when a moral order is being destroyed for being unjust, a time when the liberating subject is exposed, one could say, to the harsh elements, without cover or protection in the moral order that is falling into pieces. It proposes a morality beyond the present morality. The liberator, or liberators, the heroes that rise against the established order guided by liberative ethics, does not destroy the old moral order only to build a new one on the life and courage of the warriors, the victorious, the revolutionaries but in service to the oppressed, the poor, the alienated people. That liberator, in the end, is the people themselves, the poor, the historical "we." With their lives they build new moral orders. This is the greatest insight of liberative scholars and figures.

Current Themes and Methodologies

According to some liberative social theorists, ethics is the practical order of a critical, difficult milieu, in the process of changing toward a new order of things: from the passage of an established moral system accepted by most to another, nonnormative, liberative ethical order. Morality is the all-encompassing established praxis, triumphant, in power (reinforced by the laws of the state); whereas ethics means the practical structure born from oppression of the established order, from the morality in power, and travels the long, road of building a new practical totality that is more just, in the future horizon of an oppressed society, of liberation.

For Latin American liberative ethicists, ethics is the practical order of moving from an unjust morality to a more just future morality. It is the normative order during the dialectical passage

Possible Future Trends

As a consequence of the theory of dependence, Latin American liberative social ethics continues to deal with some urgent challenges to Central and South America; for example, the essence of capital, dependency, transnational economics, foreign debt, military buildup, struggle for peace, democracy and dictatorship, liberation of women and feminism, self-affirmation of the Latin American youth, the question of the Amerindian before the five centuries of the "intrusion," overexploitation of work, the "cultural question," and the "question of 'the people.'"

Regarding the economy, several oppressive realities have developed since the 1950s, and thus liberative social ethicists have asked further ethical questions. First, human labor, which occupies the greatest part of human existence, has been objectified in its products: human life has been turned into a commodity. Second, there has been a misappropriation of human life due to the transfer of the surplus to the central capital (neocolonizing metropolis). This is the greatest challenge of our time, the misappropriation of the being of entire peoples, an ethical problem par excellence, robbery and victimization of human life. As a corollary to both of these realities, the transnational capital appropriates unto itself the surplus, the human lives, not only of the capital of the periphery (with less development) but also of the rest of the central national capital (with higher salaries). It extracts extra work, due to competition within the periphery and in the center itself, from all the other capitals. These ethical problems, although sometimes not perceived by the majority of social ethicists, especially in the global north, define the Latin American milieu. And it is on the foundation of these realities (capital, dependency, and transnational capital) that a liberative social ethics discourse can continue to make a transforming contribution in the years to come.

These topics might not seem to belong to the field of ethics; however, if ethics is about real life, these realities weigh heavily on the shoulders of the people on the periphery, especially those in Latin America. In the same way, and related to the topics indicated above, the foreign debt of the poor countries was produced by the necessity of rich countries to loan money so that these countries might be able to buy their overproduction. The debt is the fruit of the crisis of the central capital that pays the capital of the periphery. Here one is dealing, once again, with an ethical issue by definition, a situation that allows central capital to cruelly take possession of the lives of the poor and underdeveloped. All these fall under the umbrella of ethics, if by ethics one means the thinking through of domination, both in general and concretely, which weighs heavily on those from which this ethics emerges.

Not only as a political problem but also existentially and concretely, the participation or lack thereof of the people in the decisions of their governments becomes a possibility for a liberative social ethics. The problems of democracy and dictatorship, as the liberty of the people and possibility of participation, have become central issues in the recent history of Latin America. Although, since the mid-1980s, an extremely weak form of democracy has become a reality in most countries of South America, dictatorship continues to be the rule in many states of the Western Hemisphere.

Half of humanity suffers another type of domination that has become the object of ethics and liberation. Latin American women suffer oppression from the machista ideology and the praxis of domination of the male, in sexual, cultural, economic, and political realms. The "mujerista" movement has generated a liberative ethics of womankind. This ethics is an integral part of an ethics of liberation, whether or not that has been articulated in a concrete way by both movements.

A liberative ethics cannot forget the youth in the construction of a more developed and just future Latin America. By nature, the youth are the future social ethicists, the young men or women who with their idealism desire a better, more just, more participative future world. Life within the established system, the current crisis of capitalism with its crisis of unemployment in the center and misery in the periphery, teach the youth of Latin America a harsh reality. A liberative ethics is a message of hope for that youth that can be generous and courageous in the building of a free Latin America.

Latin American liberative ethics, already begun by José Carlos Mariátegui in his reflection on indigenous identity, must also develop an ethical discourse on the nature of the Amerindians, on their mythical-rational thought, and on their place in the history before the conquest.

Amerindians see the five-hundredth anniversary of the "discovery" of the so-called new world as five centuries of domination, genocide, and death. However, they have survived and are reclaiming their lands, their dignity, their liberty, their political and cultural autonomy.

BOX 1.8

José Carlos Mariátegui

José Carlos Mariátegui (June 14, 1894–April 16, 1930) was a Peruvian journalist, political philosopher, and activist. A prolific writer before his early death at age thirty-five, he is considered one of the most influential Latin American socialists of the twentieth century. Mariátegui's most famous work, *Seven Interpretive Essays on Peruvian Reality* (1928), is still widely read in South America. An avowed, self-taught Marxist, he insisted that a socialist revolution should evolve organically in Latin America on the basis of local conditions and practices, not the result of mechanically applying a European formula.

Together with the oppressed, the peasant farmer, the Amerindian, the woman and the youth, the salaried worker of the countries of the periphery, suffers an overexploitation of ferocious dimensions. The transfer of surplus from the periphery to the center is compensated by an overexploitation of the worker in the form of low salaries that contribute to miserable standards of living or subliving. A liberative social ethics has to think ontologically, from the being of capital and dependency, about the reality of Latin American workers. And ethically, it needs to elaborate a moral theory that explains and makes known the evilness of the overexploitation this social class suffers.

Together with all of these issues and questions, there is the "cultural question." The developed nations exercise a cultural hegemony over Latin America, the dominant classes over the dominated ones, the established ideologies over the youth, machismo over women, and so on. Culture, like the totality of those phenomena, shows us another important field for current, liberative ethical reflection. A liberative ethics thinks the reality of a national culture before that of the central nations (which is imposed through the means of television, radio, cinema, publications, satellite communications, etc.), the reality of popular culture before the "illumined" culture of the hegemonic groups of dependent countries, and a culture of a consumerist society before a revolutionary popular national culture. In other words, the question of "popular culture" is a central and difficult topic that a liberative ethics must confront.

The word *popular* raises, in turn, the question of the meaning of "the people." Since "the people," the reality of this social organism and the category used by the populisms of Latin America (projects of the national elites in the countries of the periphery to unite the newly born working class), many have thought to discard the category of "people" from the agenda of social change. However, this term continues to be used by every revolutionary leader of the global south. In an established system, "the people" is the social bloc of the oppressed—classes, sectors, ethnicities, marginalized, and so on. In the dissolution of a given order, the poor are expelled from the oppressed classes. When a new order is constituted, the poor form part of the new classes; and the members of the new oppressed classes will become the people.

Joaquín Hernández Alvarado, writing in 1976, stated that liberative social ethics had reached its productive climax, and one could not expect any further developments or insights. However, it seems that this prophecy has not been fulfilled. Latin American liberative social ethics continues to deal with the threat of new oppressive challenges and ideologies by continuing to propose a liberative alternative for a more just future.

Study Questions

1. Before reading this chapter, could you have named a Latin American philosopher or thinker? Why do you think Latin Americans are associated with folklore but not with theoretical or scientific production?
2. What are the main tenants of a "liberative education" versus a "financial education"?
3. What is the difference between a "liberative analectic" and an "analectic of oppression" as presented by Enrique Dussel? Can you enumerate the elements of Dussel's liberative pedagogical schema?
4. What is the theory of dependence? How does the question of culture and "the people" come into play?
5. What is "post-Westernism" and how does it relate to the philosophy of liberation, postcolonial theory, and postmodern thought?

Suggested Readings

Barbero, Jesús Martín. *Communication, Culture and Hegemony: From the Media to Mediations.* Newsbury Park, CA: Sage, 1993.

Boff, Leonardo. *Introducing Liberation Theology.* Maryknoll, NY: Orbis, 1987.

Cámara, Hélder. *Dom Helder Camara: Essential Writings.* Edited by Francis McDonagh. Maryknoll, NY: Orbis, 2009.

Canclini, Nestor Garcia. *Hybrid Cultures: Strategies for Entering and Leaving Modernity.* Translated by Christopher L. Chiappari. Minneapolis: University of Minnesota Press, 2005.

Castro Gómez, Santiago. *Critique of Latin American Reason.* Barcelona: Puvill, 1996.

De La Torre, Miguel A. *Liberation Theology for Armchair Theologians.* Louisville: Westminster John Knox, 2013.

Dussel, Enrique. *Philosophy of Liberation.* Translated by Aquilina Martinez. Eugene, OR: Wipf & Stock, 2003.

Freire, Paulo. *Pedagogy of the Oppressed.* Translated by Myra Bergman Ramos. 30th anniversary ed. New York: Continuum, 2000.

Gutiérrez, Gustavo. *A Theology of Liberation: History, Politics, and Salvation.* 15th anniversary ed. Maryknoll, NY: Orbis, 1988.

Mariátegui, José Carlos. *Seven Interpretive Essays on Peruvian Reality.* Austin: University of Texas Press, 1988.

Mignolo, Walter. *The Idea of Latin America.* West Sussex, UK: Wiley-Blackwell, 2005.

———. *Local Histories/Global Designs.* Illustrated ed. Princeton: Princeton University Press, 2000.

Richard, Nelly. *The Insubordination of Signs: Political Change, Cultural Transformation, and Poetics of the Crisis.* Translated by Alice Nelson. Durham: Duke University Press, 2004.

2 African Liberative Ethics

Ezra Chitando

In memory of Simon Zivanai Mawondo

"A STRUGGLING (PERSON) HAS got to move. I am struggling (person) and I have got to move on!" Thus sang the reggae icon Jimmy Cliff. Africa's story remains one of continuous struggle, a "moving on." Embodying the struggling person, Africa has had to live in a state of permanent vigilance due to its often tragic interaction with the rest of the world. Abused, scalded, and discarded, Africa is on a lifelong struggle for liberation. Liberation remains high on Africa's agenda. Anything else would dishonor the memory of heroic struggle against systematic dehumanization. This chapter will focus on African liberative ethics, an ethics that emerges from the continent's consistent struggle against domination by external forces. This struggle has taken many mutually reinforcing forms. Africa has sought to assert its independence in political, economic, intellectual, and ideological spheres; in particular, African liberative ethics seeks to ensure that the rights and dignity of Africans are upheld.

African liberative ethics is informed by the conviction that Africans, as full human beings, are entitled to lead full lives. This basic tenet may seem obvious; however, due to historical factors such as the slave trade, colonialism, neocolonialism, and globalization, it needs to be restated time and again.

Historically, the world has struggled to accept the full humanity of Africans. In fact, the world's numbness to African tragedies suggests that African lives do not matter as much as the lives of other, "more human" beings. African liberative ethics thus seeks to equip Africans to attain total liberation in the face of multiple dehumanizing forces. Proponents of African liberative ethics find common ground in the struggle to overturn structures of oppression. Although these structures express themselves in diverse forms, including

> ## KEY TERM 2.1
>
> *Globalization.* The process through which various economies become integrated. African liberationists (and other critics) contend that this process continues to favor the powerful and that it does not grant equal access to all.

globalization, landlessness, political oppression, patriarchy, and HIV and AIDS, they agree on one fundamental theme: Africans must be fully released from these debilitating structures!

Basic Tenets of African Liberative Ethics

The story of Africa has been one of a hard, grim battle for survival in the face of multiple forces of death. Tragically, the integrity of Africa and Africans has never been accepted by those who wield political and economic power. Africa has always been valued to the extent that its resources can be exploited. The exploitation of African resources has left the continent bleeding and gasping for breath and has contributed to the continent's ongoing struggle against HIV and AIDS, refugees and poverty. African liberative ethics emerges from this context of wishing to ensure the total liberation of Africans from oppressive structures; however, it should be noted from the onset that this field is still evolving and it does not yet constitute a unified area of study. Consequently, this chapter seeks to consolidate into one narrative material that has been developed in diverse contexts.

The term *African ethics* is, like most other scholarly constructs, a loaded and debatable one. Due to space considerations, attention will be paid to only the key considerations relevant to the theme. First, the sheer diversity of the continent (historical, geographical, racial, linguistic, etc.) leads one to hesitate to suggest there could be a discipline that covers the whole continent. Second, the emotive significance of the term *African* is contested. Does it include nonblack citizens of the continent? For example, would it be proper to include ethical reflections by white/Asian Africans under the category of African ethics? Third, missionary religions such as Christianity and Islam now claim the membership of many African intellectuals. Does one include African Christian ethics, for example, within the classification "African ethics"?

Due to the impact particularly of Christianity on the development of African ethics, the reflections of African Christian ethicists will be included because they have emerged as the single most productive block of contributors to the discourse on African ethics. For this reason, it is legitimate to include reflections by converts to Christianity within the corpus of African ethics, a point reinforced by Samuel W. Kunhiyop in his book *African Christian Ethics*, in which he observes that "African ethical thinking did not develop in isolation, but has been richly influenced by the forces of Westernization, Christianization and Islamization." Effectively, African Christian theologians have also contributed to African ethics in general and African liberative ethics in particular.

The issues relating to the complications relating to the term *African ethics* are important, and elicit different responses from various academics. These responses are informed by the ideological standpoints of the different scholars; thus, within this chapter, an open or operational definition of *African ethics* is adopted. Open definitions do not pretend to be final. They are tentative and temporary. Or, as Martin Prozesky reminds us in his article "Cinderella, Survivor and Saviour: African Ethics and the Quest for a Global Ethic," African ethics "refers to the moral traditions embedded in the many and various cultures of sub-Saharan Africa, the moral traditions of black African cultures."

African liberative ethics has evolved from African life experiences. These include communal wisdom that has been accumulated across the years, as well as the reflections of individual philosophers (lay and professional). African liberative ethics is therefore the product of both the cumulative tradition (ideas and practices handed down from one generation to another) and personal reflections by African philosophers. In underlining this point, rapprochement between those who emphasize the communitarian nature of African ethics on the one hand and those who uphold the role of individuals (read professional philosophers) in articulating ethical theories on the other requires facilitation.

Ethical reflections are therefore products of both social contexts and individual creativity by philosophers. This helps one to avoid the tyranny of "either/or" and to embrace the inclusiveness of "both/and." African philosophy (and, by extension, African liberative ethics) is the outcome of communal and individual reflections on the meaning of life and how to achieve freedom in the face of oppressive systems. H. Odera Oruka's classic formulation of exclusive trends in African philosophy (i.e., ethno-philosophy, philosophic sagacity, nationalist-ideological and professional philosophy) needs to be deconstructed to allow for mutual influences across these categories.

This chapter does not focus on the larger "African ethics" in general; instead, it focuses specifically on "African liberative ethics." This distinction is vital since one does not imply the other. African liberative ethics represents a specific dimension, thrust, or emphasis within African ethics. Whereas African ethics is broader, African liberative ethics seeks to isolate the liberative slant within African ethics. It also follows that the works of those who have written on African ethics in general do not feature directly in this chapter. More specifically, the focus is on how African ethicists seek to provide ethical reflections that lead to the liberation of Africans from various oppressive systems.

Since the quest for full human dignity has precipitated African liberative ethics, one can argue that all struggles to secure and enhance African health and well-being have been integral to the formation of African liberative ethics. Struggles against slavery, colonial exploitation, neocolonial domination, oppression by postcolonial African leaders, gender oppression, and other struggles have all contributed to the insistence that the key

tenet of African liberative ethics is securing an acceptable quality of life for Africans in oppressive situations. African liberative ethics is built on the contention that the highest good consists in achieving freedom from oppression. When faced with ethical questions, Africans must prioritize those courses of action that achieve their liberation and contribute to their attainment of the "abundant life"—that is, life characterized by freedom from oppression and want.

As illustrated below, scholars who have contributed to the discourse on African liberative ethics place emphasis on *ubuntu*, communal solidarity.

Ubuntu is based on the conviction that, unlike in the West, Africans seek to cultivate harmonious relationships within communities rather than promoting individualism. The concept of *ubuntu* has tended to dominate ethical reflection in sub-Saharan Africa, especially after the official end of apartheid in South Africa in 1994. It is a critical tenet of African liberative ethics. According to Augustine Shutte, *ubuntu* seeks to promote personal growth within the community. The concept regards the community as indispensable in the process of ethical decision making.

History and Development of African Liberative Ethics

In terms of historical development, the "decolonizing decade" of the 1960s is particularly significant for the eventual emergence and growth of African liberative ethics. Significantly, it is the

KEY TERM 2.2

Ubuntu. "I am because we are." An African concept that describes communal solidarity, as opposed to individualism.

same decade that saw the emergence of African theology. As the African struggles for political independence gained momentum and many African countries achieved freedom, there was serious soul searching within the various disciplines. What was the role of the African intellectual in mapping the continent's total freedom? How could African academics contribute toward the Africanization of various disciplines? The decolonization of the disciplines was therefore a key consideration. Philosophy and theology could not remain untouched. The search for "African" literature, philosophy, history, theology, and so on became an urgent undertaking.

One of colonialism's most profound effects on the colonized people was to sap them of their confidence. It sought to deliberately undermine the confidence of the colonized in their history and identity by rubbishing their heroes, downplaying their collective memories, and renaming their landscapes. Colonialism thrived on the erasure of the indigenous peoples' records and identities. The search for African philosophy needs to be located within this anguished search for identity. This search was closely related to developments in fields such as African history, literature, religion, and others.

Colonialism bequeathed a legacy of divided language zones in Africa. It has become fashionable to refer to Anglophone, Francophone, and Lusophone regions to capture the use of English, French, and Portuguese as the dominant languages

---

KEY TERM 2.3

Africanization. A process through which African ideas and concepts are brought to the center of disciplines in Africa. This is in opposition to the centralization of European and American (and other non-African) concepts.

---

used (for official records) on the continent. This division according to language has had a definite impact on histories of African philosophy, as most scholars tend to focus on publications from the Anglophone region. African philosophers from the Francophone region have been equally consistent in their reflections and deserve recognition.

Current Themes and Methodologies

The oppression of the African continent is not limited to some historical colonial pass. Present-day global economic relationships continue to contribute to Africa's oppression. For this reason, ethical responses rooted in the African social location remain a continuous theme.

On the Existence of African Philosophy and the Emergence of African Liberative Ethics

One of the fundamental questions African philosophers have had to grapple with is whether African philosophy exists in the first instance. In fact, it is only after answering this question in the affirmative that the secondary issue of African liberative ethics can be entertained. There is now consensus that African philosophy does exist. The emergence of notable practitioners, including H. Odera Oruka, Kwasi Wiredu, D. A. Masolo, Tsenay Serequeberhan, Kwame Gyekye, Mogobe B. Ramose, and others, especially from the 1980s to the present, confirms that the discipline has come of age. Practitioners from the Francophone region, including Alexis Kagame, Marcien Towa, V. Y. Mudimbe, Bénézet Bujo, Paulin Hountondji, and others have also contributed immensely to the growth of the discipline. Although trained in theology, John S. Mbiti in the Anglophone region and Fabien Eboussi-Boulaga have had a notable impact on African philosophy. Significantly, as reiterated below, only a few women, such as

Sophie B. Oluwole, have emerged in African philosophy. Other women have contributed to African philosophy, but they are more grounded in theology.

Publications that focus on African philosophy, such as Kwasi Wiredu's, *A Companion to African Philosophy* (2004), Emmanuel C. Eze's *Postcolonial African Philosophy: A Critical Reader* (1997), and P. H. Coetze and A. P. J. Roux's *The African Philosophy Reader* (2003), confirm the vibrancy of the discipline. African liberative ethics has emerged from ongoing engagement with African challenges. Especially in South Africa, the establishment of centers devoted to the study of ethics, such as the Unilever Ethics Centre at the University of KwaZulu-Natal, and the Centre for Leadership Ethics in Africa at the University of Fort Hare, has facilitated ethical reflection. Edited volumes (for example, Nicholson's *Persons in Community* and Murove's *African Ethics*) that focus on African ethics have emerged from such reflections.

As with African theology, African philosophical reflection that concentrates on the dimension of culture has tended not to be radically liberative, apart from the emphasis on liberation in the context of oppressive sociocultural practices in the face of HIV and AIDS. While some philosophers have been critical of aspects of African culture and its emphasis on community (i.e., Wiredu and Gyekye), there is a tendency to celebrate the communitarian orientation of African culture. However, reflections that focus on economic and political dimensions have proved to be a rich reservoir for African liberative ethics, as will be highlighted below.

Whereas ethical reflection in some parts of the world is recondite and speculative, African liberative ethics emerges from the struggles of Africans in a world in which Africans come as third- or fourth-rate citizens. As indicated above, the themes that have occupied the attention of African ethicists have been many and varied; however, within the liberative mold, a number of themes are

recurrent. A form-critical analysis of the publications within the field shows a preoccupation with addressing pressing issues that confront Africans on a daily basis. More critically, although the ethicists might appeal to some Western writers, their primary concern is with ensuring that African interests are upheld. For them, the guiding question is whether a particular course of action results in the liberation of the African community from oppressive structures.

Africa's Economic Marginalization

"Africa is too rich to be poor" is a recurrent motif in the writings of African liberationists within various areas. Africa is endowed with natural resources and a favorable climate. While global media networks routinely flight images of poverty and chaos, Africa is incredibly rich. Regrettably and admittedly, Africa's natural riches have not translated into economic prosperity for its citizens. Tukunboh Adeyemo, an African evangelical theologian, describes the situation by observing that the land does not appear to grant maximum yield, while famine and droughts seem endemic. He bemoans the theft of mineral resources by outsiders (with the collusion of insiders). Adeyemo also draws attention to the frequent devaluation of African currencies. Granted, Africa's massive economic problems can also be attributed to internal mismanagement and corruption; nevertheless, it remains true that Europe and North America are deeply implicated in the continent's economic marginalization. Whereas globalization has been touted as a positive development, Africa remains enmeshed in its "poverty" and underdevelopment. In the meantime, African resources are being plundered with impunity. Now, China has joined the party, extracting Africa's wealth at will. African liberative ethics seeks to challenge the marginalization of Africa within the global economy, yet Africa's resources are being used to drive the same. In the context of such abuses,

Fig. 2.1. One of thousands of refugee families who arrived from Somalia to the Dadaab refugee camp in 2011 to flee the drought and conflict.

Rogate Mshana has called for justice and an alternative to globalization.

Some of the dominant questions that contributors in this area wrestle with include the following: Why does Africa remain desperately poor when it is endowed with so many resources? Why does Africa seem unable to exploit its resources for the benefit of its own citizens? What are some of the ethical guidelines that could be formulated and implemented in order to address Africa's marginalization in the global economy? What is the role of indigenous ethical values in mobilizing Africans to claim their rights in the face of greed by

outsiders? These questions have precipitated serious reflections in African philosophy.

Musa P. Filibus, from Nigeria, contends that Africa's economic marginalization and the global financial crisis are outcomes of greed and the emergence of economic dictatorship. He proposes "the principle of enough" as a strategy to address the rapaciousness that characterizes the current world order. The principle of enough will cultivate peace and justice, as well as promote service of the neighbor. Filibus stands within the tradition of African liberative ethics by suggesting that the global financial system stifles the freedom and dignity of Africans. It fuels systems of death and needs to be revamped in order for it to be guided by new ethical principles. Although he draws from the Christian ethical tradition, he is also influenced by the African notion of *ubuntu*.

In the face of gross economic injustice and wanton exploitation of African resources by outsiders, African liberative ethics calls for the adoption of new values. These new values will replace the current greed, violence, and injustice that define economic relationships during our time. For example, Munyaradzi F. Murove calls for a new economic system that embraces African indigenous values of communal well-being. More proactively, African liberative ethics challenges Africans to exert their agency. As ethical beings, Africans have an obligation to defend their resources and to ensure that they utilize these resources effectively. Instead of the dominant view that Africans are a hapless lot, African liberative ethics enjoins Africans to be informed by the ethic of responsibility. This reminds Africans that they have the responsibility to protect their resources in order to ensure the viability of future generations.

Land Hunger

Closely tied to the theme of Africa's economic marginalization is that of land hunger. Settler colonialism displaced indigenous peoples. Globally, darker skinned people have been robbed of

Causes of the African Situation

The media is dominated by negative images of Africa. Wars, disease, corruption, incompetence, and other debilitating pictures bombard readers and viewers in relation to the continent. Afro-pessimism is a term that has been coined to describe the tendency to project Africa as "the hopeless continent." Critics and cynics portray Africa as a lost cause. They routinely imply that gross mismanagement is behind the continent's apparent poverty. Although Africans are partially to blame for the continent's struggles, it is vital to acknowledge that global economic powers are also implicated directly. Africa's resources are routinely plundered by those who wield economic power. African warlords have been armed by Western powers in order to facilitate unfettered access to Africa's resources. African revolutionaries and visionaries, such as Thomas Sankara of Burkina Faso, have been physically eliminated with the assistance of Western powers. Brutal African dictators have been entertained abroad, as long as they have enabled Western companies to plunder African resources. In African liberative ethics, some key questions are raised. Why should African countries continue to be asked to repay their so-called debts when African resources have been plundered without any meaningful compensation? Since Africans literally have to die in order to repay the debt, but Europeans and North Americans will not die if the debt is not repaid, are there any ethical grounds for insisting on debt repayment?

their land by lighter skinned people. This scandal has been particularly pronounced in southern Africa, where the white minority owns vast tracts of land. On the other hand, millions of blacks struggle to eke out a living on barren land. Western philosophical concepts, such as the sanctity of private property, have been deployed to uphold such clearly morally bankrupt systems.

Some of the critical questions that have guided reflection in this area include: Why have black people remained marooned in unproductive areas after the struggles for liberation have been won? How are concepts such as healing and reconciliation related to justice in the face of black dispossession? Is it ethically sound to concentrate on the welfare of animals at the expense of human beings? What are some of the key indigenous ethical precepts that could clarify the debate on land and environmental conservation?

As is the case virtually everywhere, land is an emotive issue. In sub-Saharan Africa, it is tied to spirituality, as well as historical, legal, and racial issues. During the colonial period, black people were disenfranchised and forced off their fertile lands. The colonial state sought to protect the white settlers, and it accorded them preferential treatment in all aspects of life. Blacks were reduced to squatters in their own countries. Robin Palmer observes that most white settlers in southern Africa have presided over underutilized vast tracts of land. They lack the skills and capital to develop their farms and have relied on patronage by the state to remain dominant.

The violence, greed, and lack of consideration that have been shown in the displacement of blacks from their ancestral lands, especially in South Africa, Namibia, and Zimbabwe has precipitated serious ethical reflection on the part of some African ethicists. The late Simon Mawondo of Zimbabwe devoted considerable time and space to the issue. Mawondo questioned the emphasis on reconciliation ahead of justice. He consistently argued that the memory of dispossession and the reality of landlessness on the part of blacks had to be taken seriously. After all, blacks had embarked on a stony and demanding struggle for liberation. In the face of continued landlessness, the struggle had been in vain. Although he remained acutely aware of the complexities, such as the fact that some whites had actually bought their land, Mawondo insisted on distributive justice. Writing on the eve of dramatic fast-track land reform program, Mawondo charged that most Zimbabweans remained poor and landless. They continued to stay in the marginal lands that settler regimes had allocated them. Regrettably, the small group that benefited through colonialism continued to hold on to the land

The story of black land hunger is not confined to Zimbabwe, which is a sad reminder of the injustices wrought by colonialism. African liberative ethics insists that the rights of indigenous peoples must be prioritized in addressing the land issue. Practitioners argue that once the full humanity of black people has been accepted, it should follow with necessity that their historical claims to land be acknowledged. Still, it must be noted that more work needs to be done in terms of developing ethical reflection on the land issue. The appropriation of non-African philosophers such as Robert Nozick, while helping to broaden reflections, should not receive emphasis ahead of African concepts that could inform debates on the land issue.

Environmental Ethics

The question of African environmental ethics is also tied to the theme of land, although it requires a longer narrative to do justice to this theme. It is essential to acknowledge that the skewed distribution of land has resulted in many Africans adopting practices that are harmful to the environment. This has been unavoidable, as they are struggling for sheer survival in the face of oppressive structures. When Africans are criticized for precipitating environmental

degradation, African liberationists have argued that Africans have been left without an option due to historical processes.

African ethical reflection on the environment emphasizes the African concept of harmony with nature. Practitioners maintain that, at least in its pristine form, the indigenous African attitude toward nature is non-exploitative and reverential. In addition, they stridently attack Euro-American and Japanese technology. Africans are enjoined to retain their positive attitudes toward nature. Hence, a call is made to take this African interpretation of reality seriously if the environment is to be saved. Bujo argues that the entire cosmic community forms the foundation of African ecological ethics, and wonders what priority this specific interpretation of reality will be accorded in future. Bujo recommends dialogue between the African holistic perspective and Western rationality within the conservation debate

Although some critics charge that the reading of African indigenous values as being intrinsically ecologically friendly is rather romantic, there is a general consensus that a check is needed on the rapid expansion of Euro-American and Japanese technology if the environment is to thrive. Proponents of a specifically African environmental ethic further argue that while the African interpretation of reality is anthropocentric, its holism empowers it to preserve the environment.

Postcolonial Governance

Given the thrust of the foregoing section, one could be forgiven for concluding that all the problems Africans must contend with have an external source. One might contend that historical experiences such as the slave trade, colonialism, and globalization have led to the current situation, in which many Africans have to struggle against poverty and hunger on a regular basis. Nevertheless, many postcolonial African governments have not been paragons of virtue. In fact, a sizeable number of African governments have been responsible for

CASE STUDY 2.1

Ordinarily, the presence of natural resources should precipitate economic growth and development. However, many African states have experienced natural resources more as a curse than as a blessing. The discovery of diamonds and oil in particular has led to wars. However, the theme of environmental pollution and the subsequent depreciation in the quality of life for the majority of citizens has not received sufficient attention.

Nigeria's Niger Delta region epitomizes the challenge that citizens face when multinational companies connive with ruling elites to plunder African resources. While oil should bring prosperity, in this particular region it has brought a legacy of death. The United Nations Environment Programme (UNEP) has noted that oil contamination in Ogoniland is widespread and severely affecting many components of the environment. It also observes that although the oil industry is no longer active in the region, oil spills continue to occur with alarming regularity. This has led to massive environmental challenges in the region.

Ogoniland has experienced environmental degradation at an alarming scale. Oil pollution has left young people unable to fish or to participate in agriculture, the main occupations in the area. While the media projects militants in Ogoniland as terrorists who seek to destabilize the country, we must appreciate the need for justice in their struggle. In the meantime, Shell, the company that has contributed to the ecological and public health problems in Ogoniland, has not yet invested heavily in the reclamation of the environment.

What is intriguing about the environmental degradation that has been caused by the oil spills in Ogoniland is the connivance between a global oil company and the local ruling elite. The local ruling elite has not prioritized the needs of its citizens. Instead, personal interests and the contribution of oil to the national economy have tended to dominate. When citizens have pressed for their rights, the might of the state has descended on them heavily. The execution by the Nigerian state under military rule of Ken Saro Wiwa, the outspoken campaigner for the rights of the Ogoni people, confirms this sad state of affairs.

From an African liberative perspective, what are the people of Ogoniland entitled to? What are their rights and responsibilities? What must the state of Nigeria provide to its citizens? What should Shell do in order to mitigate the negative effects of the oil spill in Ogoniland? How would upholding African environmental ethics have helped to avoid the catastrophic situation in Ogoniland?

gross human rights violations, suppressing freedoms and corruption.

Some of the leading questions include: Why have many African governments failed to grant peace and prosperity to their citizens? How can a culture of good governance and upholding human rights be inculcated? What is the place of indigenous ethical values in postcolonial African contexts? How can a new vision of Africa be created in the wake of rampant corruption, oppression, and hopelessness?

African liberative ethics maintains that the freedom and the well-being of the generality of African citizens take precedence over the whims of the ruling elite. Many authors accuse the ruling elite of being insensitive to the plight of the majority. They charge that many African leaders are keen to accumulate wealth, pursue status symbols, and build personality cults while their citizens wallow in poverty. One may note here that the concept of greed that seeks to account for the crisis within the global economy is also applicable to the actions of many postcolonial African leaders.

Some African liberationists have exposed the abuse of indigenous concepts, such as *ubuntu*, by some African leaders. Although, as explained above, the concept seeks to provide an ethical blueprint for social justice, some leaders have exploited it to further their political agendas. Fainos Mangena also observes that some African leaders abuse the concept of patriotism. It is heartening to note the application of a hermeneutics of suspicion within writings on political ethics in Africa. Politicians are, by profession, keen to appropriate concepts that find resonance among voters and do not hesitate to deploy concepts that win them votes, even when such deployments are insincere.

In the face of the lack of imagination and the abuse of power by some postcolonial African leaders, there have been various efforts to promote new ethical standards. For example, Reuel J. Khoza of South Africa and Mandivamba Rukuni of Zimbabwe both use the concept of *ubuntu* to challenge African leaders to prioritize the well-being of their citizens. These scholars emphasize the need for African leaders to ensure that their citizens enjoy life in full. Although the concept of *ubuntu* can be abused (as cited above), it can still inform African ethical reflections in a profound way.

Writing from within African Christian social ethics, Emmanuel Katongole suggests that Africa is in desperate need of new imagination. The postcolonial African state that replaced the colonial state has tended to retain the latter's oppressive and stultifying characteristics. Citizens are butchered, resources are plundered, and hopelessness abounds. There is simply too much wastage—the

sacrifice of Africa. According to Katongole, Africa requires a new, liberating vision if it is to thrive.

Gender Oppression

African ethicists have also addressed the theme of gender oppression. Patriarchy is deeply entrenched in Africa, as it is in other parts of the world. A combination of religious, cultural, economic, and political factors has left women at the bottom of the pile. Issues of poverty, economic injustice, and landlessness assault women with devastating effects. In particular, women have demanded an end to their oppression. Consequently, there have been urgent calls for women empowerment and poverty alleviation.

African women writing from within the liberationist strand have been unrelenting and consistent in calling for the dismantling of oppressive patriarchal structures. Some of the central questions they have raised include: What are the factors that promote patriarchal oppression? How can women overthrow these patriarchal structures? What are some of the ethical values that inform the struggle against patriarchy? How can sexual and gender-based violence be overcome? What is the relationship between feminist ethics and African womanist ethics? What kind of society is envisaged after the demise of patriarchy?

A longer narrative is required to do justice to African liberative ethics in the face of patriarchal oppression; however, for the purpose of this chapter, it should suffice to indicate that African Christian women theologians have been actively involved in the struggle against patriarchy. They have drawn attention to the role of indigenous religions and cultures, Christianity and Islam, colonialism, and other factors in enhancing patriarchy in contemporary Africa.

As they struggle against patriarchal oppression, African women ethicists have placed emphasis on the ethic of resistance and transformation. They insist that the current world order is unsustainable: men should take their feet off the necks of

BOX 2.2

Gender Rights

Many African countries have made notable strides in an endeavor to promote gender equality and to minimize women's vulnerability. They have passed legislation that prohibits discrimination on the basis of gender. They have also passed various versions of domestic violence acts that seek to protect women (and men) against sexual and gender-based violence. While such pieces of legislation are progressive, the major challenge has been on the question of enforcement. A litany of religious, cultural, economic, and political factors prevents many women from approaching law enforcement agents. African liberative ethics seeks to ensure that women are empowered to act in order to safeguard their health and well-being. Although considerable progress has been made in terms of creating a legal framework to secure women's rights, patriarchy continues to prevent women from drawing maximum benefits. Patriarchy sponsors militant responses by some men who argue that the whole discourse on women's rights is alien to Africa. However, activists within the liberative tradition insist that the lives of individual African women should never be sacrificed in the name of resisting neocolonialism.

women! There is therefore a desperate need for women to resist oppression and to work for transformation. Gender justice will be attained when patriarchy is defeated and the humanity of women is fully accepted. In this struggle, men too have a role to play. As Nyambura J. Njoroge argues, African Christian women have given themselves fully

to the struggle for liberation and fullness of life. They are prepared to challenge poverty, violence, and the HIV pandemic.

The theme of violence features prominently in ethical reflections by African women. They have noted that patriarchy finds expression in sexual and gender-based violence. Faced with women who are becoming empowered, men have resorted to crude and dehumanizing strategies to reassert their power and influence. They have authored deadly forms of masculinity that unleash violence against women. African women scholars have called for an ethic of responsibility on the part of men. This has become particularly urgent in the face of HIV and AIDS.

HIV and AIDS

Ethical reflection on HIV and AIDS is intricately tied to the theme of gender oppression. In addition, it is also influenced by Africa's marginalization in the global economy, greed, and the need for solidarity with people living with HIV. Given the increasing diversity within this field, only some of the dominant themes will be summarized. Reflection on this theme has grappled with such questions as: Why does the world appear indifferent to the suffering and death of millions of Africans in the face of HIV and AIDS? Why have big pharmaceutical companies placed profits ahead of saving the lives of Africans who need antiretroviral treatment? How can stigma and discrimination be eradicated?

Musa W. Dube of Botswana, one of the leading voices in the scholarly response to HIV and AIDS, charges that globalization prevents

KEY TERM 2.4

Circle of Concerned African Women Theologians. A pan-African group of African women theologians who are challenging patriarchy and promoting gender justice.

"Culture" is a double-edged sword in sub-Saharan African contexts where HIV is rampant. On the one hand, culture gives individuals and communities identity. On the other hand, culture is open to manipulation and abuse. Unfortunately, the latter has tended to dominate. Many women have become vulnerable to HIV in the name of upholding cultural traditions. One particularly contentious practice in the wake of HIV is called "widow cleansing." In this instance, a widow is expected to engage in unprotected sexual activity with a stranger in order for the homestead to be "cleansed" of the spirit of the deceased. This practice has been persistent among the Luo of Kenya. This is the testimony of one woman:

My in-laws brought a filthy-looking stranger to cleanse me. I did not like the idea but had no option since I was protecting my children against chira, impurity. Besides, clan members insisted that I undergo all the rituals to enable my sons to marry and construct houses of their own. There was too much pressure exerted upon me so I decided to solve the immediate problem rather than fear HIV transmission that is a future possibility (Ambasa-Shisanya, 62).

The case of widow cleansing raises major issues regarding the conflict between what is perceived to be the greater common good and individual rights. In this particular instance, the woman is expected to sacrifice her personal rights in favor of the "survival" of her family and community. Sometimes the concept of *ubuntu* is deployed in order to encourage women to forgo their individual rights for the sake of the family. In particular, male brokers of culture tend to evoke "culture" to promote patriarchal views.

When the media in Africa reports on widow cleansing and other oppressive cultural practices, the emphasis tends to be on the "stubbornness" of the women who resist them. Alternatively, cultural nationalists charge that women who oppose such practices are buying into Western ideas. Such cultural nationalists tend to suggest that African women who resist death-dealing cultural practices are not being faithful to the African heritage.

African liberative ethics does not condone gender oppression in the name of African culture. It raises critical questions regarding culture and tradition. Specific questions include: Does a specific cultural belief/practice uphold the rights and dignity of women? What are the available legal, political, and social avenues that are available to women to challenge oppressive beliefs and practices? What are the underlying patriarchal values that are influencing the course of events when women are being subjected to degrading treatment?

Africans from enjoying abundant life in the face of the epidemic. She calls for a new era of compassion and justice. Indeed, the writings of the Circle of Concerned African Women Theologians demonstrate a preoccupation with justice. Justice overcomes Africa's marginalization, gender-based discrimination, and poverty. Their emphasis on liberation is informed by the conviction that African women (and men) too have the right to lead full and rewarding lives.

In summary, one may say that liberative ethical reflection HIV and AIDS in Africa places

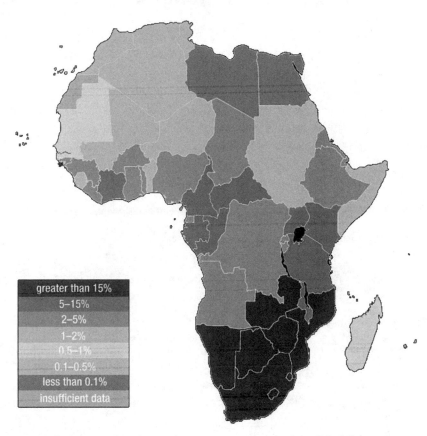

Fig. 2.2. Estimated HIV prevalence among young adults (15–49) by country in 2008.

emphasis on justice, responsibility, and compassion. In particular, it challenges men to become more responsible and caring in the face of the epidemic. Authors within this strand of African ethics are keen to counter stigma and discrimination, promote access to treatment and care, and highlight that a broader social justice perspective is more illuminating than the preoccupation with personal morality.

Leading Scholars and Figures

As previously indicated, the field of African liberative ethics is still emerging; nonetheless, as the foregoing sections indicate, scholars have

reflected on existential issues that confront Africans and have proffered some creative proposals. Some of the leading voices include Bénézet Bujo, Mogobe Ramose, and, although steeped in biblical and gender studies, Musa W. Dube. Nyambura J. Njoroge has called for a feminist ethic of resistance and transformation. Rogate Mshana has been consistent in the quest for economic justice, as have been emerging voices, which include Munyaradzi F. Murove, Fainos Mangena, Puleng LenkaBula and Domoka L. Manda. (The latter two are women ethicists.) Essentially, these are postcolonial African scholars who are determined to contribute to Africa's total liberation.

A form-critical analysis of the publications indicates that practitioners begin with a social and historical analysis. The social analysis is critical

Liberative Ethics in Action: The Issue of HIV and AIDS

Sub-Saharan Africa carries a disproportionate HIV and AIDS burden. Annual AIDS Epidemic Updates issued by UNAIDS in Geneva consistently show the region as having the highest infections and as suffering the most AIDS-related deaths in comparison to other regions. Furthermore, the number of people on life-saving medication is consistently low. The HIV and AIDS epidemic exposes fundamental injustices that characterize the contemporary world. It lays bare the rape of Africa's resources, the unsustainable character of globalization, the skewed nature of north-south relationships, the imbalances in gender relationships, unjust power structures, and poor governance systems. One of the most consistent commentators on the epidemic in Africa, Father Michael Kelly, a Catholic priest from Zambia, forcefully maintains that the epidemic emerges from an unjust world. He observes that millions of human beings have been kept in a state of captivity and have not been able to exercise their rights. He charges that the factors that sponsor the epidemic are opposed to human and religious interpretations of justice, as these put emphasis on liberation from oppression.

During the early phase of the HIV and AIDS epidemic (1980s–1990s), there was an emphasis on individual morality. It was believed that individuals simply needed to uphold high levels of discipline in the area of sexuality. The formula was: avoid casual and irresponsible sexual behavior, and you will not get infected. In particular, religious organizations sought to promote the model of abstinence and faithfulness in relationships. The same religious organizations have generally been opposed to the use of condoms. Liberative ethics challenges the preoccupation with individual morality. Instead, it places emphasis on structural factors that make individuals vulnerable to HIV. It undertakes social and historical analysis to understand vulnerability. For example, it examines patterns of labor migration in sub-Saharan Africa and the region's economic marginalization in order to appreciate its vulnerability. It also looks at historical factors that have given rise to migrant labor and how these have influenced the spread of the epidemic.

African liberative ethics asks critical and rather uncomfortable (to those in power) questions, such as: Why do most people living with HIV in Europe and North America tend to live, while those in sub-Saharan Africa die? Who gets antiretroviral therapy and who decides when treatment should be stopped? Who dies and who cares? Why are women more vulnerable to HIV? Why is there a reduction in funding when millions of black Africans are staring death in the face?

Liberative ethics is therefore concerned with "structures of sin" that render individuals vulnerable to HIV and AIDS. It seeks to move from scorn and pity to justice. Liberative ethics therefore seeks to ensure that the rights and dignity of people living with HIV are upheld, that all those who must have access to treatment do so, and that communities and nations become more responsible in addressing the epidemic. In this quest, liberative ethics challenges the stigmatization of people living with HIV and the resistance to the use of life-saving preventive strategies. Its central preoccupation is to ensure that all human beings have a high-quality life in the present. Integral to its approach is the conviction that human beings should not die while we wait for convincing ethical theories to be crafted!

because it lays bare the contemporary situation in which Africans find themselves. However, the historical analysis is equally vital. From there, ethical precepts that promote liberation are proffered.

Possible Future Trends

There are new voices emerging within the field, as noted above. These younger scholars seek to retain contextual relevance. They are likely to continue to reflect on the significance of indigenous ethical concepts to Africa's liberation and development. Since the question of postcolonial governance remains critical, they are likely to address it in their research and publication. However, they are also likely to tackle emerging issues such as masculinity. What does it mean to be a man in contemporary Africa? What are some of the key ethical values that a contemporary African man needs to embody?

European and American philosophers have been quite influential in the teaching of philosophy in Africa. As African philosophy continues to decolonize, African traditions are likely to gain greater acceptance. One can therefore surmise that in the future, scholars will pay greater attention to liberative practices and concepts within African traditions. More African liberative ethics will emerge, even as African scholars will continue to relate to scholars in other settings.

Earlier on in this chapter, a passing reference was made to the fact that there are very few women in African philosophy. Although most disciplines in Africa are male-dominated, in the case of African philosophy the situation is worse. Historical, cultural, and religious factors that lie beyond the scope of this chapter are responsible for this unacceptable situation. As more women gain access to higher education, it is likely that feminist reflections will increase and deepen African liberative ethics.

African liberative ethics summons Africans to shake off their lethargy, deploy their agency, and work for their total liberation. Addressing themes such as the continent's economic marginalization, land hunger, postcolonial governance, patriarchy, and HIV, scholars in this area have sought to mobilize Africans to continue to fight for freedom and dignity. In this chapter, we have examined the battles within these sites of struggle as well as the ethical principles that have been proffered. In the face of many options for death, Africans continue to steadfastly choose life.

Study Questions

1. Discuss the contention that African history provides the basis for African liberative ethics.
2. "If African philosophy does not exist, it follows with necessity that African liberative ethics is non-existent." Debate this assertion.
3. "Excluding ethical reflections by nonblack scholars who are based in Africa is discriminatory, driven by ideology, and therefore unacceptable." Critically examine this statement.
4. Using examples, illustrate how the theme of HIV and AIDS brings together issues relating to Africa's marginalization in the global economy, land hunger, postcolonial governance, and the struggle against patriarchy.
5. Identify reasons why there are very few African women scholars operating within African philosophy.

Suggested Readings

Adeyemo, Tokunboh. *Is Africa Cursed? A Vision for the Radical Transformation of an Ailing Continent.* Nairobi: WordAlive, 2009.

Ambasa-Shisanya, Constance. "Widowhood and HIV Transmission in Siaya District, Kenya." In

Compassionate Circles: African Women Theologians Facing HIV. Edited by Ezra Chitando and Nontando Hadebe. Geneva: World Council of Churches, 2009.

Bujo, Bénézet. "Ecology and Ethical Responsibility from an African Perspective." In *African Ethics: An Anthology of Comparative and Applied Ethics.* Edited by Munyaradzi F. Murove. Pietermaritzburg: University of KwaZulu-Natal Press, 2009.

Chitando, Ezra. "Towards Land Answers? Spirituality, Reconciliation and Resettlement in Zimbabwe." *Bulletin for Contextual Theology in Africa* 5, no. 3 (1998): 55–60.

———. *Troubled but Not Destroyed.* Geneva: World Council of Churches, 2009.

Coetze, P. H., and A. P. J. Roux, eds. *The African Philosophy Reader.* 2nd ed. London: Routledge, 2003.

Dube, Musa W. "Theological Challenges: Proclaiming the Fullness of Life in the HIV/AIDS & Global Economic Era." *International Review of Mission* 91, no. 363 (2002): 535–49.

Esack, Farid, and Sarah Chiddy, eds. *Islam and AIDS: Between Scorn, Pity and Justice.* Oxford: Oneworld, 2009.

Eze, Emmanuel C., ed. *Postcolonial African Philosophy: A Reader.* Malden, MA: Blackwell, 1997.

Filibus, Musa P. "Justice not Greed: Biblical Perspectives on Ethical Deficits of the Present Global Financial System." In *Justice Not Greed.* Edited by Pamela Brubaker and Rogate Mshana. Geneva: World Council of Churches, 2010.

Katongole, Emmanuel. *The Sacrifice of Africa: A Political Theology for Africa.* Grand Rapids: Eerdmans, 2011.

Kelly, Michael J. *HIV and AIDS: A Social Justice Perspective.* Nairobi: Paulines Publications Africa, 2010.

Khoza, Reuel J. *Attuned Leadership: African Humanism as a Moral Compass.* Johannesburg: Penguin, 2011.

Kunhiyop, Samuel W. *African Christian Ethics.* Nairobi: WordAlive, 2008.

Manda, Domoka L. "Religions and the Responsibility of Men in relation to HIV and Gender-Based Violence: An Ethical Call." *Journal of Constructive Theology* 15, no. 2 (2009): 23–40.

Mangena, Fainos. "Aristotle, Patriotism and Reason: Reflections on MacIntyre's Question—Is Patriotism a Virtue?" *Phronimon: Journal of the South African Society for Greek Philosophy and the Humanities* 11, no. 2 (2010): 35–48.

Mawondo, Simon. "In Search of Social Justice: Reconciliation and the Land Question in Zimbabwe." In *The Struggles after the Struggle: Zimbabwean Philosophical Studies.* Edited by David Kaulemu. Washington, DC: The Council for Research in Values and Philosophy, 2006.

Mshana, Rogate R., ed. *Poverty, Wealth and Ecology: The Impact of Economic Globalization: A Background to the Study Process.* Geneva: World Council of Churches, 2008.

Murove, Munyaradzi F., ed. *African Ethics: An Anthology of Comparative and Applied Ethics.* Pietermaritzburg: University of KwaZulu-Natal Press, 2009.

New African. January, Issue 513. London, 2012. Cover Story, Niger Delta, 10–22.

Nicholson, Ronald, ed. *Persons in Community: African Ethics in a Global Culture.* Scottsville: University of KwaZulu-Natal, 2008.

Njoroge, Nyambura J. "Daughters and Sons of Africa: Seeking Life-Giving and Empowering Leadership in the Age of HIV/AIDS Pandemic." In *Women, Religion and HIV/AIDS in Africa: Responding to Ethical and Theological Challenges.* Edited by T. M. Hinga et al. Pietermaritzburg: Cluster, 2008.

Palmer, Robin. *The Context of Land Management and Reform in Southern Africa.* London: The Royal Institute of Surveyors, 1995.

Prozesky, Martin H. "Cinderella, Survivor and Saviour: African Ethics and the Quest for a Global Ethic." In *African Ethics: An Anthology of Comparative and Applied Ethics.* Edited by Munyaradzi F. Murove. Pietermaritzburg: University of KwaZulu-Natal Press, 2009.

Rukuni, Mandivamba. *Being Afrikan: Rediscovering the Traditional Unhu-Ubuntu-Botho Pathways of Being Human.* Arcadia, SA: Mandala, 2007.

Shutte, Augustine. *Ubuntu: An Ethic for a New South Africa.* Pietermaritzburg: Cluster Publications, 2001.

Wiredu, Kwasi, ed. *A Companion to African Philosophy.* Oxford: Blackwell, 2004.

Asian Liberative Ethics

Keun-Joo Christine Pae

ASIA, THE LARGEST CONTINENT on earth, embraces more than three billion people, seven different language zones, and diverse political and cultural systems and religions, including but not limited to Buddhism, Hinduism, Christianity, Islam, Confucianism, and Taoism. Since racial/ ethnic, linguistic, cultural, and religious diversity is what makes Asian liberative discourse distinctively Asian, it is impossible to summarize or generalize Asian liberative ethics. Therefore, this chapter explores Asian liberative ethics revolving around the Christian theology of liberation.

Asian liberative ethicists understand (1) that the heart of religious ethics is justice, and (2) that justice is revealed through people's concrete experiences of oppression. Liberation specifically highlights the political and theological visions and activism (praxis) practiced by those whose works are grounded in grassroots movements in various Asian regions. Many theologians of liberation are from South Korea, Taiwan, Hong Kong, India, the Philippines, and Sri Lanka, where strong local churches have played important roles in leading political and economic liberation movements. In addition, Asian liberation ethics is communal by nature—Asian liberationists articulate

their identities, theologies, and political activism within their particular communities, in solidarity with others who struggle for liberation.

BOX 3.1

Asian Social Justice

Social justice has been a driving force for Asians, both religious and secular, in creating political activism for liberation from (neo)colonialism, globalized capitalism, military dictatorship, sexism, racism, religious authoritarianism, and so on. As a religious minority (3 percent of the Asian population is Christian), Asian Christian liberationists have also found resources for liberation in other religions practiced by the Asian majority. In Asia, religion involves a way of living rather than merely academic discourse. Therefore, any Asian Christian liberationists appreciate the presence of religious diversity and its impact on Christian thought concerning social justice and liberation.

Basic Tenets of Asian Liberative Ethics

Christian theology in the Asian context is politically theological and ethical. For many Asian liberationists, theology must respond to the political context in which people have lived and shown a liberative way of being. The beginning of Asian liberative ethics corresponded to the oppressed Asian masses—their reading of the Bible and critiques of the social structures. These people are Dalits (India), Minjung (South Korea), indigenous people, colonized women and men, factory workers, sex workers, and landless farmers, to name but a few.

Between 1945 and 1960, most Asian countries won independence from their European, American, and Japanese colonialists. These newly independent Asian countries aimed to autonomously affirm Asian identity, specifically culturally, religiously, and politically. The Bandung Conference of 1955, sponsored by Indonesia, Pakistan, Burma (Myanmar), Ceylon (Sri Lanka), and India was the defining event for newly independent countries. Asian and African leaders strategically adopted the self-affirmative identity of the "third world." Unfortunately, the spirit of Bandung declined in the 1960s, for most political leaders who were present at the conference no longer held political power, and the Vietnam War ultimately succeeded in dividing Asia between Communist and the capitalist blocs. Nonetheless, the self-determined identity of the third world has been generally circulated among liberation theologians. Asia's "third worldness" connects Asia to other continents in the struggle for liberation.

The Second Vatican Council and the emergence of Latin American liberation theology in the 1960s and in the early 1970s stimulated Asian liberation theologians to articulate liberationist voices in various Asian contexts. For the last four decades, Asian liberation theologies have

BOX 3.2

Bandung Conference

In the Indonesian city of Bandung, twenty-nine Asian and African countries participated in the Bandung Conference. The conference helped these countries found the modern identity politics of race, religion, and nationality by declaring and accepting third world status, aligning neither with the USSR-led Communist bloc nor with the US-led free market democratic bloc.

contributed to worldwide theological discourse. Various Christian faith-based organizations born in the 1960s through the 1980s proliferated Asian liberation theologies, rooted in various popular resistances of neocolonialism, military dictatorship, gender-based oppression, and so on. These organizations include the Ecumenical Association of Third World Theologians (EATWOT), Christian Conference of Asia (CCA), the World Student Christian Federation (WSCF) Asia-Pacific Region, the Asia and Pacific Alliance of YMCAs, Asian Women's Resource Center, Indian Social Institute, Christian Institute for the Study of Religion and Society, and the Center for Society and Religion, as well as various grassroots organizations. The history of these organizations suggests that Asian liberation theologies are a collaborative work, and in consistent dialogue with liberation theologies from Africa, Latin America, and racial/ethnic minorities in North America.

The global network of third world liberation theologians, EATWOT, was born in Dar es Salaam, Tanzania, in 1976. Various revolutionary movements in Asia, Latin America, Africa, and the United States in the 1960s spiritually awakened the third world theologians, who expressed rebellion against unjust domination and exercise of power. EATWOT Asian theologians have provided a strong challenge to Christian theology by drawing out the particular differences of Asia compared to other parts of the world. Asian theological issues are articulated based on the critical observation of socioeconomic, political, and religious-cultural realities that have affected the lives of the people for centuries. These realities include the persistent poverty of the majority of Asians, diverse colonial experiences, political and military tension between political ideologies (e.g., Communism vs. capitalism), and religious diversity and conflict. Among the EATWOT, Asia's theological issues were human dignity, theo-ethical methodology, liberation spirituality, interfaith praxis, and indigenous peoples' liberation.

Before the birth of EATWOT, the CCA had supported Asian liberation theologians' collaborative work and struggles for liberation. Having first begun as the East Asia Christian Conference (Kuala Lumpur, Malaysia, in 1959), the CCA focused on the ecumenical movements among denominationally diverse Asian churches; the liberative practices of Christian worship; the contextualized and liberative interpretation of the Bible with focus on the meanings of Jesus Christ and Christianity in Asia; and the church's roles in liberation for the marginalized and the oppressed in Asia.

The WSCF Asia-Pacific has been working especially on ecumenical leadership of young Asian people, specifically student empowerment for social and personal transformation, human rights and solidarity work, and gender and sexual equality. Founded in 1895, the WSCF is the oldest Christian ecumenical organization. Its Asia-Pacific chapter includes the sixteen members of Student Christian Movement, which began as a grassroots organization for sociopolitical liberation in various Asian countries. Not surprisingly, college students have been vital forces in various political-revolutionary movements in Asia when repressive regimes restricted people's freedom and equality.

Asian feminist theology and movements have been active in the major international organizations mentioned above. Refusing to consider women's liberation and feminist theology secondary to theological reflection on political and economic liberation, Asian feminist theologians have articulated their particular experiences of oppression caused by patriarchal interpretation and practice of major world religions, poverty, patriarchal culture, the caste system, and so on. In response to Asian women's need for a safe space for theological work and feminist activism, the Asian Women's Resource Center (AWRC) was born in 1987. The AWRC and the Asian women's commission at EATWOT and WSCF Asia-Pacific have expressed special theological concerns for ecofeminism, human sexuality, ageism, women's bodies, military sexual exploitation of women, reproductive choices, and other issues that have not been discussed enough in most Asian countries.

Asian liberative ethics have been developed not only through national and international institutions but also and more importantly through local churches, grassroots theological institutes, small Bible study meetings, and peoples' movements for liberation. These grassroots movements have made Asian liberative ethics productive and practical.

Need for Liberation

Although the faces of oppression vary according to region, the common issues for liberative ethics include the economic structure and its resulting poverty, the political system, gender hierarchy, ecological destruction, religious conflict, racism, transnational migration, and militarism.

Liberation from Systemic Poverty

More than 80 percent of the Asian population lives in poverty, often without clean water, sanitation systems, decent houses, or enough food. Women and children are the most vulnerable in this exploitive market system. Asia's systemic poverty, originating from European colonialism, has been sustained by globalized capitalism (neocolonialism) since World War II. Systemic poverty is what connects Asia to the rest of third world. During the colonial periods, Asia offered raw materials for the industrial development of European colonialists and became the market for their finished products. Asia's economic dependence on the European market did not end with the Asian countries' independence. The International Monetary Fund and the World Trade Organization have controlled the Asian market economy through development projects and international loans. The Asian economic crisis of 1997 that began in Malaysia demonstrated Asia's economic dependency on the global money market. Asia still offers cheap labor and raw materials for developed countries in Europe, North America, and now in the more developed countries of Asia itself.

For the last three decades, several Asian countries' economic development has been dramatic. Besides Japan, whose economic progress is well known, South Korea, Singapore, Hong Kong, and Taiwan have been referred to as "four little dragons" for their miraculous economic development. Malaysia, Indonesia, and Thailand have modestly increased their national wealth. The economic development of China has turned the country into an emerging market with high purchasing power, yet the country is the world's factory, sustained by cheap labor and raw materials. The increasing gap between the rich and the poor threatens social security and sustainability in China. India's economy has grown fast, and has emerged as a new power in information technology. The economic disparity in India is scandalous: while India's richest man built the world's most expansive house for his family, 25 percent of the world's poor who are hungry live in India.

In sum, Asian liberative ethicists consider at least four major faces of systemic poverty in their critical theological reflection: (1) the Asian economy's dependency on exploitative international capitalism; (2) economic disparity among Asian countries; (3) the increasing gap between the rich and the poor on a domestic and on an international level; and (4) the persistence of scandalous poverty among Asian masses.

Authoritarian Political System

Most Asian countries have experienced military coups and autocratic governments that severely oppress freedom of speech, of publication, and of assembly. Burma has been ruled by the military authoritarian government since the military coup d'état in 1962. Burma's neighboring countries, including Pakistan and Bangladesh, faced bloodless military coup d'états followed by military dictatorships. South Korea experienced brutal military regimes led by three dictators from 1961 through 1992. Both Indonesia and the Philippines went through more than twenty years of dictatorial rule, Suharto (1967–1998) and Ferdinand Marcos (1965–1986) respectively. From 1950 to 1975, Taiwan was under Chiang Kai-shek's martial law, which restricted political freedom. Pol Pot conducted the killing of three-quarters of the Cambodian population from 1975 through 1979. China, North Korea, Vietnam, and Laos also add restricted political freedom to the Asian history of human indignity.

These authoritarian regimes have often been supported by religious powers, who led the massacres for ethnic, class, and religious cleansings. Since most Asians share the tragedies caused by repressive political regimes, their liberative ethics expresses people's collective desire for justice, freedom, and peace, and articulates how to embody these values within their respective societies.

War, Armed Conflict, and Militarism

Before emerging as an economic market or tourist destination, Asia was considered a war zone. During the Cold War period, Asia was the battleground where the two different political ideologies of capitalism and Communism violently clashed, causing the Korean War (1950–1953) and the Vietnam War (1955–1975). Civil wars, small and large armed conflicts due to territorial disputes, different religious ideologies, and racial/ethnic conflicts, military coup d'états, and ongoing wars in Iraq and Afghanistan are all additions to the history of war in Asia.

For the second half of the twentieth century, Asian countries were competitively militarized. The United States has been deeply involved in militarization of the Asia-Pacific region. United States armed forces have been stationed in Japan and South Korea since World War II. The Subic Bay of the Philippines was an important naval base for the United States until 1992. Poor Asians in the rural areas and in Pacific Islands lost their land and property to the military bases. Hence, liberative ethics in the Asian context cannot ignore the suffering of human beings and other living creatures caused by war and militarism.

Oppressive Religious Ideologies

Although religious diversity gives Asia the appearance of a mystically spiritual place, these diverse religions have caused sociopolitical and economic exploitation and gender hierarchy for centuries.

Fig. 3.1. My Tho, Vietnam. A suspected Viet Cong base camp is being torched. In the foreground is Private First Class Rumpa, C Company, 3rd Battalion, 47th Infantry, 9th Infantry Division, with a 45-pound 90mm recoiless rifle, April 5, 1968.

Violence against the Muslim minority in India and in the southern Philippines, against Christian and Hindu minorities in Pakistan, Buddhists in Nepal, as well as the tension between Buddhists and Christians in South Korea are the realities of Asia's religious situation.

Liberation from Asia's religious realities is four-fold. First, liberation from religious conflict and the development of peaceful engagement among the different religions is necessary for ordinary people, who have been exposed to religious violence. Second, Orientalist approaches to Asian religions, especially Hinduism and Buddhism, and Western-biased understandings of Islam must be liberated through Asians' critical analysis of their religious texts and practices, as well as through the redis-covery of the liberative powers in these traditions. Third, Asian churches should be liberated from missionary Christianity, which portrays Asians as an inferior race due to their non-Christian ori-gins, emphasizes individual salvation, and is inter-linked to bourgeois morality and to economic and political powers. Fourth, religious ideologies, doctrines, interpretation, and rituals that sustain the exploitative political and economic structure must be liberated both through scholarly analysis and through social movements. Although Chris-tianity has been the main subject of criticism and transformation by Asian liberation theologians, they agree on the importance of scrutinizing all religions practiced in Asia. Asian feminist theo-logians in particular have successfully analyzed how patriarchal ideologies ingrained in religion have sustained the cultural and structural violence against women. Their analysis, however, is often criticized by the nationalists, who view feminism as a Western colonialist influence.

Exploitation of Women — Patriarchal Oppression

Not only Asian feminist theo-ethicists but also male liberation theologians accentuate the impor-tance of women's liberation from religious, cul-tural, economic, political, and sexual violence in order to transform Asia into a more just society. Asian feminists illustrate the various faces of inequality and exploitation that women experi-ence. In Pakistan and Nepal, 80 percent of women are illiterate, and in some parts of India and Ban-gladesh, about three-quarters of women can barely read.

Economic exploitation of female labor is com-monly found in Asian countries. Women are employed in mostly low-skilled or semiskilled manufacturing jobs, in retail, and in the service sector. Even in industrialized Asian countries, the wage system illustrates gender inequality. In Korea, women earn 70 percent of what men earn in the same business sector, in Taiwan about 60 percent, and in Hong Kong, 74 percent. In the agricultural sector of the world market, many Asian women are producing large-scale cash crops such as rice, fruit, flowers, and vegetables for export and are working on tea or sugar plan-tations without dreaming of going to school or enjoying a cup of the finest Ceylon tea.

In addition, many Asian women are sexually exploited. The economy of Thailand, notoriously known as the world's brothel, has been sustained by sex tourism at the cost of the bodies of poor women and girls. Around US military bases in South Korea, Japan, and the Philippines, local women sell their bodies for American soldiers and Western tourists. Although these women are consistently exposed to sexual and physi-cal violence, psychological abuse, and economic exploitation, they have been silenced for the sake of international security. Even in the 1970s, the South Korean government secretly supervised US military prostitution and sex tourism in order to secure the influx of foreign currency for the country's economic development. Similar govern-mental intervention occurred in both the Philip-pines and Thailand. The boom of the sex industry in various Asian countries accelerates transna-tional migration of sex laborers and exacerbates human trafficking of poor young women and girls, especially from South Asia, Central Asia, and Southeast Asia.

Religious and cultural ideologies often make economic and sexual exploitation of women possible. The mainstream teachings from major institutionalized world religions indoctrinate inferiority of women and name the virtues of women in relation to chastity and responsibilities for family. The doctrinal teaching of women's inferiority forces women to be submissive to social, economic, political, and family authorities. This perception of the virtues of women ostracizes female sex workers while simultaneously forcing women to find any available jobs, including sex work, in order to support their families.

Ecological Destruction

Asian liberation theologies articulate the importance of protecting the environment from ruthless economic development. Differently from the anthropocentric perspective on nature in mainstream Christian doctrines, Buddhism, Hinduism, Taoism, and indigenous-folk religions teach unity between humanity and nature.

Uncontrollable economic development in most Asian countries has destroyed the environment, polluting the air quality, drinking water, and soil. Environmental deterioration exacerbates poverty—landless farmers join the urban slums or find low-skilled factory jobs; factory workers are exposed to the hazardous environment, losing their health for a meager earning; and poor people make their lives in landfills, where global trash is imported. Besides economic development at the cost of environmental destruction, excessive militarization and armed conflicts have destabilized the ecological system. Most recently, the explosion of the nuclear power plant in Fukushima revealed the danger of nuclear power that requires theo-ethical reflection and action.

The "theology of life" articulated by Asian liberative ethicists accentuates the necessity of liberating all living beings from ecological destruction.

BOX 3.3

Waste

China is the world's dumping ground. In 2004, the country imported 4.1 million tons of waste plastics, 12.3 million tons of used paper, 10.22 million tons of scrap iron, 3.95 million tons of copper scrap, and 1.2 million tons of aluminum scrap, accounting for more than 90 percent of imports from Asia (34.8 percent), Europe (15.2 percent), North America (34.2 percent), and neighboring countries (8.3 percent).

The liberative message of theology of life is deeply rooted in traditional Asian religious teachings of "reverence for life."

Racism and Transnational Migration

While "Asian" is a single racial category in the United States, this Western generalization of the diverse Asian population does not reveal the particularities and racial discrimination found in the real Asian context. In India, the caste system is interwoven with whiteness. The whiter skin a person has, the nobler she or he is. In East Asia's metropolitan cities, white skin is desired among young women.

Migrant workers are the victims of Asian racism. For example, Filipina, Thai, and Indonesian domestic workers in Singapore, Hong Kong, and Saudi Arabia experience racial discrimination. Recently, the execution of an Indonesian domestic worker in Saudi Arabia escalated the diplomatic conflict between the two countries. Dark-skinned migrant workers and Southeast Asian women who immigrate to South Korea through marriage often endure severe racism and anti-immigration law. Japan continues to discriminate against foreign migrants by denying them naturalization or legal protection from violence, and by calling them "third world people." Racism in relation to transnational migration is a recently emerging issue and awaits critical theological reflection.

Indigenous tribes in India, the Philippines, Taiwan, and Japan experienced near genocide. In the 1980s, Japanese liberation theology arose in the context of the Ainu, Okinawans, Korean residents, and the Burkakumin people (the so-called invisible race or outcasts), who are discriminated against on the basis of the concept of "ceremonial pollution."

Issues and Questions in Asian Liberative Ethics

Critically approaching the systemic injustice against human beings and nature, Asian liberationist ethicists accentuate that different forms of injustice are interconnected. At the general assembly in Oaxtepec, Mexico, in 1986, EATWOT Asian liberation theologians delineated the theological task for the liberation of the Asian people from exploitative sociopolitical, economic, patriarchal, and ecological systems. This theological task leads Asian liberation theologians to contemplate the meanings of "doing theology." "Doing" has at least two basic meanings: First, Asian liberation theology comes out of life in practice; and second, "doing" means that something is always in process. "Doing theology" highlights the theological methodology, namely praxis, commonly shared among diverse liberation theo-ethicists across the globe.

The Asian masses' experiences of injustice require Asian theologians to seek an alternative way of articulating and practicing theology. Seeking out this alternative way, Asian liberative ethicists must first wrestle with the meanings of sin and salvation in the Asian context. Criticizing privatized sin and redemption based on the image of a retributive God, they pay attention to

social sin—that is, the collective human participation in exploitative social structures that requires the redemption of humanity as a whole from the vicious cycle of oppression. God is revealed and met in the collective human commitment and effort to redeem and to transform social structures.

Second, this understanding of social sin and redemption further expands the perspective of liberative Christology. Asian liberation theologians arduously contemplate Jesus Christ; his salvific roles in the history of people's struggles for liberation in Asia; as well as the historical realities of the liberationist movements of the marginalized in Jesus' own time. The historical Jesus becomes transcendental, as Asian people are transforming the exploitative social structures into more just forms. These Asian margins' liberation movements liberate Jesus from the Eurocentric doctrine of privatized sin and redemption. Furthermore, Jesus becomes the Christ, the savior in the process of liberation; when Christianity empowers those in the Asian margins to liberate themselves from the multiple layers of oppression.

Third, Jesus Christ, the liberator, inevitably leads Asian liberative ethicists to articulate who Jesus is within Asia's diverse religions and cultures. Jesus does not liberate Asians from non-Christian religions or cultures. As the liberator, who shares suffering and redemption with Asian masses, Jesus encounters diverse Asian religions and cultures. In the process of liberation, other religious individuals meet and understand Jesus through their own religious experiences of liberation. Here, Asian liberationists emphasize that Hinduism, Buddhism, Islam, Taoism, and others also have potential resources of liberation for the marginalized. Therefore, the Christian missionary zeal should be liberated from the narrow-minded notion of conversion into institutionalized Christianity. Jesus, however, can convert the minds of Asians into liberation through the notion of the transformation of society into the kingdom of

God. Just as Gandhi rediscovered Hindu nonviolent resistance through the studies of Jesus, this form of conversion should allow other religious Asians to articulate who Jesus is to them in the process of their journeys to liberation.

Fourth, Asia's religious and cultural realities further enable Asian liberation theo-ethicists to practice interfaith dialogue and activism. They wrestle with the liberative roles of the church in multireligious and cultural contexts. In their theological reflection, Christians do not stand against or over Asian religions or cultures but cooperate with and respect Asia's old religious traditions. Liberation of people, especially from oppressive religious ideologies, is only possible through interfaith dialogue and social activism.

Fifth, Asian liberationists, both the secular and the religious, have been delineating the postcolonial identity of Asia since World War II. Postcolonialism is an effort to liberate Christianity from European colonialist interpretation. Criticizing the Western church's biased concerns for enculturation of the gospel in Asia, Asian liberationists debunk the early church's appropriation of Hellenistic philosophy and Greco-Roman culture. The postcolonial lens enables Asian liberative ethicists to liberate the Bible from colonialist interpretation. Imperial desire and the nationalist agenda in the Christian Bible must be analyzed in order for the Bible to deliver the message of liberation for the colonized, articulate the margins as the autonomous moral agents in the history of liberation, and destabilize colonialist power. Since colonialism is a political, economic, religious, cultural, and ideological process, liberation requires the transformation of both the whole person and the whole society.

Furthermore, postcolonialism generates a transnational lens. Due to globalized Westernization, twenty-first-century Asia is not the "authentic" Asia and, at the same time, is not "Western" enough. Asian culture, religion, and people are falling in between. As Kwok Pui-Lan says, this "in-between" space opens up new possibilities for negotiating identity, exploring cultural hybridity and articulating different cultural practices and priorities.

Sixth, all of these ways of doing theology should be scrutinized through gender analysis. Asian women know the meanings of justice and liberation through their experiences of poverty, sexual exploitation, religious oppression, and so on. Women's liberation is not a token to Asian liberation alone, but it should be at the core of the liberation of all humanity. Furthermore, Asian feminist ethicists have contributed to theological contemplation on the liberation of nonhuman entities. Specifically, Asian ecofeminists articulate life-saving wisdom ingrained in Asian folktales, religions, dancing, arts, and literature. For example, Korean ecofeminists, *salimist*, rediscover that women's everyday house chores (*salim* in Korean) such as cooking, washing dishes, cleaning, taking care of the plants and animals, growing vegetables, and so on are activities to revere and nurture these various living beings. *Salim* in Korean means "keeping things alive." Analyzing the similarity between exploitation of mother earth and that of women, these feminists accentuate that human liberation is intrinsically connected to that of all living creatures.

Finally, Asian liberative ethics has wrestled with how to achieve liberation regarding practicality and efficacy. While various forms of violence, including that of military power, are present in Asia, an ongoing theological question is whether to resist through nonviolence. Although the majority of Asian liberative ethicists advocate nonviolence as a desired way to achieve peace and justice, the use of violence by the powerless is ethically justified by some. Even among the advocates of nonviolence, the methods of nonviolence are varied. Nonetheless, Asian liberation theologians agree that nonviolent peacemaking requires not only physical practice but also spiritual changes in the activists. In addition, nonviolent peacemaking is the space where interfaith praxis happens in a productive way.

Current Themes and Methodologies

Asian liberation theologians consider methodology central to theology. Most Asian ethicists agree that (1) commitment to social justice is the first act of doing theology, (2) social analysis is an indicator of the signs of the times, and (3) the process of doing theology is action-reflection-action. Common methodology helps Asian liberative ethicists respond to their particular social, political, and economic situations. Since Asian liberationists articulate their theological and ethical concerns through collaborative work, and the political situations are varied from country to country, it is difficult to pin down the leading Asian liberation theologians, ethicists, or schools. Only a small number of Asian liberation theo-ethicists are to be introduced here, with a focus on four political-theological-ethical trends in the Asian context: Korean Minjung theology, Indian Dalit theology, Asian feminist theology, and interfaith/enculturated approaches to liberation.

Minjung Theology

The Korean term *Minjung* means "common people," or the masses of Koreans who are deprived of basic human rights in both the political and socioeconomic realms. During the regime of military dictator Park Jung-Hee in the 1960s and 1970s, Minjung theology arose out of a theological commitment to the people's movement for human rights, democratization, and social and economic justice. Historically speaking, the Japanese occupation (1910–1945), the Korean War (1950–1953), the division between North and South Korea, the US military's presence in South Korea, the massacre during the Gwang Ju revolution for

democratization (1980), and the economic domination of superpowers in Korea exacerbate the Minjung's suffering. Methodologically, Minjung theology uncovers the suffering and liberative stories of the Minjung (or Minjung biography) in its critique of the so-called Western logical way of theologizing.

In the 1970s–1980s, the Korean students' movements were assimilated within the concept of Marxist social revolution toward a classless egalitarian society and working-class-dominated democracy. While using Marxist social analysis, Minjung theologians question the theological appropriation of Marxism. In the Korean context, Marxist social analysis and its vision of a proletariat society do not effectively correspond to the theopolitical task for the reunification of the Koreas beyond their ideological differences. Marxist hostility toward religion is also considered inadequate to articulate social changes in South Korea, where Confucianism, Buddhism, Shamanism, and Christianity are culturally and religiously alive. A Marxist class analysis does not properly uncover the multiple layers of the suffering the Minjung have experienced, specifically politically, culturally, religiously, colonially, and militarily.

As an analytic tool of historically accumulated suffering of the Minjung, Korean theologians propose the concept of *han*—accumulated deep sorrow of people. *Han* is a terrible physical and spiritual injustice committed against a person or groups of people. Where sin is committed, *han* arises as its corollary; therefore, by naming the realities of *han*, we can begin to heal the victims of sin rather than condemn them, which will initiate a new journey of solidarity toward a theology of *han*-liberation.

Distinguishing political messianism from messianic politics, Kim Yong-Bock argues that the Minjung transcend the narrow and self-contained entity of the proletariat (which is ultimately political messianism propagandized by the Communist elites). The Minjung realize their subjectivity in social transformation, while their suffering and struggling for liberation unfold the history between the times of "not yet" and "the already." The politics of Jesus and other messianic traditions in Korea make the Minjung the subject of their own historical destiny, struggling for justice, *koinonia*, and *shalom* to come (messianic politics lived by the Minjung). Proposing Minjung-dominated liberation, Kim avoids both Communist totalitarianism and the Western/Korean trap of anti-Communism.

Minjung theology is indebted to Kim Chi-Ha, a Catholic lay writer and political activist in the 1970s. Kim's short play *The Golden-Crowned Jesus* inspired Korean theologians to meditate on the suffering and liberation of the Minjung in light of Jesus' suffering and liberation. In this play, Jesus is forced to be confined in a cement statue with a golden crown by the political, economic, and religious powers. He is liberated from his deep silence and sorrow when the downtrodden, such as beggars, factory workers, and poor peasants, challenge his salvific roles in their society. Although Jesus asks the downtrodden to share his golden crown that imprisons him, political, economic, and religious authorities snatch the crown from the hands of people and put it back on the cement statue of Jesus. Jesus returns to the prison of the expressionless cement statue, and those who had liberated Jesus are arrested. *The Golden-Crowned Jesus* satirically described South Korea in the 1970s; although political authorities suppressed people, and religious authorities silenced them, the Minjung never ceased to speak loudly with their cry for liberation.

Incorporating Kim's play in his Minjung theology, Ahn Byung-Mu compares the *ochlos* ("crowd" in Greek) frequently used in the Gospels (Mark, Luke, and Matthew) to the Minjung. Ahn argues that Jesus shared his life with *ochlos*, the crowd (beggars, prostitutes, tax collectors, lepers, peasants, etc). Refusing to be bound to religious doctrines, Jesus chose to be with the Minjung in the midst of their struggle for liberation. Unlike the Christ of kerygma (the doctrinal Jesus Christ), Jesus' life of suffering and resurrection and liberative message can be fully understood only through his association with the *ochlos*'s liberation movement.

Hyun Young-Hak and Suh Nam-Dong are also leading Minjung theologians whose works are rooted in the 1970s political movements in Korea and in Korean folk tales. Notably, Hyun's major contribution is the discovery and reinterpretation of the Korean mask dance of the Minjung as the faces of the resolution of *han*. Hyun distinguishes the Minjung's *han* as "priestly" (for resignation and adjustment) and "prophetic" (for struggle and justice), while "servant-king" holds these two together with satire and laughter. The traditional mask dance of the commoners illustrates the symbols that show that the Minjung mock their oppressors and transcend their *han* in dreaming of the new society of justice.

Dalit Theology

"Dalit" is the self-affirmative identity declared by the lowest-caste people (Pariahs or Harijans) in India, often translated into English as "the untouchables," the "depressed class," or "outcasts." Dalits cannot even belong to the four social castes (Brahmins, Kshatryas, Vaisyas, and Sudras), and are the servants to upper-caste people and are considered pollution to society. Under the religious and cultural code of purity and pollution, Dalits have been ostracized from India: they are not allowed to dress like others, to drink water from the same wells that other people use, or to worship in the same temples.

Dalit theology emerged in the 1970s as Indian theologians began to take socioeconomic injustice more seriously. Both James Masey and M. E. Prabhakar, leading Dalit theologians, define Dalit theology as a prophetic theology for identification with the oppression of Dalits and as a political theology for social action toward the transformation of unjust, undemocratic, and oppressive structures. Dalits often convert to Christianity, dreaming of a casteless society. Although they make up the majority of Indian Christians, Dalits have been discriminated even in the Christian church due to the caste system's being so deeply ingrained in Indian society, as well as Indian Christian theology interpreted in light of the Brahmanic philosophy of the Hindu Vedas of the Indian elites.

For this reason, Arvind Nirmal, a pioneer in Dalit theology, argues that Indian Christianity did not bring liberation into the lives of Christian Dalits, who are the most oppressed in India. Furthermore, Indian liberation theologians who were in dialogue with Latin American liberation theology overlooked the complex socioeconomic realities of India beyond the Marxist analysis of haves versus have-nots. Critically reflecting the

Deuteronomic creed (Deut. 26:5-9) between the postexodus Israelites and God in the Dalit context, Nirmal elaborates on Dalit theology of the Trinity. Dalits' conversion to Christianity is compared to the Israelites' promise to be God's people after the exodus from the slavery in Egypt. Through conversion (the Dalits' experience of exodus), Dalits who were oppressed under the Hindu caste system become conscious of their "humanness" as beings created in the image of God (*imago Dei*). God becomes the God of Dalits. Jesus was also a Dalit in his time; just as Dalits were rejected, mocked, and ostracized, Jesus was crucified, and associated with outcasts. The Holy Spirit is the healer of all oppressed people, including Dalits. Nirmal's Dalit theology is a normative voice concerned with why the goal of Dalits' liberation is to reclaim their human dignity; why Dalit theology

Fig. 3.2. Member of Dalits in Jaipur, India.

should be articulated by Dalits and their experience of indignity; and why Dalit Christians must liberate themselves from the caste system.

To seek liberation, Dalit theologians articulate the Dalit consciousness of humanity and injustice through exploring Dalit literature, folktales, poetry, Dalit movements, and Indian mythologies. Sathianathan Clarke's studies of the communal religious life of the Paraiyar of Tamil Nadu in southern India demonstrate the community's creative interpretation of Ellaiyamman, the independent goddess to the Hindu caste system. In addition, since the drum is the symbol of resistance and of the self-affirmative collective identity of Dalits, Clarke proposes a Dalit Jesus—drum as Christ and Christ as drum.

Asian Feminist Theology

Asian feminist theology has been prolific for the last four decades. While sharing the universal goal of women's liberation for justice and equality, Asian feminist theologians pay attention to the

LIBERATIVE ETHICS IN ACTION 3.1

Liberative Ethics in Action: Operation Green Hunt

Thousands of innocent citizens are being ruthlessly killed in the name of so-called development in India. The Maoist, the forgotten people of India, are being killed and humiliated under Operation Green Hunt, using sophisticated weapons and equipment (i.e., laser range finder, thermal imaging equipment, and unmanned drones) bought from Israel to kill its own poor tribesmen. At the same time, the government-owned training camps were established to turn street dogs to hunt the poor Gondis (tribesmen). Indigenous people's lives are systematically threatened in India.

According to World Food Project, nearly 50 percent of the world's hungry live in India, a low-income, food-deficit country with "extremely low" nutritional and health indicators. Thirty-five percent of India's population—350 million people—are malnourished and do not know when or from where their next meal will come. This is India, where a third of the world's poor live, and which has worse rates of malnutrition than sub-Saharan Africa.

In terms of India's internal security, the aftermath of Hindutva (Hindu nationalists) power in Delhi was catastrophic. Hindutva fascists planted their own cronies in various governmental institutions. Although the government made enormous changes in social governance, the legacy of Hindutva's masculinist-powered nationalism continued. A large number of non-Hindus have been killed in the past few years across the country, and the numbers are steadily rising.

In response to injustice against indigenous people, poor people, and non-Hindus, Dalit theologians and interfaith grassroots organizations such as World Faith India work together for liberation. The Chipko Movement (also known as Tree Hugging Activism) is Indian women's historical movement against exploitation of natural resources in the Himalayan region. Fighting against deforestation of the Himalayas, this local women's nonviolent movement has brought ecological awareness tied with the protection of the poor, the indigenous, and women to the world.

particular historical contexts that different groups of women face. They also agree that Asian feminist theology must emerge out of Asian women's own cultural resources.

A leading Asian feminist theologian, Kwok Pui-Lan from Hong Kong elaborates on postcolonial Asian feminist theology. Kwok emphasizes the importance of Asian women's concrete experiences of injustice in their particular socioeconomic contexts. Yet, these women's issues are not merely local or particular but also transnational/global. Kwok argues that the globalized economy, militarism, and patriarchal ideologies all work hand-in-hand to exacerbate the oppression of Asian women. Therefore, Kwok accentuates the importance of global networking (transnational feminist activism) in order to peel away the multiple layers of patriarchal oppression against women.

Kwok also applies postcolonialism to biblical hermeneutics. In order to allow the Bible to be liberative for Asian women, the politics of the Bible must be examined from a feminist perspective. In other words, the biblical hermeneutics and interpretation must be scrutinized through the eyes of women, who experience European colonialism, sexism, and racism. Even feminist hermeneutics developed in the West must simultaneously consider women of color.

A Korean feminist theologian, Chung Hyun Kyung, utilizes Asian women's own cultural and religious resources in her theological thinking of liberation. In the context of Korea, Chung delivers the stories of Korean "comfort women" used by the Japanese military for sexual slavery, ostracized Korean female shamans, and so on. Chung's feminist theology articulates how these women physically and spiritually liberate themselves through their own survival wisdom, popular Buddhism, and the shamanist ritual of *Han-Pu-Ri*. Syncretism is another method used by Chung, as her keynote speech at the General Assembly of World Council of Churches in 1991 presented Kwan In

---

BOX 3.4

Postcolonial Feminism

Kwok Pui-Lan's postcolonial feminist imagination consists of three phases: historical, dialogical, and diasporic. Each phase highlights women's subjectivity to interweave different stories of suffering and liberation historically and dialogically. Dialogical and diasporic imagination particularly emphasizes a "contact zone" created by historical, cultural, political, and religious interactions among the groups of people. Although a contact zone is often created through unequal power relations (e.g., colonial occupation and forced migration), Kwok argues that diasporic consciousness arising in the contact zone enables people to see similarities and differences among their cultures and identities so that they can move toward solidarity in the struggle for liberation.

(female divinity of Bodhisattva in Mahayana Buddhism) as the image of the Holy Spirit.

Chung elaborates on an Asian Mariology with emphasis on the virgin as an autonomous woman, liberated from patriarchy, as well as on an Asian Christology, with the images of Jesus as a factory worker and as food to be shared. Chung accentuates that the future of Asian feminist spirituality is "life-centric" enough to empower poor Asian women to be liberated from Christocentrism.

Various Asian contexts further foster Dalit women's liberation theology, Filipina feminist theology, and others. The Philippines, the only Christianized country in Asia, boasts a militant feminist movement organized by grassroots organizations, such as Gabriella. Filipina feminist theology is rooted in ordinary women's political activism for peace and justice.

Guru. A spiritual teacher chosen by God for the visible embodiment of truth and in some cases worshiped as an incarnate deity. A Guru is responsible for the transferral of knowledge of God to people and is invariably related to the process of salvation.

Interfaith/Enculturated Liberationist Theology

While India's sophisticated philosophy, religion, and culture have long enchanted Western scholars, Indian theologians debunk Western scholars' Orientalism and attempt to make sense of Christianity in India. M. M. Thomas, a pioneer in Indian liberation theology, and Sebastian Kappen interpret Jesus in the Indian context where the caste system, ancient religions and cultures, and tribal conflicts are present. In their Christology Jesus

A South Korean man killed his Vietnamese wife when she was attempting to leave the house with their nineteen-day-old son. Hoang, the murdered Vietnamese woman, asked for a divorce many times after having moved to South Korea in August 2010. To escape poverty, this twenty three-year-old woman was married to Lim, a thirty-seven-year-old Korean man who was mentally challenged. When officers arrived at Lim's house, they found the couple's baby lying next to his bleeding mother and his father outside the house with a knife in his hand. Hoang was one of four Vietnamese women murdered by their Korean spouses between July 2010 and June 2011.

In South Korea, four out of ten rural men are married to foreign women, mostly from China, Mongolia, Vietnam, Cambodia, Laos, the Philippines, and Thailand. Poor young Asian women in rural areas choose to marry Korean men in order to escape poverty and support their families. International marriages between Korean men and foreign women are conducted through marriage agencies. Marriage agencies send the catalog of women to Korean single men, who are not able to marry Korean women because of their poverty, lack of education, or disabilities. The majority of these men are in their forties and married to foreign women in their early twenties. The marriage agencies charge the man between eight thousand and eleven thousand dollars. Due to the high cost of marriage, some men consider their wives private property. The South Korean government recently tightened control over matchmaking agencies and opened premarriage education centers for those who plan to marry foreign people.

Does the mail-order-bride system oppress women more than men? Why or why not? Is the system ethically tolerable? Is it right for a poor woman to choose marriage for economic benefit? Why or why not? Is it better for a poor woman to choose to marry or to find a low-paying job in manufacturing? What should be considered in order to help a poor Vietnamese woman autonomously choose her future? Is the Korean government's regulation enough to protect a woman like Hoang? What should the Korean government do for both foreign wives and for Korean men, who are not able to find the wives in Korea? What religious resources did you find in this chapter for liberation of a woman like Hoang?

is in solidarity with the poor and in resistance to economic and political exploitation, and is also the Christ of other religions and cultures. Michael Amaladoss, Indian Catholic liberationist, further portrays popular images of Jesus that are familiar to Asian people: Sage, Way (Taoism), Guru (Hinduism), Avatar (incarnation of the divine), Servant, Compassionate One, Dancer, and Pilgrim.

A Sri Lankan Jesuit priest, Aloysius Pieris, also contributes to the sophistication of interfaith liberation theology. For Pieris, poverty is the distinctive character of Asia's third-worldness. Compared to Latin American liberation theology, which deals with poverty within a relatively homogeneous linguistic and religious region, Asian liberation theology must consider liberation of the poor across their linguistic, religious, cultural diversity. Pieris's contribution to liberationist theo-ethics is

not only an interpretation of the Second Vatican Council in the Asian context of poverty but also a rediscovery of Buddhist and Christian spirituality and monasticism in resistance to the economic exploitation sustained by political and religious ideologies.

Distinguishing voluntary poverty (monastic practice of poverty) from structured poverty, Pieris argues that poverty as a physical and spiritual practice in solidarity with the poor is what religious people should do. Needless to say, even monastic poverty without concern for the poor has no spiritual or ethical meaning. Pieris's interfaith theology further elaborates on the relation between what he calls "cosmic religion" and "metacosmic religion." Metacosmic religion is concerned about human salvation (soteriology) on an ontological level and is found in all religions

CASE STUDY 3.2

When Zen Master Thich Nhat Hanh was finally allowed to visit Vietnam from thirty-nine-year exile, he founded a monastery, Prajna. During Nhat Hanh's first visit to Vietnam in 2005, Abbot Thich Duc Nghi offered his monastery as a training and practice center in the tradition of Plum Village, the monastery established in France by Thich Nhat Hanh. Since then, elder monks from Plum Village have traveled to Prajna and trained and ordained over three hundred young people. Most of these youth are from poor families and come to search for the meanings of life.

In September 2008, three disciples of the abbot led a group of twenty men in a raid on the monastery residence, where the monks' belongings were thrown outside. Despite an apparent resolution to the dispute in early October, the Religious Affairs Committee of Vietnam denounced Thich Nhat Hanh and reiterated a call for the monastery to be cleared out. Regular harassment by the religious police followed, culminating in mobs of several hundred people attacking the monastery in June and July with no police intervention. Sister Chan Kong, Thich Nhat Hanh's foremost adviser, told BBC News, "The government fear that we are too dynamic and they can't control us. Local police in every province have been paying visits to the parents of our young disciples, telling them to get their sons and daughters out of Bat Nha [Prajna] because we are 'political.'"

Does Sister Chan Khong argue that the Prajna monastery is not political? What is your interpretation of her comments? Why does the Vietnamese government consider Buddhists monks political? What should the Prajna monastery do? Should they close their monastery or fight for religious freedom, and why? What can non-Buddhists or non-Vietnamese do in order to serve justice in this case? What would liberation mean in this case?

in Asia. Cosmic religion, however, focuses on the liberation of social structures, such as political and religious orders. These two characters of religion are intertwined in serving human dignity. Asian Christianity can articulate its identity marked with liberation when the church liberates herself from the Eurocentric Christ against non-Christian religions and cultures, and practices poverty in solidarity with the poor in their resistance of economic and political exploitation.

Similar to Piers's religiousness of the poor, Tissa Balasuriya finds empowering spirituality of the poor in popular devotion to Mary. Examining Sri Lanka's colonial experience, Balasuriya argues that Sri Lankan Catholics could discover the liberative power of Mary due to their experience of oppression during Dutch colonialism. Mary is not merely the submissive mother of God, but is an autonomous woman who worked with Jesus for the liberation of the poor and the oppressed so that these people would recover human dignity. Through devotion to Mary, the poor endure and resist exploitative social structures. Balasuriya's Mariology further suggests interfaith liberationist theology grown out of popular religious practices.

C. S. Song, a Taiwanese liberation theologian, expands the ideas of Jesus, identifying him with the crucified people through Christian-Buddhist-Asian folk religious dialogue. Song portrays God, the biography of suffering people, and Jesus as the collective story of people's suffering and liberation

---

KEY TERM 3.2

Confucianism. A cultural philosophy and religion that originated in China but that has also influenced East Asia and Southeast Asia. As moral and cultural philosophy, Confucianism emphasizes the importance of hierarchical social order and one's duty within social systems.

KEY TERM 3.3

Taoism. Popular religion in China that teaches that Great Tao (the Way) transcends all human knowledge of truth. Tao Te Ching is the written collection of Taoism.

---

especially in the Asian context. Although Jesus' crucifixion and liberation enable Christianity to communicate with Asians, Buddhism and Asian folk religions also illustrate Asians' liberative resources. Song compares Jesus to Bodhisattva, the savior for the suffering masses in popular Buddhism, and to the lotus flower, the Buddhist symbol of emancipation of suffering. In Song's theology, Jesus does not exist as an individual hero or leader of liberationist movement. Rather, following the Asian emphasis on the communal identity as an individual identity, Song emphasizes Jesus as the collective identity of all Asian people, who again and again rise up against structural oppression.

Possible Future Trends

Asian liberative ethicists in the twenty-first century will continue to contemplate emerging issues including the following. First, a critical question is whether or not liberation theology is the proper terminology. Filipino/a theologians prefer the term of "theology of struggle," while Korean feminist theologians suggest *salimist* theology" in order to include salvation of all living beings. Furthermore, liberation theology is likely to fail to address liberative powers in other Asian religions such as *Ummah* in Islam (community of brotherhood), interbeing in Buddhism, the harmonious universe in Confucianism, unity in nature in Taoism, and so on. Some liberative ethicists suggest "theology of life" or "life-centric liberation" for future generations.

Second, whether Asian liberation theologies are effective and practical is an important question in itself. Although for the last four decades Asian liberation theology has found its particular location within academia, specifically in Christian theology, it is questionable whether it has contributed to social transformation in real Asian contexts beyond academia. Just as Minjung theologians lived with poor factory workers and peasants in the 1970s and 1980s, Asian liberative ethicists should reexamine their practice of liberation and seek out practical ways to be part of people's struggle for liberation. Moreover, as an academic discourse, Asian liberation theology has been written predominantly by East and South Asian theologians, who are trained in the West or able to speak English. Stories of ordinary people's liberation and suffering from central Asia should also be heard.

Third, interfaith liberative ethics should be practiced more actively. Currently, interfaith dialogue is dominated by mainstream Christian theologians in the West, who create typologies of exclusivist, inclusivist, and pluralist approaches without considering Asian people's religiously syncretistic lifestyle. Asian liberationists should continue to critically analyze Eurocentric assumptions of interfaith dialogue and articulate an Asian way of syncretism. Furthermore, non-Christian perspectives on interfaith liberation must be incorporated more actively in Christian liberationist praxis.

Fourth, while liberation from poverty, militarism, and political oppression should continue to receive attention, how to achieve peace (e.g., how to resist continuous militarization and nuclear power) needs deeper analysis and practice. Asian liberationist ethics is searching for this vision and practice of peace from a bottom-up approach.

Last, global and transnational perspectives will help form new praxis in Asian liberationist ethics.

BOX 3.5

Thich Nhat Hanh

Thich Nhat Hanh, a Vietnamese Zen Master and peace activist is the best-known leader of Engaged Buddhism. This liberationist movement, born out of poverty and war in Southeast Asia, is based on Buddhist teachings on loving-kindness and compassion, or Bodhisattva vows that articulate the salvation of all sentient beings. Based on the reinterpretation of the Buddhist five precepts or ethical living in light of the suffering masses' experience, Nhat Hanh has taught the five mindfulness trainings. Emphasizing interbeing, or interconnectedness all living beings, the five mindfulness trainings include the reverence for life, generosity, sexual responsibility, deep listening and loving speech, and right nutrition for body, spirit, and society. During the Vietnam War, Nhat Hahn accentuated the Buddhist middle path, supporting neither North Vietnam nor the United States and demanding the immediate end of war and human suffering. Due to his nonpartiality, the Vietnamese Communist regime persecuted Buddhists and barred Nhat Hanh from entering Vietnam until 2005. Nhat Hanh has influenced nonviolent peacemaking and interfaith dialogue in the West.

Along with a gender analysis in power relations in Asian situations, a global and transnational analysis will continue to reveal the complexity of power relations and social issues in Asia as well as evoke international collaboration for peace and justice.

Study Questions

1. What aspects of Asian liberative ethics stood out to you the most and why?
2. What similarities and differences do you find as you compare Asian liberative ethics and contexts to other chapters in this book?
3. Asian liberative ethicists claim Jesus as the collective identity of suffering people? Do you agree or disagree? Why?
4. How does US economic, ecological, military, and sexual violence relate to the suffering of Asian masses?
5. From your own social location, how can you participate in Asian peoples' liberative struggles religiously and/or nonreligiously?

Suggested Readings

Amaladoss, Michael. *The Asian Jesus.* Maryknoll, NY: Orbis, 2006.

———. *Life in Freedom: Liberation Theologies from Asia.* Maryknoll, NY: Orbis, 1997.

Chung, Hyun Kyung. *Struggle to Be the Sun Again: Introducing Asian Women's Theology.* Maryknoll, NY: Orbis, 1990.

Hyun, Young-Hak. *Mask Dance of Jesus.* Seoul, Korea: Korean Theological Institute, 1998.

Kwok, Pui-Lan. *Introducing Asian Feminist Theology.* Cleveland: Pilgrim, 2000.

Pieris, Aloysius. *An Asian Theology of Liberation.* Edinburgh: T&T Clark, 1988.

Rajkumar, Paniel. *Dalit Theology and Dalit Liberation.* Burlington, VT: Ashgate, 2010.

Song, C. S. *Jesus: The Crucified People.* Lima, OH: Academic Renewal Press, 2001.

Sugirtharajah, R. S., ed. *Frontiers in Asian Christian Theology.* Maryknoll, NY: Orbis, 1994.

Economic Liberative Ethics

Laura Stivers

RELIGION, ACCORDING TO KARL Marx, is the "opium of the people." Marx felt that humans create religion in response to alienation in material life. One form of alienation that Marx identifies in the capitalist economic system is the purchase of, and inevitable exploitation, of human labor to achieve profit for those who own the means of production. While exploitation of humans predates capitalism, the scope of this chapter will focus on economic ethics in the United States both before and after the introduction of liberation theology. In the late nineteenth and early twentieth centuries, when industrialization and increasing capitalist relations were taking hold in the United States, Christian ethicists and theologians were writing about, and often active in organizing efforts to address, problems associated with economic exploitation and marginalization. These thinkers were aware of the ways in which religion was used to pacify people by focusing their attention on salvation and a heavenly realm separate from the material realm of their present lives and economic reality. Yet these thinkers all felt that religion could be more than an opium of the people, that it had the seeds for prophetic

criticism of economic injustice based on Christian understandings of a liberating God, on the Hebrew prophets' attention to economic justice for those on the margins, and on the example of Jesus' ministry and hospitality to all.

History and Development of Economic Liberative Ethics

Early industrialization is often associated primarily with the early factories in the Northeast that employed native whites and immigrants, but in reality the northern factories relied on the cotton plantations of the South and the African slave labor that made the plantations profitable. Although churches and religious folk were involved in the Abolitionist movement, the first well-known religious thinkers addressing economic exploitation of labor in the capitalist system focused mainly on white male workers in the increasingly industrialized cities of the North in the 1900s. While poverty and economic exploitation were always issues for African American leaders in the black community, for these leaders class oppression was connected to race oppression. Overcoming key facets of racial oppression, such as lack of education, access to decent jobs, ability to joins unions, and violence against blacks, would go a long way in improving economic conditions for the black community. Attention to the plight of Native Americans was not acknowledged by any religious leaders for economic justice, and Hispanics and Asian Americans were not even on their radar screen.

Protestant Social Gospel Movement

The most widely recognized religious leaders to relate religion to economic justice were white Protestant males (and a few females), and while they were aware of racism, they did little to address race oppression. Some of the leaders critiqued the effects of capitalism in American cities but continued to champion American imperialism and missionary Christianity. They did break new ground, however, in bridging the gap between personal piety and concern about economic injustice.

Walter Rauschenbusch, the most well-known social gospeler, argued that personal salvation and social salvation go together. He was trained to focus on saving souls in his parish ministry, but after paying pastoral calls to crowded New York City tenement buildings and conducting numerous funerals for his parishioner's children, he began to rethink his conception of the kingdom of God. His new perspective was based upon his belief that Jesus stood in line with the prophets of the Hebrew Bible and that Jesus' teachings centered on the revolutionary transformation of this world. He felt the church settled for less than the kingdom of God—and even thwarted it—by focusing only on heaven and life after death.

Rauschenbusch argued that Christianity should be prophetic rather than hierarchically based on priests and power. He uplifted the prophets in Scripture for speaking of a God who wants justice and goodness, not sacrifice, and he emphasized a

---

BOX 4.1

Social Gospel Movement

The "father" of the social gospel movement was Washington Gladden, who was born in 1836, but the movement was not referred to with the words *social gospel* until near the end of his life, in 1910. In addition to Gladden, some key leaders were Richard Ely, Walter Rauschenbusch, Vida Scudder, and Reverdy Ransom. Their main claim was that Christianity has a mission to change the unjust structures of society. Associated with liberal Protestant Christianity, it was an attempt to apply biblical teachings to problems associated with industrialization, such as inequality, slums, child labor, and exploitation of workers. The social gospel movement embodied a belief in social progress and optimism in human nature to love one's neighbor and support social and economic justice. Many reformers opened settlement houses to meet the needs of the poor, especially immigrants. The most notable was Hull House in Chicago, run by Jane Addams. The social gospel movement was radical in its notion of "social salvation" and paved the way for ecumenical and social justice ministries that continue today.

Jesus who taught with parables against an apocalyptic (end of the world) worldview of his time and in favor of "new life" in this world. For Rauschenbusch, the true kingdom of God is connected to the physical, moral, and spiritual uplift of humanity. To this end, he strongly critiqued the capitalist system for its predatory and corrupting nature, even connecting it to the "superpersonal forces of evil." Private property and profit-making were

KEY TERM 4.1

Social salvation. In 1902, Washington Gladden wrote a book called *Social Salvation*, in which he decried evangelical Christianity's focus on individual salvation without attention to the social problems that weaken the bonds of solidarity among all people. He argued that no person can be converted without obeying the laws of love.

not the central problems, in Rauschenbusch's view, but rather the lack of checks and balances on the system. Thus he advocated for democratic socialism in which property rights are expanded and the process of investment is democratized, a socialism with decentralized and cooperative forms of ownership rather than centralized government ownership. Rauschenbusch hoped that a revival of religion and a Christian transformation of society could bring us closer to the kingdom of God. While not wholly naive, he was optimistic that such transformation could occur apart from class struggle/war. One of his contemporaries, Vida Scudder, had a similar vision of collective ownership of the means of production and redistribution of material wealth, yet she took seriously the need for class struggle and the limits of moral idealism—that is, people being virtuous without being forced to be.

The social gospel movement was not confined to white Protestants. Reverand Reverdy Ransom opened the first black-owned and black-controlled settlement house (modeled off those begun by Jane Addams Hull) in Chicago in 1900 to minister to the over fifteen thousand blacks on Chicago's south side and the many more arriving daily. Blacks were doing the lowest-paying, backbreaking jobs and were confined to the poorest neighborhoods, often near railroad yards, river docks,

stockyards, or waste dumps. While Ransom was an advocate of democratic socialism, solidarity with the labor movement was difficult because of the movement's racism. As his social gospel ministry proceeded, Ransom began to focus more on black pride than socialism because racism continued to be the most prevalent force of oppression for his community.

Catholic Perspectives on Economic Justice

While Catholics were not part of the social gospel movement, they were not silent on issues of economic injustice. Beginning in 1891, the Catholic Church began a tradition of social teachings through papal documents. The first document issued by Pope Leo XIII called *Rerum Novarum* or *The Condition of Labor* paved the way for social ethics in relation to political economy. Further documents addressing economic ethics came out in 1931, 1961, and 1981. In all of them, Christians are called to pursue justice by protecting the weak and poor and by promoting the dignity of work. While the documents promote the right to private property and steer clear of advocating socialism, they are quite critical of unbridled capitalism that benefits a few rich men and lays "upon the masses of the poor a yoke little better than slavery itself." In *Rerum Novarum*, there is a call for a "just wage," for government regulation of working conditions in factories, and for the right of workers to unionize. In all of the documents addressing economic injustice, there is an emphasis on the dignity of human nature as well as the promotion of a common good. Later influence from Latin American liberation theology in the 1960s led to the language and concepts of an "option for the poor" and "solidarity" of those who are well off with people on the margins.

An American Catholic social ethicist, John Ryan was influenced both by the work of social gospeler Richard Ely and by the 1891 social encyclical *Rerum Novarum*, despite the fact that it barely registered with the American Catholic

KEY TERM 4.2

Natural Law and Natural Rights. Catholic ethicists often use natural law moral reasoning; that is, a system of law determined by nature and known universally by reason. Natural law standards can be used to critique human-made laws of particular societies. Natural rights are universal and inalienable rights that people possess by nature.

church at the time. In his 1906 book *A Living Wage*, he argued that all humans have a right to a wage that allows them a decent standard of living, and that this right is a natural right, not simply a right granted by society or civil authority.

Since humans are endowed by God with this right in support of human dignity and personhood, he argued that it is the obligation of the state to ensure the welfare of its citizens. Ryan held that a just wage would in effect be a "family living wage," as he believed male wage earners had the right to be the head of a family.

He made no mention of the many female wage earners, especially women of color and single women. Nevertheless, Ryan was way ahead of his colleagues in critiquing unjust private land

KEY TERM 4.3

Living wage. A living wage was developed in the United States because the minimum wage set by law was not sufficient for people to afford basic needs, such as housing, food, transportation, and medical care. A living wage is relative to the costs in particular geographical areas and is calculated based on what is necessary to meet basic needs if a person is working forty hours a week with no additional income.

and capital ownership, business practices, and wage systems, and he was a leader in promoting just distribution of wealth through tax and wage policies and regulation of businesses. While Ryan consistently maintained that private ownership was a natural human right, he argued that the right of tenants and employees to a decent livelihood should take precedence over the landowner's and capitalist's right to the highest return on their investment.

Another influential Catholic figure who promoted economic justice was Dorothy Day. In 1933, Day opened her first "House of Hospitality" and was at the same time writing to lay Catholics about economic injustices in the first edition of the *Catholic Worker*, a paper that paid attention to economic exploitation and worker strikes as well as spiritual and theological foundations for alternative visions to capitalism that embraced worker ownership and decentralized local community economies. In the Houses of Hospitality, people were welcomed and treated as equals unlike other street missions that only opened the doors to those who were willing to be helped and/or evangelized. Day always taught that every person is an image of God, and therefore that everyone has importance.

The "Catholic workers," as they were called, generally adopted voluntary poverty and manual labor and lived in the houses of hospitality in community with those whom they served. They took Jesus' message to heart that you cannot serve God and money at the same time. Day rejected the Catholic Church's accommodation on matters of money. They called religious brothers or sisters to embrace poverty, but allowed others to accumulate wealth as long as they supported the church and practiced charity. She argued that all Christians have a call to practice self-emptying love and to be co-creators in the work of God, that we are all called to be "saints." In her early years as a socialist, Day railed against charity measures. In her later years, she believed that separating justice and charity was a dualistic response that did not solve problems. In her activism, she always sought to change the world, but at the same time she continued to feed, clothe, and shelter her sisters and brothers. In terms of social policy, she and her Catholic Worker cofounder, Peter Maurin, while always critical of capitalism, championed decentralization of local economies over a social welfare state with increased bureaucracy.

Christian Realist Contribution to Economic Ethics

The social gospel paved the way by connecting concern for economic injustice with God and salvation, yet Rauschenbusch's emphasis on human goodwill to bring about social and economic justice and his adoption of missionary evangelism undercut the liberatory potential of the movement. Reinhold Niebuhr, while heavily influenced by the movement, argued that more attention to power dynamics and the reality of social sin are necessary to effect liberating political change. Later leaders such as Martin Luther King Jr. and César Chávez took Niebuhr's insights to heart in their organizing for racial and economic justice. Niebuhr was especially critical of the American myth of unending progress and the idea that capitalism can be made kinder and gentler as long as individuals are educated about the economic injustices in their midst. He argued instead that private ownership gives social power, and as long as such social power in unequally distributed, there will be inequality and injustice. Calling people to emulate the love of Jesus is not adequate. Rather, justice requires promoting and sustaining a balance of power, which in turn requires pressure and coercion, as no social group will willingly give up its power, despite the social gospel call for religious goodwill. As the civil rights movement illustrates, whites went to all lengths to protect their privilege (and still do).

Niebuhr pointed out that people with power and privilege who benefit from economic injustice are less capable of understanding the effects of oppression and are quick to hide economic injustice by celebrating their gestures of philanthropy (and consequently are outraged when its recipients respond cynically to their efforts). The attitudes of privileged groups, he held, are characterized by self-deception and hypocrisy; these groups will go to all lengths (albeit often unconsciously) to morally justify inequalities of privilege. Niebuhr held that Jesus offers a model of pure religious idealism and moral perfection that we can lift up as an ideal (what he calls an "impossible possibility"), but that this social ideal of Jesus is a personal ethic. A Christian social ethic that addresses economic injustice will require, according to Niebuhr, nonviolent forms of resistance and coercion to achieve an equilibrium of power so that equality and justice might prevail.

Movements for Economic Justice

One of the most important connections of Christianity to economic justice was found in the movements for change that posited Niebuhr's insights on coercion as a means of balancing power. Many Christians in the social gospel movement were connected to the first organized labor movements in the United States that brought about substantial changes in the workplace, such as the end of child labor, eight-hour workdays, paid overtime, minimum wage, right to collective bargaining, workplace safety regulations, workers' comp for injuries on the job, and health and pension benefits; but the labor movement also existed outside the church. In contrast, the next big movement for change—the ongoing struggle of blacks for basic civil rights and integration—was organized primarily from within the black church. While racial justice was the core focus of the movement, Martin Luther King Jr., near the end of this life, focused increasingly on economic justice, as he was well aware of the link between racism and classism.

In his 1967 talk titled "Where Do We Go From Here?" he showed the interconnections between racism, economic exploitation, and war. Making segregation illegal and granting formal equal opportunity, while important, were not sufficient for liberation and the building of King's "beloved community." Social policies that create greater equality of condition are also needed to empower American blacks and others to participate in opening opportunities. Therefore, King urged a war against poverty, and consistently argued that a country spending so much money on war would not invest to alleviate poverty. King critiqued American society not only for its racism but also for its economic exploitation of developing nations, and argued that we must support the revolutions of the poor around the world.

King argued that we need to transform structures, not simply be good Samaritans to those who cross our paths. That is, we must see that the "whole Jericho road must be transformed so that men and women will not be constantly beaten and robbed as they make their journey on life's highway." He argued that we rely on the myth of the bootstrap philosophy, that people can rise up on their own. Yet he points out that it is a "cruel jest" to tell people who have no boots that they can lift themselves by their own bootstraps. For King, true compassion goes beyond charity and changes the structures that produce poverty. The beloved community will be one in which the essential worth of each person is uplifted—a "person-oriented" society rather than a "thing-oriented" society. Each person's dignity and worth as created in God's image will be more important than profit and property rights.

Following the civil rights momentum, César Chávez, along with Dolores Huerta and others, began organizing Chicano agricultural workers in the fields of California. Chávez also emphasized human dignity rooted in the truth that God made us all. He felt that the face of God is revealed in each human person, and therefore the failure to recognize and promote the humanity of farmworkers is a failure to recognize and praise God.

Influenced by Catholic social teaching, Chávez saw work as sacred and deserving of just wages, as God is a God of justice. Chávez was contemptuous of attempts to pity the farmworkers and called instead for solidarity with them in their struggle for bargaining and workplace rights. His goal was for the farmworkers to generate their own economic and political power. To this end, he organized the United Farm Workers Union and worked to develop the skills of farmworkers to organize democratically and nonviolently for their rights. He always taught them, however, that their true empowerment is measured by service to one another and the promotion of community.

Faith and prayer were at the heart of Chávez's organization efforts. Just as the civil rights movement emerged out of and was nourished by the black church, the Chicano farmworker movement was rooted in Mexican popular Catholicism. Labor rallies always began with Mass and prayers to Our Lady of Guadalupe; and prayer vigils, shrines, and the singing of spirituals offered sustenance to continue the struggle. Several times when dissension occurred in the ranks over the strategy of nonviolence, Chávez went on a multiday fast (the longest was for thirty-six days in 1988), both to bring workers together in solidarity and to enact personal prayer, purification, and penance.

Liberation Theology's Critique of Capitalism

While liberation movements were happening in the United States in the 1960s, a new "liberation theology" was being developed in Latin America in response to grinding poverty and the idea that developing countries could achieve modernization in progressive stages of growth similar to developed countries. Peruvian theologian Gustavo Gutiérrez argues that liberation theology has its roots in the poor's organizing themselves in defense of their right to life, and that it is the poor who challenge the church, calling it to conversion and to a new consciousness. Gutiérrez insists that the poor must be artisans of their own liberation because only they will be fully committed to liberation. Thus liberation theology begins through involvement and solidarity *with* the poor in their reality of poverty, with theological reflection on that involvement second. The church often starts with theology first and does not employ the use of social sciences in relation to theology, nor does it reflect theologically from the perspective of those on the underside of society.

Gutiérrez replaces the term *development* with the concept of "liberation." He argues that development should not simply be equated with economic growth but must be a "total social process" that includes economic, social, political, and cultural aspects. Gutiérrez outlines three interconnected levels of liberation. The first level is external liberation from unjust social situations. Theologically, this aspect of liberation is about addressing structural sin.

Gutiérrez argues that global economic policies and capitalism benefit a handful of wealthy people through the exploitation and marginalization of large numbers of poor people in Latin America and other colonized areas of the world. He challenges the idea that economic growth benefits the poor and sees that "developmentalism" or the idolatry of mammon (money and wealth) in Latin America was actually causing the death of the poor. Liberation at this level entails eliminating the *root causes* of poverty and injustice. Historically, he says, the church has paid the least attention to this meaning of liberation.

The second level is an inner liberation from the power of fate. This meaning of liberation is about people taking hold of their own destiny and in doing so having an inner freedom despite various servitudes. Historically the church has promoted fate, especially of poverty and suffering, as the will of God. Gutiérrez believes that God is working for justice along with people actively oriented and struggling toward a just future and that poverty and oppression are never the will of God. The third level is a theological liberation from personal sin. Gutiérrez claims that personal sin is a major cause of poverty, injustice, and oppression. He critiques the church for not connecting personal sin to structural injustice, and thereby falling into spiritualist approaches that avoid harsh realities. Development, Gutiérrez argues, should entail integral liberation of the poor and oppressed, whereby they create their own history, participate in establishing just institutions, and work with all people in solidarity and communion with God. This integral notion of liberation entails both the changing of hearts as well as structures, and challenges the traditional view that spirituality and politics do not mix. Liberation is not just the struggle for political or economic rights but is also about a new self-consciousness in which affectionate and caring relationships among all are important.

Solidarity and a preferential option for the poor are the two moral norms most associated with liberation theology. Their meanings, however, are often misinterpreted. Solidarity can be misconstrued as "doing for" rather than "struggling with," and a preferential option for the poor can become simply an ethical demand rather than a call for making the struggle an actual option. In other words, a preferential option is often about charity *for the poor* instead of about becoming

---

KEY TERM 4.4

Structural sin. A larger, social dimension of sin beyond individual wrongdoing. Individual biases are institutionalized and legitimized by particular structures in society that in turn lead to oppression and marginalization for particular groups. An emphasis on structural sin entails that we have corporate responsibility for sinful actions that originate from social systems.

a church *of the poor*. For Gutiérrez, making an option for the poor in the church is more than joining the struggle for social justice. For him, "the church of the poor *is* the church." The entire Bible, Gutiérrez claims, "mirrors God's predilection for the weak and abused of human history." Making an option for the poor means confronting powerful interests, and the church must make a choice not to be neutral. Neutrality is neither ethical nor Christian since it means siding with injustice and oppression.

Feminist Economic Ethics

While women have always been at the forefront in addressing economic injustice, theoretical work in Christian feminist economic ethics did not emerge until the 1980s. Drawing on insights from Latin American liberation theology and ethics, Christian feminist economic ethicists analyze ethical issues from the perspective of women and explore the interconnections between sexual and economic injustice. Beverly Harrison's feminist take on political economy paved the way for a number of later feminist economic ethicists. Harrison pays explicit attention to how power is structured in society, especially in economic institutions, and its impact on the concrete lives of people. She shows how the economic realm both shapes and is shaped by the interstructuring of race, gender, class, and sexual identity.

Christian feminist economic ethicists begin with the material and sexual realities of women's lives and address what it would take to develop communities and social structures in which women have effective moral agency for meaningful participation and decision making. Harrison's first book on abortion connected a sexual ethic of procreative choice to women's ability to have full agency in both the personal and public (economic) realms. The experiences of women and the embodied reason and emotion that stems from these experiences are important sources of moral knowledge, but often get devalued in traditional ethics. Also important to Christian feminist economic analysis is an emphasis on the interlocking nature of different oppressions such as sexism, racism, classism, and heterosexism. Challenging dominant ideologies that serve to keep oppression in place becomes paramount. For example, Traci West shows how ideologies devalue and dismiss the personhood of black women, justifying sexual and economic violence against them. Gloria Albrecht claims that the rhetoric of "family values" ignores real family arrangements and serves to bolster white male power and privilege.

Still another characteristic of Christian feminist economic ethics is attention to practical issues that women face in both the so-called public and private realms. Issues within the home, like child rearing and elder care, as well as domestic violence, affect women in the workplace. Opening up opportunities for women in the public realm is not enough if oppressive cultural assumptions about gender roles and the value associated with them are not challenged. Increasingly, these scholars are focusing on interconnections between women globally and how capitalist political economy, in conjunction with oppressive ideologies, both exploits and marginalizes the productive and reproductive labor of women. Attention to the material realities in both the home and workplace is important.

KEY TERM 4.5

Reproductive labor. Activities involved in carrying out the jobs assigned to families (e.g., child rearing, housework, cleaning, cooking). Reproductive labor has most often been performed by women. It often contributes to their oppression, as it is not paid and can negatively affect their success in the paid workforce.

Environmental Justice Movement

In the United States, the environmental movement began in earnest in the 1970s, but the environmental focus in Christian circles was primarily on sustainability and preserving God's good creation. While links between economic and environmental injustice were made, racial justice was not a central focus in environmentalism. In the late 1980s, the environmental justice movement, as well as increasing class analysis of environmental destruction by scholars in other fields, began to influence the work of Christian social ethicists. Scholars in the movement pointed to environmental racism, which refers to several things: (1) disproportionate impact of environmental contamination on communities of color, especially hazardous waste facilities and unwanted land uses; (2) racial and class discrimination in formulating and carrying out environmental policy; (3) adverse health effects from environmental destruction in these communities; (4) narrow focus on what issues are considered of environmental concern; and (5) lack of people of color in leadership of the environmental movement. While the environmental movement tends to picture us all in the same boat when it comes to environmental destruction, the environmental justice movement argues that we are not all equally affected. For example, those with the least power drink the most polluted water and work in the most dangerous jobs.

The Latin American collective of ecofeminist theologians called *Co-spirando* ("breathing together with others") brings to light many of the interconnections between environmental and economic injustice. The daily suffering of countless people in Latin America (and other areas in the two-thirds world), from the absence of sewers to toxic pollution due to oil drilling or mining, has led these women to reflect theologically on evil and the human desire to take possession of life and make it our own, noting that certain groups have had the power and privilege to be the "self-appointed proprietors of the earth." The negative effects of environmental destruction have been disproportionately borne by women in Latin America, as they are responsible for the reproductive labor in the household, which in poor households includes gathering water and ensuring the health of children against numerous environmental threats.

Latina ecofeminists have outlined an embodied theological ethic that highlights spiritual wholeness with an emphasis on healthy relatedness to ourselves, to other bodies, and to the larger web of life infused with divine energy. In addition, they claim that these embodied and environmentally sensitive relationships draw sustenance from the ancestors and extend to future generations. Ecofeminist theologians see all material bodies as part of divine energy and thereby sacred. Therefore, their embodied spirituality tends to the healing of bodies that have suffered and celebrates the beauty of the natural world and the intricate and complex web of relationships within it.

Need for Economic Liberation

Americans tend to be proud of their economic system and believe that the United States is a place of opportunity for those who work hard, but many individuals are finding that they are working harder and harder and slipping further behind economically. Others are not even getting the opportunity to work. Wages for the bottom 80 percent of the population have gone down since the 1970s. The minimum wage set in 1938 had its peak value in 1968, when it was worth $10.04 an hour in 2010 dollars, as compared to our current minimum wage of $7.25 an hour. According to the Center for American Progress, almost 60 percent of minimum-wage workers are female and 40 percent are people of color. While not everyone makes minimum wage, it sets the bar for all other wages, giving a fair indicator of the falling value of wages for most families. Families avoided falling behind for a number of years by having more family members work and by putting in longer work hours, often at more than one job, but at some point these strategies are no longer options, as there are only so many work hours in a day and only so many work-age family members.

Not only have wages fallen, but the cost of living has increased substantially. One of the biggest economic struggles for families is the cost of health care. Health insurance has become prohibitively expensive for many people, resulting in 50 million people uninsured in our country in 2009, as per the US Census Bureau. Even for those who are insured, however, health-care costs that insurance does not cover are more than many families can financially handle. A recent study in the *American Journal of Medicine* shows that over 60 percent of all bankruptcies these days are linked to medical expenses. Another economic hurdle for families is the cost of housing. As per the Joint Center for Housing Studies of Harvard University, 39 million households paid more than 30 percent of income on housing (traditionally 30 percent has been considered "affordable") and almost 18 million paid more than 50 percent of their income on housing in 2007. The national hourly wage needed to afford rental housing in 2009, as calculated by the National Alliance to End Homelessness, was $17.84 (much higher than any state's minimum wage). It is not only the poor who are struggling to get by, but increasingly the middle class is feeling the pinch.

The Economic Policy Institute reveals that while incomes have decreased for the bottom 80 percent, both wealth and income have increased exponentially for the top 10 percent. After World War II up until 1979, the United States had a period of strong economic growth and productivity, and the richest 10 percent of families accounted for 33 percent of average income growth, while the bottom 90 percent accounted for 67 percent. For those three decades, the distribution of wealth was stable, in large part due to strong unions that were organized in the 1930s and the Wagner Act of 1935, which protected workers' right to unionization. In the 1980s, with the advent of "Reaganomics"—supply-side economic policies that President Ronald Reagan instituted to shift money to the top with the justification that the rich would invest the money efficiently and wisely to create jobs—wealth distribution was substantially widened. These policy changes included drastically lowering taxes on the wealthy and corporations, defunding social services, deregulating the finance industry and corporations, privatizing industries and services, and instituting antilabor initiatives.

While it was not clear any economic growth "trickled down" to the bottom, these policies did a great job of amassing wealth at the top. Some of that wealth might have been invested in endeavors that created jobs, but some of it was also used in ways that decreased jobs, such as taking over other companies (called "leveraged buy-outs") or shifting companies overseas in search of cheaper labor and less environmental and labor regulations. As a result of these policy changes, as well as increased globalization that placed workers in competition with one another, the rich reap the majority of the gains even when we have an economic upturn. For example, the Economic Policy Institute shows that between 2000 and 2007 when the US economy was expanding, the richest 10 percent received all of the income growth. Sociologist G. William Domhoff documents how by 2007, the top 10 percent of Americans brought in almost half of all reported income, most of it money made from investments (not salaries), as they own more than 80 to 90 percent of all stocks, bonds, trust funds, and business equity. Even more shocking is that the top 1 percent of the American population now owns more than the bottom 90 percent combined (see http://www2.ucsc.edu/whorulesamerica/power/wealth.html).

LIBERATIVE ETHICS IN ACTION 4.1

Liberative Ethics in Action: Housing Bubble to Jobs Crisis

Many commentators chalked the housing bubble and ensuing home-mortgage-foreclosure crisis and recession up to "pure and simple greed" of individuals. While greed certainly played a part in the crisis, poor economic choices and mismanagement of our economy was a bigger piece of the puzzle. Economic choices were made over the last forty years that precipitated the economic crisis. In particular, policies causing the income of America's working families to decline prompted them to borrow against the equity in their homes, and dismantling of regulations in the financial sector allowed investors to extend riskier loans (a trend of increasing "financialization"—profit-making from the financial economy in contrast to the real material economy). In addition, new homeowners were lured into loans that they normally could not afford through offers of low "teaser" interest rates that were later readjusted to much higher rates (called "subprime loans"). As housing prices stopped rising, millions of families were left with mortgages they could not afford. Financiers combined these bad home loans with other assets into "collateralized debt obligations" (CDOs) and unloaded them to other banks and institutional investors. These new home loans and refinancing loans were made on an overinflated housing market, and therefore the system was basically a bubble ready to pop. The financiers made money even when the mortgages went bad through what are called "credit default swaps," basically insurance policies for CDOs. In effect, speculators sold the credit risk on debt and stood to gain from adverse developments concerning the debt. Since companies who issued these credit default swaps were not required to keep a reserve of money to cover bad CDOs (result of deregulation), the whole house of cards came down when enough loans went bad.

Policy makers allowed this unsustainable housing bubble to develop because it benefited the rich and powerful. They made off like bandits, while average working families suffered the fallout by losing their homes or being evicted as renters and by losing their jobs since businesses contracted and spending drastically declined. The job loss and unemployment has been the highest since the Great Depression, with the most vulnerable suffering the most. For example, according to the Center for American Progress, the unemployment rate for African Americans rose 50 percent faster than the rate for white workers. High unemployment further reduces the bargaining power of workers, especially in nonprofessional jobs, and has increased the number of people living in poverty and without health insurance.

Some Americans do not see inequality of wealth as a problem. After all, they claim, if people work hard and become wealthy, who are we to punish them for their initiative; the American Dream should be open to all. The truth, however, is that the American Dream is served on a platter to a handful and is an elusive myth for the majority.

On the top side, over one-third of the rich inherit their wealth, while another third benefit from inheritance. On the bottom side, many families have little or negative wealth. Race and gender also play a factor. Although the income of poor households is significantly below the median, in 2009, as per the US Census Bureau, the median income for white households was $51,861; for Hispanic households, $38,039; and for black households, $32,584. Further, even if rich people have worked hard to amass their wealth, their profit-making was not made simply through individual initiative but relied on the work of many people employed in our global capitalist system, many of whom do not make a living wage and do not have safe and stable working conditions.

Not only is massive wealth accumulated on the backs of the poor, but the resulting inequality has a negative effect on the common good, both nationally and globally. Wealth in the hands of a few gives disproportionate power at the expense of everyone else. One of the reasons our economic systems have seen little to no reform that would help the poor or even the struggling middle class (even with Democrat presidents in office) is that the elite, often in the guise of corporate interest, have put their interests first with their heavy influence on our political system and control of major media outlets and money. Through the media they have managed to convince much of the American public that universal health care, labor unions, and taxes are bad, and through corporate lobbying and campaign contributions they have stopped any sort of progressive change on these fronts.

This powerful elite includes the top 10 percent of wealthy people in other countries as well, and has had a huge influence in what policies have been enacted globally to both protect corporate interests and keep the financial sector extremely profitable. Ever since 1982, when Mexico became the first developing country to say they could not manage the interest payments on their debt, the International Monetary Fund and the World Bank, influenced by the global elite, set up structural-adjustment programs that forced indebted countries to change key aspects of their economy in exchange for debt rescheduling and further loans.

These changes are part of what is called "neoliberalism" and include privatization, deregulation,

---

KEY TERM 4.6

World Bank. An international financial organization that is the single largest source of international development financing, lending money for things like building bridges, dams, and factories. Its efforts were at first directed successfully to rebuilding Japan and Europe, and only later did its focus shift to middle- and poor-income countries.

KEY TERM 4.7

International Monetary Fund (IMF). An intergovernmental organization that oversees the global financial system. Its goal is to prevent financial instability and promote global economic trade and development. It increasingly offers loans to poorer countries with debt payment problems, with the condition that they reshape their economies according to a neoliberal agenda.

---

liberalization of trade and finance, decrease of social subsidies, and devaluation of currency to promote exports.

Some of the free-trade agreements, such as the North American Free Trade Agreement (NAFTA) and others, along with decreased regulation on corporations enacted by the World Trade Organization (WTO), further much of this agenda to promote a so-called free market.

Neoliberalism adopts the theory of comparative advantage that each country should specialize in what it is good at and a free market ideology that increased trade without restrictions should benefit everyone. The result, however, has been increased access by corporate and financial interests to cheap labor and resources and decreased

Fig. 4.1. A man holds up a George W. Bush street puppet outside the World Bank in Washington, DC, for the A16 demonstrations. Photo taken on April 16, 2005, by Ben Schumin.

ability of nations to structure their economies in ways that promote sustainable economic development that benefits the majority of their people.

It is not simply the phenomenon of economic globalization that has led to worker disempowerment, but also deliberate domestic and international policies. Unions in the United States have had to contend with threats of corporations going overseas as well as antilabor and procorporate governmental policy. The development of corporate models like that of Wal-Mart and others big box retailers—a large economy of scale with the ability to force suppliers to cut prices—has also led to declining wages and benefits for many. Even public employees are facing cuts to their wages and benefits in the face of shrinking state and

KEY TERM 4.8

Neoliberalism. A market-driven approach to economic and social policy based on neoclassical economic theory that emphasizes private enterprise, liberalized trade, and relatively open markets. Neoliberalism aims for private- versus public-sector control over the economy in the belief that the private sector is more efficient. Critics of neoliberalism argue that any increased efficiency is due to labor exploitation and environmental degradation.

KEY TERM 4.9

Privatization. Placing assets and services that have been owned and/or managed by the government into the hands of private business.

KEY TERM 4.10

Deregulation. The elimination of governmental regulations that affect the business community and financial sector.

KEY TERM 4.11

Liberalization of trade and finance. The removal or reduction of barriers that thwart the free flow of goods, services, and financial interactions between nations. Liberalization includes the dismantling of subsidies, taxes, and tariffs on goods as well as nontariff barriers such as regulatory legislation and quotas.

KEY TERM 4.12

World Trade Organization (WTO). An organization that aims to liberalize international trade. It regulates trade between countries and guides trade agreements. It also has a dispute resolution process to enforce adherence to WTO agreements signed by member governments. Critics claim it promotes a free-trade agenda of multinational corporations at the expense of local communities, the environment, and democracy.

KEY TERM 4.13

Top tax rate. The tax percentage on the highest bracket of taxation for personal income. Not all of one's income is taxed at the top rate; only the income that falls into that income bracket.

federal budgets, yet no move has been made to cut corporate subsidies or increase taxes on corporations or the rich. The Tax Policy Center shows that our top tax rate is 25 percent today, as opposed to 92 percent in 1953. The percentage of federal tax revenues from corporate tax, as per the Center on Budget and Policy Priorities, has fallen from an average of 28 percent in the 1950s to around 10 percent today.

Current Themes and Methodologies

The emphasis in liberation theology and ethics on social analysis of issues from the underside of society continues to be central, with theological reflection in relation to the lived reality of those on the margins as the second step. In liberation theology and ethics, several key moral norms have traditionally been developed in this theological reflection—namely, justice, preference for the poor, solidarity, subsidiarity, community, and increasingly sustainability.

Where one begins ethical analysis—that is, what loyalties and worldview one starts with—determines in large part what issues are identified as ethical problems. In turn, one's social location influences both what questions are asked and who is asked, further influencing what options are identified as possible strategies for addressing ethical problems.

A liberative economic ethics will start with subjugated voices and analyze particular practices in addition to developing moral norms. Such an ethic, in giving preference to the experiences of those on the margins, will pay attention to both the way people are victimized and the ways they have courageously resisted oppression. Power analysis will be central, especially with a historical focus, to be aware of the changing guises of oppression. Economic and social justice will always be an end goal of a liberative economic ethics, but an adequate concept of justice will truly challenge unjust structures and not simply advocate minor reforms that distribute resources more equally without transforming the structures that created inequality in the first place. Last of all, in conjunction with God's purpose of salvation and liberation for all of creation, a liberative economic ethics will emphasize solidarity with one another in the perpetual unfolding of God's love and compassion. A deep faith in God and a holistic spirituality that embraces all of God's creation

KEY TERM 4.14

Subsidiarity. A principle of social doctrine that claims matters ought to be handled by the most local or least centralized competent authority.

will nourish movements to promote both love and justice in our communities both locally and globally.

Subjugated Voices and Analysis of Practices

A liberative economic ethics will not limit analysis to economic data and consult only the "experts." The starting point for a liberative economic ethic will be the experiences of everyday people, especially the lives of those who are so often seen as "problematic" in our economy (e.g., the unemployed, homeless, immigrants, women on welfare). The information that experts and professionals can offer will be important, but equally as important will be the embodied experiences of those who suffer economic injustice in our global capitalist economic system. Their experiences will add knowledge about the effects of economic systems and practices that are often overlooked, and can offer strategies for resisting structural conditions of exploitation and marginalization in our economic system.

A liberative economic ethic will also examine particular economic practices in conjunction with broad universal norms. For example, traditional ethics might emphasize the values of justice, hard work, or love of neighbor without assessing how these values might play out in particular situations. For example, emphasizing a work ethic for women on welfare without analyzing the obstacles they face, such as lack of affordable child care, flexibility in the workplace, transportation to good jobs, or sufficient education, would be counterproductive and would serve to simply blame the women for their failure to take initiative and pull themselves up by their own bootstraps. When a policy change like welfare reform is proposed, a liberative economic ethical analysis would query how justice is being defined and would broaden the picture to assess all the factors that lead to women's opting for welfare over work. Liberative economic ethicists argue that if we truly want people to have full agency, that is, the freedom to make rational decisions based on a variety of choices, we must examine whether our societal practices actually support agency.

Victimization and Agency

While people on the margins have little political or economic power, this does not mean they are simply victims without the ability to effect change. A liberative economic ethics must pay attention to both the obstacles people face as well as the courageous responses they make despite oppressive realities. Approaches that focus solely on oppression can be used to support stereotypes and to legitimate interpretations that claim the supposed pathologies of a group are the cause of their suffering, thereby avoiding any systemic analysis of economic injustice. Approaches that emphasize the full agency that people on the margins have can negate the victimization and unjust realities they face. Such approaches also ignore the ways in which exploitation and marginalization affect people's psyches. The depression and self-doubt that poverty and oppression can engender are realties that limit full agency. It is easy to fall into the trap of calling people to an ethics of virtue based on the assumption that everyone has full moral agency. A liberative economic ethic is aware that we cannot completely separate individual moral action from environmental circumstances. For example, many would cite crossing a national border illegally as

> ### KEY TERM 4.15
>
> *Maquiladoras.* A manufacturing operation that gets duty- or tariff-free treatment on its import of materials and equipment for assembly of products that are then reexported to the originating country. The North American Free Trade Agreement spurred the growth of maquiladoras. US firms are attracted to the cheaper labor and lower labor and environmental regulations.

CASE STUDY 4.1

Josseline was one of 183 migrants who died in Southern Arizona in 2008. She was a fourteen-year-old girl from El Salvador whose mother was working in the United States without proper documentation. Her mother had saved money to have a coyote bring Josseline and her ten-year-old brother from El Salvador to Los Angeles. In southern Arizona, Josseline became ill and could no longer walk, and so the coyote left her behind. Her brother made it to LA but had to tell his mother that Josseline was left in the Arizona wilderness. Activists found her dead body several days later, identifying her by the green shoes her brother had said she was wearing.

People from Central America and Mexico are immigrating to the United States out of financial necessity. Inability to make enough to raise a family and high underemployment fuel a constant stream of poor people to make the hazardous trek north through Mexico, where they face gangs that prey on immigrants and injuries from riding the train to the US border. If they make it that far, they must cross a perilous river and dessert to circumnavigate the US border patrol. Many get caught and deported back to their countries; others suffer sometimes serious injuries. Human rights violations can happen to immigrants at any stage of their journey. A few manage to enter the country undetected to face the struggle of making it on low-wage work and the instability of being in a country without proper documentation. The money they make sustains their families back in their home countries, however. Remittances (money sent home) account for at least 16 percent of gross domestic product (GDP) in El Salvador, for example. Estimates are that anywhere from 400 to 750 Salvadorans leave the country each day (with or without proper documentation) in search of greater economic security.

These immigrants are victims of a global capitalist system that both marginalizes and exploits them. The neoliberal emphasis of current global economic policy continues to fuel the underdevelopment of poor countries (referred to as neocolonialism). Structural-adjustment programs and free-trade agreements in countries like El Salvador serve to bolster transnational investment in maquiladoras, where wages and working conditions are abysmal, and in export agriculture at the expense of subsistence farmers. These immigrants are not simply victims, however. They exhibit resourcefulness and resiliency in the face of grinding poverty and high unemployment and underemployment. They calculate both the perils of staying and leaving their country of origin and decide accordingly. Some, like Josseline, have little choice in the matter; nevertheless, they show extreme courage in facing the dangers of journeying north. How does focusing one's ethical analysis on neocolonialism over illegal border crossings frame the issues and the solutions differently? How might individual Christians and religious communities be in solidarity with migrants from Central America and other areas? Can you identify both local and global strategies?

Fig. 4.2. Two undocumented immigrants caught by the US Border Patrol in the process of being arrested for future deportation. Photo taken on August 27, 2008, by Miguel A. De La Torre.

unethical, but a liberative economic ethics would analyze how people are exercising agency amid unjust economic circumstances.

A liberative economic ethics will also be aware of the tendency for society to divide the poor into the "deserving" and "undeserving" poor. The label "undeserving poor" refers to people who are perceived as being poor due to their own inferiority and/or bad behavior, whereas the deserving poor are seen as having simply run into some bad luck. However, many people are labeled as undeserving even when structural causes of poverty are primarily at issue. Destructive individual behaviors such as addictions, teen pregnancies, or gang involvement can be a response to grinding poverty. Further, racial stereotypes prompt people of color to be labeled as undeserving despite any behavior they might exhibit. The deserving/undeserving labels serve to keep the structures of power in place, as people can be denied charity or other forms of help and instead punished if they do not go along with the status quo. For example, the homeless people on the street who refuse to enter shelters or other programs can be arrested for loitering. These labels are also used to justify cutting social programs. For example, the 1996 welfare reform law that curtailed welfare entitlements was based on an inaccurate and racist image of black women as having more kids to increase their welfare payments.

Power Analysis

To do economic analysis of our global capitalist system from the perspective of those on the underside, one must connect the dots to follow where power lies. That means asking key questions of any economic system or policy: Who benefits? Who loses? And how? The tendency in traditional analysis is to look only at individual power relations within a current time frame. To do an adequate power analysis of economic relations, it is imperative to look at groups and to give attention to historical foundations for current relationships of inequality and oppression. Without a historical analysis of discrimination and oppression, it becomes too easy to blame the victims for the poverty they face. Too often, equal opportunity is touted without noting that some people are born on third base while others are not given a bat. The income of one's father is still the strongest predictor of one's future income level despite the rhetoric of America as a place where anyone can achieve the American Dream of moving from rags to riches.

Most institutions claim race, class, and gender neutrality but are in fact influenced by dominant social understandings that privilege white, male, heterosexual, and middle-class perspectives on the world. Thus the mantra of neutrality can be a convenient crutch for keeping unjust power relationships in place. We do not have a level playing field, and until we uplift those who are routinely disadvantaged by "neutral" attitudes and systems, we cannot equate neutrality with justice.

One way we act in denial of power inequities is to assume that social problems like poverty, homelessness, and inequality are simply inevitable features of human society. To the contrary, all of these problems are a result of choices about economic policies and structures. More often than not, focus is not on the unjust policies and structures that create the problems but on the moral failings of the victims. For example, some programs addressing poverty work with people to overcome the "culture of the poor" by adopting middle-class values but pay no attention to the actual options people in poverty have for jobs, housing, transportation, and such.

Power analysis must be done at both a local and a global level, as the two are intricately connected. The United States has built up an "empire" through massive military spending. According to the *Stockholm International Peace Research Institute Yearbook 2010*, the US military budget is six times the next largest military budget, of China, and accounts for over 40 percent of global arms spending. Military might in conjunction with economic policies that favor developed countries and transnational corporations keep the majority of people at or below a subsistence level of survival. Many middle-class and even working-class Americans have benefited from the oppression of the world's poor, but increasingly, even they are not immune to the effects of empire and a global capitalist system that serves to benefit a small elite minority at the expense of everyone else. Being able to identify these power relations will help people critically analyze calls for increased patriotism or nationalism that serve to bolster the power of those on the top and pit groups of people at the bottom against one another. Engaging a liberative economic ethics means valuing solidarity with one another and with the earth and other species through policies that equitably distribute power among humans and that promote and support sustainable living.

Forms of Justice

We often think of economic injustice as a distributive problem; that is, wealth, income, and resources are unequally distributed. While distributive justice should clearly be an emphasis of liberative economic ethics, addressing other forms of oppression is equally important. Most importantly is challenging the institutional

BOX 4.2

Five Faces of Oppression (Iris Marion Young)

1. Exploitation. Exploitation is built into the market economy and entails the transfer of the wealth that workers create through their labor power to the capitalists who own the means of production. Redistributing wealth does not necessarily change the institutional practices and structural relations that created the unequal distribution.

2. Marginalization. Marginalization refers to people who are left out of the labor market. Those who are marginalized often experience further oppression in welfare systems that curtail rights and freedoms and shamefully mark people as "dependents."

3. Powerlessness. Powerlessness refers to the ways in which workers have little or no work autonomy, exercise little creativity or judgment in their work, and have no technical expertise or authority.

4. Cultural Imperialism. Cultural imperialism occurs when the dominant experiences, meanings, cultural expressions, and history of a society are seen as "normal," rendering the particular perspectives of some groups invisible while simultaneously stereotyping them and marking them as the "other."

5. Violence. Systemic violence is used to keep groups in their place. Members of oppressed groups end up fearing random unprovoked attacks on their persons and property that are meant to degrade, humiliate, and stigmatize group members. Compounding the oppression is societal acceptance of such violence.

practices and structural relations by which exploitation, marginalization, and all forms of oppression are sustained. Simply redistributing wealth will not bring about justice if these structural practices and relations are not radically transformed. For example, the Jubilee 2000 campaign organized by religiously affiliated groups was successful in getting debt relief for twenty-two of the most highly indebted poor countries, yet without a change to global trade policies and international structures, such achievements toward distribution of wealth are limited. With the deck stacked against them, these countries will simply go back into debt.

Usually charity and reform efforts are emphasized over deep and broad structural change. They are much easier to enact, and they do not generally entail much sacrifice for those with power and privilege. In fact, those in power sometimes see the benefit of allowing small reforms to quell unrest. For example, many in the business community supported Roosevelt's New Deal policies as they kept those organizing for socialism at bay and in many ways allowed capitalism to continue to flourish. While reform efforts such as regulations and safety nets are clearly something to be supported from a liberative standpoint, they do not challenge the logic of domination by which capitalism is structured. That is, they do not challenge the idea that the goals of economic activity are growth and profit. Increased economic growth in the insatiable search for profit can only be wrought at the expense of workers and the environment. Charity is even more insidious, as it puts on a pedestal the "hospitable" philanthropists who made their wealth through the exploitative capitalist system. Charity also creates a divide between the giver and the receiver, keeping the status quo of power relations in place.

Solidarity and Social Movements

Liberation theology highlights the norm of solidarity and working together to effect liberative change. While liberation theology has always placed economic oppression at the forefront, it is clear that all forms of oppression are interconnected and need to be addressed simultaneously on various fronts. Further, human oppression and environmental destruction are intricately linked, and should not be addressed separately. Advocates of liberative perspectives must find ways to engage the participation of groups from various theological spectrums, as economic injustice is clearly a reality for many people, no matter their theological beliefs. While not all Christians envision a liberation God, many embrace a God of love and compassion. The challenge is to encourage people to work as partners with God in bringing about love and justice within and between communities rather than using religion to justify oppressive structures and practices (what Marx was decrying).

There are many examples of the power of religion in movements of justice. Two notable examples—the civil rights movement and the farmworker movement—were discussed earlier in this chapter. Both of these movements drew on deep spiritual resources of particular communities and existing church networks in their organizing. While economic globalization and resulting social and environmental injustices often feel too big to tackle, multiple small-scale movements of resistance can fuel one another to create a larger social movement for economic, social, and environmental justice. These movements need not all be religiously motivated, but clearly a deep faith and spiritual connection can nourish and strengthen such movements. Rather than religion being used by those in power as a disempowering opium of the people, we can have faith in a God of justice, compassion, and love, and make religion a liberating sustainer of and for the people and for all of God's creation.

Study Questions

1. Identify ways a Christian liberative approach might promote economic and social justice in solidarity with people on the margins. Contrast this with a direct-charity approach.
2. Identify and discuss how liberative economic ethicists offer a deeper understanding of sin as structural as well as individual, and salvation (or liberation) as material as well as spiritual.
3. Discuss what it means to place subjugated lives and voices at the moral center in relation to economic policy, and why participation and recognition in society is equally important to just distribution of social goods.

4. Identify stories and values within the Christian tradition and told within faith communities that offer alternative theological visions to some of the American ideologies that stigmatize and idealize particular groups of people in our society and that support inequality.
5. Envision and strategize ways to encourage and spiritually nourish both individual and collective responsibility for promoting economic and social justice.

Suggested Readings

Albrecht, Gloria H. *Hitting Home: Feminist Ethics, Women's Work, and the Betrayal of "Family Values."* New York: Continuum, 2004.

Beckley, Harlan. *Passion for Justice: Retrieving the Legacies of Walter Rauschenbusch, John A. Ryan, and Reinhold Niebuhr.* Louisville: Westminster John Knox, 1992.

Brubaker, Pamela K. *Globalization at What Price? Economic Change and Daily Life.* Cleveland: Pilgrim, 2001.

Brubaker, Pamela, Rebecca Todd Peters, and Laura A. Stivers, eds. *Justice in a Global Economy: Strategies for Home, Community, and World.* Louisville: Westminster John Knox, 2006.

De La Torre, Miguel A. *Doing Christian Ethics from the Margins.* Maryknoll, NY: Orbis, 2004.

Dorrien, Gary. *Social Ethics in the Making: Interpreting an American Tradition.* West Sussex, UK: Wiley Blackwell, 2008.

Estey, Ken. *A New Protestant Labor Ethic at Work.* Cleveland: Pilgrim, 2002.

Grau, Marion. *Of Divine Economy: Refinancing Redemption.* New York: T&T Clark, 2004.

Harrison, Beverly Wildung. *Justice in the Making: Feminist Social Ethics.* Louisville: Westminster John Knox, 2004.

Martin, Joan. *More than Chains and Toil: A Christian Work Ethic of Enslaved Women.* Louisville: Westminster John Knox, 2000.

Rieger, Joerg. *No Rising Tide: Theology, Economics, and the Future.* Minneapolis: Fortress Press, 2009.

Robb, Carol S. *Equal Value: An Ethical Approach to Economics and Sex.* Boston: Beacon, 1995.

Snarr, Melissa. *All You that Labor: Religion and Ethics in the Living Wage Movement.* New York: New York University Press, 2011.

Stivers, Laura. *Disrupting Homelessness: Alternative Christian Approaches.* Minneapolis: Fortress Press, 2011.

Todd Peters, Rebecca. *In Search of the Good Life: The Ethics of Globalization.* New York: Continuum, 2004.

Todd Peters, Rebecca, and Elizabeth Hinson-Hasty. *To Do Justice: A Guide for Progressive Christians.* Louisville: Westminster John Knox, 2008.

Tooley, Michelle. *Voices of the Voiceless: Women, Justice, and Human Rights in Guatemala.* Waterloo, ON: Herald, 1997.

Young, Iris Marion. *Justice and the Politics of Difference.* Princeton: Princeton University Press, 1990.

———. *Responsibility for Justice.* Oxford: Oxford University Press, 2011.

PART TWO

The US Racial and Ethnic Context

5 Hispanic Liberative Ethics

Rubén Rosario Rodríguez

ALTHOUGH THERE HAS BEEN a Hispanic presence in North America since before the founding of the United States, the contributions of Latino/a religion to American culture are often overlooked, perhaps because until recently Latino/as have resisted the tendency to identify themselves as a single group with a common history. Hispanics in the United States represent a diversity of nationalities and political perspectives from no less than twenty-two Latin American countries, with Mexicans (63 percent), Puerto Ricans (9.2 percent), and Cubans (3.5 percent) constituting the largest subgroups. Recent polling finds that while more Latina/os prefer the term *Hispanic* to *Latino* or *Latina*, most still identify themselves by country of origin (even when born and raised in the United States), saying, "I am Puerto Rican" or "I am Colombian" rather than, "I am Latino/a" or "I am Hispanic." This suggests that to self-identify as "Latino/a" or "Hispanic" is an intentional act of political empowerment for all Hispanics.

Given the growth of the US Hispanic population, it is unavoidable that Hispanic perspectives are transforming North American religion, politics, and ethics. According to the 2010 census, the Hispanic population accounts for over half the growth of the total population in the United States between 2000 and 2010, with Hispanics now constituting over 16 percent of the general population.

KEY TERM 5.1

Hispanic. A person of Latin American or Spanish ancestry born and/or raised in the United States; emphasizes the linguistic base of a common Latino/a identity.

KEY TERM 5.2

Latino/a. A gender inclusive (albeit clumsy) term for a person of Latin American ancestry born and/or raised in the United States; quickly becoming the preferred term for self-identification by Latino/as in the academy.

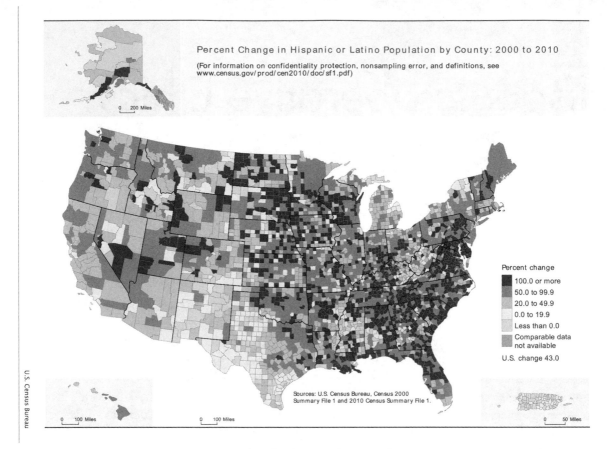

Fig. 5.1. Census data for the United States of America, 2010.

Over two-thirds of Latino/as (68 percent) identify themselves as Roman Catholics, more than 35 percent of the Roman Catholic Church in the United States, while the second largest religious grouping, evangelical Protestants, makes up an estimated 15 percent of the US Hispanic population. Since over 90 percent of Latina/os self-identify as Christian (Roman Catholic, Pentecostal, evangelical, mainline Protestant, etc.), and less than 1 percent of the Hispanic population self-identifies with Judaism, Islam, or other world religion, an analysis of Latino/a religion in public life will of necessity focus primarily on Christian expressions of political and social action.

Within the academy, the field of Christian ethics has begun to address the demographic shifts that are transforming North American Christianity. Yet, in spite of efforts by the Society of Christian Ethics (SCE), the Association of Theological Schools (ATS), and the American Academy of Religion (AAR) to foster cultural and racial diversity, the discipline of Christian ethics remains bound to a primarily Eurocentric academic canon. Nowhere is this more evident than in the nominal presence of racial-ethnic faculty as a percentage of total full-time faculties in theological education. In 1999, the percentage of Hispanic full-time faculty in ATS member schools was approximately 4 percent.

In 2011, that number still hovered at under 4 percent. This stark reality is most noticeable within the discipline of Christian ethics, where only a handful of Latino/a scholars, Ismael García, Ada María Isasi-Díaz, Eldin Villafañe, Michael Manuel Mendiola, and Miguel A. De La Torre, have obtained their doctorate in and teach Christian ethics. Many factors account for the dearth of Hispanics in this field, aside from documented patterns of discrimination that have historically excluded racial-ethnic minorities from the mainstream academy, such as the multidisciplinary approach embraced by Hispanic scholars of religion that holistically integrates ethical analysis and action into their work, and the current lack of an extensive body of literature written by Hispanic ethicists defining Hispanic or Latino/a Christian ethics as a distinct discipline.

While there are few Latino/a scholars working within the field of Christian ethics as defined by the Society of Christian Ethics (aside from the five senior scholars already mentioned, there is a growing but still small number of junior scholars and graduate students being mentored through the Latino/a Working Group of the SCE), almost all Hispanic scholars of religion, regardless of area of specialization, engage the ethical in their work. Accordingly, there is a forty-year history of Latino/a religious scholarship that can serve as a resource for constructing a distinctly Latino/a Christian ethics. To that end, this chapter will provide a brief overview of the existing literature in order to identify key figures, major themes, methodological contributions, and pressing moral concerns that distinguish Hispanic moral reasoning in the United States in the new millennium.

History and Development of Hispanic Liberative Ethics

While the canon of works by Hispanic ethicists exploring and articulating a distinctly Hispanic Christian ethics is small, there is a rich body of work by several generations of Latino/a scholars

of religion that can inform the construction of an indigenous US Hispanic method of ethical analysis. Drawing on a shared experience of living as a marginalized minority within a dominant majority population, Latino/a theologians have developed discourses that build bridges between different cultures, languages, and perspectives. US Latina/o theology, while recognizing its indebtedness to Latin American liberation theology, has struggled to create its own distinct identity as a North American theological movement.

Over the last thirty to forty years, Hispanic theologians have articulated an intentionally ecumenical (Roman Catholic, mainline Protestant, evangelical, and Pentecostal), multicultural theology known as *teología de conjunto* (or *teología en conjunto*, meaning "theology done jointly"): a communal approach to theology that involves the cooperative efforts of theologians, pastors, and laypersons.

In order to facilitate the task of "mapping" the landscape of North American Latino/a theology, several important themes serve as guideposts: (1) the development of a theological understanding of *mestizaje*, (2) the role of popular religion in nurturing people's faith in their struggles for liberation, (3) a liberating reading of the Bible grounded in God's preferential option for the poor and oppressed, (4) respect for theological traditions in

---

KEY TERM 5.3

Teología de conjunto/Teología en conjunto ("theology done jointly"). A communal method of doing theology characteristic of the US Latino/a theology movement that originates in and reflects the lived reality of the Latino/a community and entails a process whereby theologians, pastors, and laypersons gather to reflect together.

KEY TERM 5.4

Mestizaje ("mixing"). Racial and cultural mixing, or hybridity, originally referring to the people of European (Spanish and Portuguese) and Amerindian ancestry.

a spirit of ecumenism, and (5) a theological commitment to creating just social structures.

Mestizaje has become a central category for US Latino/a theological reflection. Originally a denigrating label for the offspring of Amerindians and their Spanish conquerors, *mestizaje* has been appropriated by Latino/as as a term of self-identity and cultural pride. Influenced by the pioneering work of Father Virgilio Elizondo, whose *Galilean Journey: The Mexican-American Promise* (1983) interprets *mestizaje* as God's means of positively transforming a racially and culturally divided world, theologians employ the term to describe the US Hispanic ethos of radical inclusion (*mulatez* signifies the offspring of African slaves and the Caribbean Spanish overseers). Without romanticizing *mestizaje*, US Latino/a theology has reinterpreted the preferential option for the poor in the North American context to include not just the economically impoverished but also the ethnically and gendered other, as evidenced by the contributions of US Latina scholars like Ada María Isasi-Díaz, Jeanette Rodríguez, and María Pilar Aquino, who have underscored the movement's theological commitment to not only explain and interpret the faith but also transform social reality itself. By refusing to separate questions of class, race, and gender, the Latina reimagining of the concept of *mestizaje* challenges US Latino/a religion to become truly inclusive by encompassing the fullness of humanity in its theological discourse and its social ethics.

A second marker that distinguishes US Latino/a theology is its use of popular religion as a *locus*

theologicus in recognition of the fact that popular religious practices serve as a source of communal identity and political empowerment. In other words, due to the Latino/a experience of cultural marginalization in the United States, of existing in an in-between space referred to as *nepantla*, our religious experiences and theological reflections about these experiences are necessarily distinct from official ecclesiastical structures and traditions.

While existing alongside dominant beliefs and practices, these religious experiences and theological reflections are not always recognized or sanctioned. By defining popular religion as a concrete expression of resistance by a marginalized community within a larger religious tradition, Latino/a theologians acknowledge that popular religious practices exist in both Protestant and Catholic communities but differ in their form of expression.

KEY TERM 5.5

Nepantla. A Nahuatl word meaning *tierra entre medio* ("in-between land"), used by Chicana feminist scholar and poet Gloria Anzaldúa to refer to the liminal spaces between cultures inhabited by *mestizo/as* who cross and transgress geographical, cultural, economic, and racial/ethnic borders.

KEY TERM 5.6

Popular religion. A term descriptive of the practices, worldviews, beliefs, political commitments, and so on, originating with the people as opposed to the officially recognized ecclesial authorities.

CASE STUDY 5.1

In 1999, the United States Equal Employment Opportunity Commission (EEOC) and Tanimura & Antle, one of the largest lettuce growers/distributors in the United States, reached a $1,855,000 voluntary settlement, approved by US District Court on behalf of two employees and a class of current and former Tanimura & Antle employees who were allegedly subjected to sexual harassment and retaliation in Salinas, California, and Yuma, Arizona. In its federal court complaint, the EEOC alleged that a Tanimura & Antle production manager subjected a female employee, Blanca Alfaro, to quid pro quo sexual harassment—that is, required sexual favors as a condition for employment and the receipt of job benefits. The EEOC alleged that Alfaro was subsequently subjected to a hostile work environment, which included constant unwelcome sexual advances by that production manager and another management employee. The commission further alleged that Alfaro was discharged in retaliation shortly after complaining about the unwelcome advances. Based on its investigation, the EEOC also alleged that other workers were subjected to similar types of harassment by managerial and supervisory personnel and were retaliated against for complaining about the repeated harassment. The company's retaliatory conduct allegedly included the creation of a hostile work environment and, in some cases, actual discharge.

The United States is a leading market for sexual trafficking, and hostile work environments like the one described above are part of the mainstream ("white") workplace. Is the category of *machismo* useful for dismantling gender discrimination in the United States, or does it merely perpetuate harmful racist stereotypes about Latina/os? How does it affect the situation when the targets of sexual harassment are undocumented workers? Does the law protect their rights too? How does the Christian doctrine of *imago Dei* aid in resisting oppression?

Nevertheless, Latina/o Christianity in all its forms is indelibly shaped by the Iberian Catholic conquest of the New World that gave birth to a distinctly *mestizo* Latino/a culture that brings together European, African, and indigenous traditions. Given this understanding of popular religion, as explored and articulated in Orlando Espín's *The Faith of the People: Theological Reflections on Popular Catholicism* (1997), personal and communal stories are an important source for establishing and preserving a shared theological identity. Latino and Latina theologians draw on the rich cultural memory of Hispanic peoples manifested in popular devotions like *La Virgen de Guadalupe* to articulate a distinct

theological perspective that has survived in great part through the efforts of lay women acting as keepers of tradition. Methodologically, this highlights the importance of what María Pilar Aquino has termed *lo cotidiano*, meaning "the day-to-day," as the context in which Hispanic ethical reflection occurs and from which liberative social praxis originates.

Accordingly, the study and analysis of popular Christianity remains an important trope for Latino/a theologians and ethicists seeking to convince the academy that dominant forms of theology ought to pay methodological attention to the people's faith and praxis or risk becoming an insular dialogue among a handful of specialists.

KEY TERM 5.7

Lo cotidiano ("the day-to-day"). A Spanish-language expression for reality as it is experienced in daily life.

It is axiomatic for Christian theology that the Bible is a record of the acts of God in human history, and provides reliable knowledge about the character and nature of God. Still, Hispanic theology recognizes that all knowledge is contextual and so views the Bible as a collection of narratives from the collective human religious imagination that gives meaning to some (but not all) people's existence. Therefore, US Latino/a theology's commitment to Scripture as the primary source of theology is not an uncritical Biblicism, for while the event of revelation is at the core of all our human talk about God, believers have access only to interpretations of this event and not to the event itself.

When this popular reverence for the Bible as sacred word is coupled with a liberating reading of the Scriptures, Latino/a communities are empowered to take part in socially transformative action. As Justo L. González contends in *Santa Biblia: The Bible Through Hispanic Eyes* (1996), Latino/as read and interpret Scripture from the perspective of a fundamental theological commitment to God's preferential option for the poor and oppressed, demonstrating the influence of and

KEY TERM 5.8

Preferential option. The theological commitment to live and act in solidarity with the most oppressed, marginalized, and powerless members of society in order to transform the structures that created their unjust situation.

relationship to Latin American liberation theology in the work of both Protestant and Catholic Latino/as (especially in light of the resurgence of Scripture following the Second Vatican Council). This liberating reading of Scripture brings together the theological themes of history and eschatology in recognition of the fact that the church lives "between the times," working for historical liberation but grounded in the hope of the eschatological fulfillment of God's promises.

As a movement, US Latino/a theology has consistently critiqued dominant Christian traditions; nonetheless, Latino/a theologians also affirm the normative role of tradition in Christian theology. While US Latino/a theology occupies the "borderlands" between official church structures and popular practices, and given that most Latino/a churches survive either at the periphery of major denominations or become "free churches" that empower local congregations and nurture "homegrown" leadership (but still remain marginalized within the broader society), Hispanic theologians acknowledge their individual confessional commitments and locate their work within the broader ecumenical Christian tradition.

Thus Virgilio Elizondo writes as a Mexican American Catholic priest, Justo L. González as a Cuban-born ordained Methodist minister, and María Pilar Aquino as a Latina Catholic lay theologian; yet all three move beyond their "local" audience by intentionally engaging the ecumenical church across boundaries of class, ethnicity, gender, and denominational affiliation. Employing a "hermeneutics of suspicion," Latino/a theology concedes the interested perspective of every theological narrative and encourages intersubjective conversation as a corrective against the tendency to universalize particular points of view, defining the task of theology as inherently communal and interdisciplinary. In other words, Hispanic theology and ethics is methodologically committed to intercultural dialogue as the means of attaining increased understanding between different

BOX 5.1

Virgilio Elizondo, a Mexican American priest from San Antonio, Texas, is perhaps the most influential figure within Roman Catholic Hispanic theology and is an important contributor to the development of *teología en conjunto*. The discourse on *mestizaje* within US Latino/a theology cannot be understood without reference to his seminal text, *Galilean Journey: The Mexican-American Promise* (1984). Cuban-born historian and theologian Justo L. González, an ordained Methodist minister, stands as the progenitor of Protestant Latino/a theology. His vast theological corpus has been described as the most cogent statement of US Hispanic theology to date, and his systematic theology, *Mañana: Christian Theology from a Hispanic Perspective* (1990), undertakes a critical hermeneutic of the Scriptures, theology, and history from a distinctly Latino/a perspective.

While neither figure is strictly speaking an ethicist, an ethic of liberative praxis grounds both men's work. Elizondo was the first to articulate *mestizaje* as a primary theological locus (a typology now used by most US Latino/a theologians), in which *mestizos*—while experiencing marginalization and subjugation—are called by God to build bridges between the oppressor and the oppressed. Thus *mestizaje* becomes an empowering and positive cultural and theological identity with concrete political consequences. González contends that the major theme unifying US Latino/a theologies is a liberating reading of Scripture that embraces God's

BOX 5.1 (continued)

preferential option for the poor ("poor" understood as encompassing issues of race, gender, and class) and leads the church to make political commitments in solidarity with the oppressed and marginalized to positively transform repressive social orders.

---

peoples by fostering genuine conversation and mutual exchange.

The fifth and final guidepost for navigating the landscape of US Latino/a theology explicitly addresses the church's social ethics. Ethicist Ismael García in *Dignidad: Ethics Through Hispanic Eyes* (1997) identifies the concept of *dignidad* ("dignity") as a guiding virtue of Hispanic ethical reflection. A Hispanic understanding of justice begins with an understanding of what it means to be a human being created in the image of God: a person is a child of God endowed with basic human dignity. Theologically speaking, the

KEY TERM 5.9

Hermeneutics of suspicion. A term coined by philosopher Paul Ricoeur to describe a critical methodology that attempts to decode and uncover the hidden political interests served by a text.

KEY TERM 5.10

Dignidad ("dignity"). A theological principle that all human beings, by virtue of their innate humanness, are deserving of certain basic conditions necessary for sustaining life.

value and dignity given to us as a gift in the act of Creation can never be lost or taken away but arises from the fact that we are created to live in covenant with God.

As an act of grace, the gift of life is unmerited, and our value as God's creatures is independent of our moral choices, our physical and mental abilities, or our social status. This fact prescribes how we must treat others and how we can expect others to treat us. Simply put, there are ways of relating to others that violate the covenant between God and God's creation since the value and dignity we possess as God's creatures entitles each and every human being to be recognized as the image of God and treated with the appropriate respect and care. Thus a guiding principle of Latino/a moral reasoning is the question, What are persons due in order to sustain their basic human dignity? Minimally, justice requires that essential needs be met: food, shelter, clothing, health care, and so on. Underlying this view of humanity is the conviction that justice does indeed take sides because God's justice, as the witness of Scripture reveals and the liberation theology movement reminds

BOX 5.2

History and Development of US Latino/a Theology

US Latino/a theology emerged as a distinct movement in the 1970s with the establishment of the Mexican American Cultural Center (MACC) in San Antonio, under the guidance and direction of founder Virgilio Elizondo. Other programs soon followed, including the Mexican American Program at Perkins School of Theology, which, in cooperation with the United Methodist Publishing House, founded the first journal exclusively dedicated to Latino/a theological reflection in

BOX 5.2 (continued)

1981, *Apuntes*, with Justo L. González as editor. During the late 1980s and early 1990s, Latino/a theology established itself within the academy through a proliferation of publications and the establishment of various organizations devoted to Latina/o theological reflection, scholarship, and theological education. These include the Hispanic American Religion, Culture, and Society Group and *La Communidad* within the American Academy of Religion; the Academy of Catholic Hispanic Theologians of the United States (ACHTUS), which began publishing the *Journal of Hispanic/Latino Theology*, with Orlando Espín as editor; and *Asociacíon para la Educacíon Teológica Hispana* (AETH), which focuses on the theological education of Hispanics. These various groups and institutions embodied the spirit of *teología de conjunto*, cooperating across denominational lines in programs like the Hispanic Summer Program, an annual intensive summer workshop where Hispanic students and professors of religion and theology gather at member institutions to reflect theologically on the challenges facing the Latino/a church, and the Hispanic Theological Initiative (HTI), funded by the Pew Charitable Trust, which promotes and nurtures advanced theological studies by creating a network of support for Latino/a doctoral students and junior faculty.

us, has always demonstrated a preferential option for the poor and oppressed.

From this brief overview of some of the major themes and innovations of US Latino/a theology, a clear picture begins to develop as to how to construct a distinctly Hispanic Christian ethics. In most cases, US Hispanic theologies are liberationist in their methodology and praxis, but even when they are not explicitly liberationist, most Latino/a theologies embody a liberative ethos. Like Latin American liberation theology, Hispanic theologies demonstrate a commitment to the interdisciplinary analysis of social reality in order to expose how present social structures perpetuate racist, sexist, and classist agendas. What they share is an emphasis on the lived experience of the believing community, a communal praxis grounded in liberation, and a biblical hermeneutics that questions dominant power structures and privileges the perspective of the oppressed. Where US Latino/a theology differs is in broadening its understanding of God's preferential option for the poor to include those who suffer social and cultural marginalization. Accordingly, while Latin American liberation theology has emphasized political and economic liberation, US Latina/o theology has, in coming to terms with the complexities of cultural, racial, and ethnic *mestizaje*, linked political and economic liberation to issues of cultural and ethnic identity.

The commitment of US Latino/a theologies to a contextual approach reinterprets the history of Christianity as the history of many local traditions rather than the history of one monolithic tradition. The experience of biculturalism suggests that US Hispanics, while subjected to marginalization, exclusion, and exploitation on the basis of race, are also comfortable navigating the dominant Western Christian tradition. Thus Latina/o theology arises from two equally and deeply held convictions: the particularity of Hispanic identity as a marginalized minority and the sense of belonging to the global ecumenical church. By conversing with the plurality that is the Christian tradition, past *and* present, along with critical perspectives from non-Christian sources, US Latino/a theology is rescued from

solipsism and provincialism and avoids dogmatically rejecting or denying potential avenues of God's revelation.

The implications for ethical methodology are clear. Choosing to do Christian ethics from a Hispanic perspective begins with an intentional act of solidarity with, by, and for the poor, marginalized, and disenfranchised. Not only does this faith commitment entail a critique of the dominant political and economic structures, but it also involves questioning the dominant Eurocentric paradigms that govern the academic discourse of ethics. Broadly speaking, the problem with the dominant discourse is that even when it is open and receptive to liberationist perspectives, by insisting that scholars of color (and other marginalized groups) employ long-standing models of ethical reasoning, the academy undermines the emancipatory agendas of oppressed communities. Quite simply, the Eurocentric narrative that establishes supposedly color-blind, universal, and objective ethical norms reflects a hermeneutical naïveté that fails to account for the interestedness of its own point of view. When the dominant point of view is racist, sexist, and/or classist, fine-tuning existing models of ethical analysis cannot overcome prevailing structural inequities, and some form of revolutionary praxis is called for.

Need for Hispanic Liberation

A liberationist perspective argues that Christian ethical thought, not just Hispanic Christian ethics, is inherently revolutionary. Not in terms of violent revolution but insofar as it seeks the salvation of both the oppressor and the oppressed by subverting and overcoming sinful structures and relationships. We are all sinners. Poverty or victimization does not make us saints. Real, concrete liberation can only occur when both the oppressor and the oppressed confront and overcome their sinfulness, guilt, and complicity in perpetuating relationships of oppression. And for Christian ethics, this radical transformation occurs only in and through Christ.

Unlike a political understanding of revolution in which the party in power is ousted, usually through violent means, stripped of power, and replaced by a new revolutionary party whose raison d'être becomes maintaining its hard-won power, the Christian conception of revolution (grounded in the doctrines of grace and forgiveness) recognizes that both the oppressor and the oppressed have need of liberation from the oppressive worldview and sinful social structures that facilitate relationships of oppression. This by no means implies that the victims of repression in some way merit their victimization. Rather, it merely recognizes the fact that the only way to overcome the historical vicious circle of revolution in which the oppressed becomes the oppressor is to overcome and reject the values that rationalize relationships of domination and exploitation. The revolutionary who struggles against repression because he or she wants what the oppressor has—power, wealth, status—does not seek to inherently transform exploitative social structures; he or she merely wants to change his or her social location within a given set of exploitative relationships for his or her own benefit.

Therefore, Christian ethics from a Latino/a perspective is not only revolutionary; it is also explicitly Christocentric, meaning that its understanding of liberation and salvation is inseparable from its understanding of who Jesus Christ is and what he does for us. God became incarnate as Jesus of Nazareth. If we take seriously every aspect of the humanity of God, it is in the history of this particular person, Jesus of Nazareth, a marginalized Galilean who transgressed social boundaries to bring good news to the poor and oppressed, that God is most fully known. Within this conceptual framework, Jesus' crucifixion is a direct result of the life he lived, not because he was a criminal, but due to the fact that as the Christ of God, Jesus of Nazareth challenged the dominant values of the religious and governing authorities of his day. They in turn executed him for sedition. In other words, a Christocentric, praxis-oriented, social ethics views the work of the Christ as adversarial politics: God's preferential option for the poor and oppressed of history demands that the church, as the body of Christ, choose sides.

At the same time, a Christology promising historical liberation without also overcoming sin and death is as vacant as a Christology that promises eternal life without addressing human suffering here and now. In light of the centrality given to Christ's praxis in Hispanic ethics, it is appropriate to look to the teachings of Jesus for guidance in the realm of social ethics. Yet, what we find is that the New Testament presents a range of ethical instruction. Nevertheless, a consistent, unifying narrative unites the Gospels: only Jesus Christ brings genuine liberation from every kind of bondage.

Temporal powers led Jesus to the criminal's cross, but God's power raised Jesus from death and glorified him at the right hand of the Father; temporal powers tried to take the life of the early church martyrs, yet God raised them to eternal life and preserved the church against persecution; temporal powers continue to legislate life and death without any consideration given to preserving basic human dignity, but Jesus' teaching and actions still stand as an unwavering countercultural example. During Jesus' time, many Jews expected a political messiah, yet Jesus, in his own self-understanding as the Messiah of God, superseded their expectations by rejecting nationalistic patterns, interpreting his mission through the lens of the Suffering Servant portions of the book of Isaiah. Granted, by choosing to follow the paradigm of Isaiah's Messiah, the King (Isa. 1–37), the Suffering Servant (Isa. 38–55), and the Anointed Conqueror (Isa. 56–66), Jesus still understands his ministry in political terms, embracing the calling and anointing of God to bring justice and liberation to the poor and oppressed (Luke 4:16-30).

Yet by interpreting kingship in terms of the Suffering Servant, Jesus subverts dominant views that expected God's anointed leader to bring about change through political rule. Jesus discards the false god of the state in recognition of the absolute sovereignty of God over all nations and empires through a radical reevaluation of values in which divine rule is embodied in the Suffering Servant, who was oppressed and afflicted "like a lamb that is led to the slaughter" (Isa. 53:7 NRSV). Accordingly, we find in Jesus' life and ministry only broad guidelines for our political life together under the Word of God, not in terms of a particular political agenda, but more a general orientation toward what any temporal government needs to be and do in order to be a just and righteous government in the eyes of God. As a result, an ethic guided by Jesus' messianic mission is necessarily adversarial, countercultural, and willing to take a costly stance in following Christ.

Always striving for tangible social justice, US Latino/a ethics begins by naming *la realidad* ("reality") through an interdisciplinary analysis of the historical and cultural context of Latina/os in the United States.

Hispanics are not only the largest minority group but also the fastest-growing segment of the US population, the youngest, and among some subgroups, the poorest. According to the National Council of La Raza, a Hispanic research and advocacy group, the socioeconomic disadvantages facing Latino/as include the lowest high school graduation rate in the nation (43 percent of Latino/as twenty-five years old and older graduated high school, compared to 84.8 percent graduation rate among whites and 78.7 percent among blacks, with only 11.1 percent of Latino/as graduating from college), and the highest rate of working poor, given that 68.4 percent of the Hispanic population sixteen years old and over are in the labor force, slightly higher than whites (66.2 percent) and blacks (63.5 percent), yet 22.8 percent live in poverty, a rate three times higher than white families. Furthermore, more than one quarter (28.6 percent) of Hispanic children live in poverty, while Hispanic families headed by a single mother have the highest rate of poverty among all census categories.

Yet, contrary to popular misconceptions, the rapid growth of the Latino/a population since 1990 is not due solely to illegal immigration, but is attributable to Hispanics having the highest birth rate among all ethnic groups. In fact, 60.9 percent of US Hispanics are native-born, among those who are foreign-born 10 percent are naturalized citizens, and of the remaining new immigrants, almost half entered the country legally. Census data also disproves further stereotypes by revealing that the majority (71.8 percent) of Latino/as who speak Spanish at home are also proficient or fluent in English.

This demographic snapshot of US Latino/a experience illuminates why our church communities promote and develop bilingual and bicultural theologies grounded in *lo cotidiano* (the day-to-day life experience of our people) that are informed by grassroots efforts to embrace the gospel in a society still defined in terms of racial, gender, economic, and ethnic inequalities. The Latina/o experience in the United States can be understood in terms of navigating the poles of assimilation and resistance. Latino/as are part of American culture, shaped by it but also shaping it. They have intermarried; they have a long and distinguished history of public service in politics,

---

KEY TERM 5.11

La lucha ("the struggle"). Recognition that the lived reality of most Latino/as in the United States entails a daily struggle for basic human dignity and all this entails.

CASE STUDY 5.2

Fifteen years ago, the United States Court of Appeals struck down affirmative action at the University of Texas Law School. In the intervening years, the state of Texas has implemented a supposedly race-neutral admissions policy known as the "Top 10 Percent Law," in which the top ten percent of high school classes across the state automatically receive admission to the University of Texas. While the policy has led to increased enrollments of African American and Hispanic students, it has failed to meet the university's stated diversity goals in university admissions. Furthermore, even with increased enrollment of Latino/a students, these students tend to cluster in certain programs like education and social work. In 2011, the same court that struck down affirmative action in 1996 has now upheld the use of race-conscious admissions by public universities in Texas.

The Fifth US Circuit Court of Appeals in New Orleans upheld the use of race as an admission factor at the University of Texas at Austin. The current ruling upholds a 2008 decision that ruled the university did not violate the civil rights or constitutional right of equal protection of two white students denied admission. The university's position is that the 10 percent plan failed to keep up with the demographic changes in the state of Texas, in which 39 percent of the population is Hispanic but only 23 percent of U.T. Austin students are Latino/a. This discrepancy is widened in certain disciplines, as is the case in the Business School at U.T. Austin, where only 10 percent of students are African American and 14 percent are Latino/a.

The rationale and legal basis for affirmative action is that certain minority populations have historically been denied access to educational and employment opportunities. As certain states, like California and Texas, become what some are calling "majority-minority" states, does it make sense to continue allowing for race-based admissions at state universities? Given that the state university system in Texas failed to create a student body representative of the state population *without* race-based admissions (under the 10 percent plan), what factors do you see contributing to this disparity between the student and the general population? Does a demographic majority necessarily entail equal access to political and economic power?

education, and the military; and they have contributed a unique flavor to the religious life of this country. Yet this shared identity as Latino/as is always in flux.

Hispanics now occupy every rung of the socioeconomic ladder, from undocumented farmworkers and day laborers to CEOs of large multinational corporations. Latino/a activism and political affiliations range from labor organizers, to Puerto Rican clergy opposing American militarism, to socially and religious conservatives who vote Republican. (Although a highly disputed figure, as many as 44 percent of Hispanics voted for George W. Bush in 2004.) Therefore, as the presence of Latino/as in the United States continues to grow, and with it the ability to influence and transform society, as demonstrated by the efforts to court the Hispanic vote in the 2008 Presidential election, Hispanic Christian ethics is informed and guided by this history of marginalization and disenfranchisement in order to embody the biblical imperative to be advocates for the voiceless and powerless inhabiting the margins of society.

LIBERATIVE ETHICS IN ACTION 5.1

Liberative Ethics in Action: The Issue of Immigration

The most contentious immigration debates have centered on the issues of undocumented immigration, border control, and the burden undocumented workers then place on public services. The National Council of La Raza has chronicled on their website (http://www.nclr.org/) many misconceptions about immigration—documented and undocumented—that continue to be presented as fact. One common misconception is that immigrants take jobs away from US citizens. A recent study by the National Federation of Independent Businesses shows that immigrant labor is needed to fill jobs that the older, better-educated American workforce is not willing to fill in the areas of agriculture, food processing and production, and the hotel and food service industry. In fact, American small businesses rely on undocumented labor but are often obstructionists when it comes to comprehensive immigration reform.

Analyzing the morality of immigration reform from the perspective of a Latino/a Christian ethics, with its emphasis on preserving basic human dignity, it is imperative to shift the discussion away from the undocumented worker and onto the business owner. The root cause of illegal immigration is the market demand for an undocumented and therefore easily exploitable workforce. In 2009, Giant Labor Solutions and two other midwestern companies were indicted under the federal Racketeer Influenced and Corrupt Organizations Act (RICO) for turning their workers into slaves, outsourcing them to housekeeping jobs in hotels and other businesses in fourteen different states while forcing them to live, sometimes eight at a time, in small apartments for which they were charged exorbitant rent.

Most of the workers, primarily from the Dominican Republic, Jamaica, and the Philippines, were in the country without proper documentation and were threatened with deportation and physical harm. This case, and others like it, reveals a pattern of predatory exploitation of undocumented workers by American businesses as a means of not only filling undesirable jobs but also of reducing operating costs for the sole purpose of maximizing profit. Hispanic ethicists need to respond to those pundits willing to trample on the basic human rights of undocumented workers on the basis that they entered the country illegally by shifting the focus of the public debate onto the corrupt and oppressive hiring practices of American small business owners. (For examples of Latino/as who critique how the mainstream media covers the issue of immigration, see the work of David-James Gonzales, a staff writer for *Prospect, the Journal of International affairs at UCSD*, and Ruy Teixeira, a senior fellow at the Center for American Progress.)

Preserving the basic human dignity (*dignidad*) of all persons as creatures made in the image of God (*imago Dei*) leads Latino/a ethicists to criticize the free-trade policies of global capitalism. While supporters of neoliberalism (an approach to economic and social policy that emphasizes free trade and relatively open markets in order to maximize the role of the private sector in determining the political and economic priorities of the state) argue that globalization has improved wages and working conditions for workers in underdeveloped nations, detractors contend that the

Fig. 5.2. Pro-immigration protest in Los Angeles, May 2004.

exploitation of weaker nations by the first world has led to an increased wealth gap between developed and underdeveloped nations, has caused unchecked environmental degradation, and when factoring for inflation, has actually resulted in reduced workers' wages.

In Latin America, trade liberalization has led to the destruction of jobs and falling real wages, leading to the commoditization of human labor to the point that the exportation of human labor (legally or illegally) has become a significant part of many nations' gross domestic product (GDP). In fact, the World Trade Organization includes remittances (the transfer of money by a foreign worker to his or her country of origin) when calculating a nation's GDP since remittances now account for 10 percent or more of the GDP in seven Latin American and Caribbean nations (Guatemala 9.8 percent, Nicaragua 10.3 percent, Jamaica 13.8 percent, Haiti 15.4 percent, El Salvador 15.7 percent, Guyana 17.3 percent, and Honduras 21 percent).

While a Hispanic Christian ethics is not necessarily adverse to capitalism, an ethic that espouses universal human liberation cannot allow market forces to become more important than preserving basic human dignity. Latin American liberation theology is arguably the most influential theological movement of the last forty years, in no small part for demonstrating the potential "power" of those who are economically poor and politically powerless. Liberation theology's preferential option for the poor and oppressed has weathered many substantial critiques but remains relevant in today's world because, in spite of the economic gains of neoliberal policies, the dehumanizing and lethal effects of global poverty remain. In the context of global poverty, liberation theology is like triage. In a crisis situation with limited resources, the prioritization of patients receiving medical treatment is a necessary course of action. Those beyond help are given palliative care to ease their dying; those whose vital signs are stable are made to wait; those with the most pressing injuries are treated first. Making a preferential option for the poor does not imply that God loves the poor more; it simply acknowledges that the poor have more immediate and pressing needs.

Accordingly, Christian ethics born from the margins of Latino/a experience in the United States seeks to expose the root causes of economic injustice but also recognizes that the depth of human suffering cannot be reduced to economic relationships. The many moral dilemmas present themselves, if left unaddressed, can undermine the liberative goals of the Latino/a community. By looking closely at the everyday reality of Latino/as in the United States, the reader is encouraged to engage in ethics *en conjunto*, seeing particular moral issues through the eyes of the marginalized, in order to articulate concrete social praxis that can transform currently oppressive situations.

Possible Future Trends

It should become evident from reading this chapter that doing Christian ethics from a Latino/a perspective entails more than being born ethnically Hispanic. The discipline of Hispanic Christian ethics begins with an intentional act of political activism on behalf of the marginalized and oppressed; Latino/a ethical analysis is grounded in the lived experience of Latina/o communities through an organic relationship between the faith community and the academic professional, who is an active member of that community. In other words, embodying an approach *en conjunto*, the "intellectual property" of the Latino/a ethicist

BOX 5.3

An Ethic "Para Joder"

In *Latina/o Social Ethics: Moving Beyond Eurocentric Moral Thinking* (2010), ethicist Miguel A. De La Torre suggests a new direction for Hispanic liberative ethics defined as an ethic *para joder*. Employing the Spanish verb *joder*, a not-too-polite colloquialism that roughly translates as "to screw with," De La Torre calls for the disenfranchised "to screw with" the powers that be as a way of destabilizing existing unjust power structures and exposing institutionalized white, Eurocentric privilege. Given that societies tend to perpetuate oppressive structures for the sake of preserving the status quo, an ethic that prioritizes destabilizing the status quo through satirical social commentary—in which a "trickster" figure like Juan Bobo in Puerto Rican folktales exposes hypocrisy through his childish innocence—seems a necessary component of a liberative praxis of nonviolent political resistance. De La Torre draws parallels to biblical "tricksters" like Abraham or Jacob who employ deception as a means of self-preservation, arguing that even Jesus can be seen as a paradigm for an ethic *para joder*, insofar as Jesus' preaching destabilized the status quo through his use of parables and his actions placed him and his followers into conflict with the reigning religious and political powers.

also belongs to *la comunidad* ("the community"). Accordingly, certain themes highlighted above, like *mestizaje*, *lo cotidiano*, and *la dignidad*, have characterized Latino/a theological and ethical reflection and action.

In his latest book, *Latina/o Social Ethics: Moving Beyond Eurocentric Moral Thinking* (2010), Miguel A. De La Torre, the 2012 President of the Society of Christian Ethics, challenged the Latino/a community to revisit its discourses and reconsider many of its now outdated concepts. These words were not intended to disrespect or diminish the accomplishments of Latino/a scholars that preceded him, but were written in the spirit of *teología en conjunto* as a catalyst for continued ethical reasoning rooted in radical social activism motivated by a faith commitment to liberation and the preferential option for the poor. As a new generation of Latino/a scholars of religion establishes itself within academia, attains tenure, and perhaps moves into academic administration, it becomes harder and harder to claim to speak from the margins of the academic mainstream. De La Torre's comments serve to remind Latino/a theologians and ethicists that living in solidarity with the poor requires us to accompany the poor in their daily struggles, and for the scholar-activist this entails personal risk and professional sacrifice.

Study Questions

1. Is there a universal and objective model of ethical reasoning? If not, upon what basis can we establish a common moral discourse? How would a contextualized engagement with the Hispanic experience differ from other forms of ethical moral reasoning?

2. What is the relationship of Latina/o liberative ethics to public policy? In other words, what is the role of a religious belief like *imago Dei* in shaping the public discourse on issues like abortion, immigration reform, and affirmative action?

3. Why do people choose to emigrate (leave their homelands)? Are better economic opportunities worth the risks of illegal immigration?

4. Several Latino community advocacy organizations in California have joined forces to sue the Environmental Protection Agency (EPA) for what they are labeling as "environmental racism." California Latino/as living in low-income farming areas thinks the EPA is poorly managing three state dumps, which in turn has negatively affected their health. Read Genesis 1:26-28. What does it mean that humankind has been given dominion "over every living thing that moves upon the earth"? What is the responsibility of businesses toward the environment?

5. Hispanics have a 53.2 percent high school graduation rate, compared to a 75 percent graduation rate among white students. What practical steps can Latino/as take to effect long-term change within the academy, especially in a field like Christian ethics, when Hispanics continue to be so underrepresented?

Suggested Reading

Aquino, María Pilar. *Our Cry for Life: Feminist Theology from Latin America.* Maryknoll, NY: Orbis, 1993.

Aquino, María Pilar, Daisy L. Machado, and Jeanette Rodríguez, eds. *A Reader in Latina Feminist Theology: Religion and Justice.* Austin: University of Texas Press, 2002.

De La Torre, Miguel. *Doing Christian Ethics from the Margins.* Maryknoll, NY: Orbis, 2004.

———. *Latina/o Social Ethics: Moving Beyond Eurocentric Moral Thinking.* Waco: Baylor University Press, 2010.

Elizondo, Virgilio. *Galilean Journey: The Mexican-American Promise.* 2nd ed. Maryknoll, NY: Orbis, 2000.

García, Ismael. *Dignidad: Ethics through Hispanic Eyes.* Nashville: Abingdon, 1997.

Goizueta, Roberto. *Caminemos con Jesús: Toward a Hispanic/Latino Theology of Accompaniment.* Maryknoll, NY: Orbis, 1995.

González, Justo L. *Mañana: Christian Theology from a Hispanic Perspective.* Nashville: Abingdon, 1990.

———. *Santa Biblia: The Bible Through Hispanic Eyes.* Nashville: Abingdon, 1996.

Isasi-Díaz, Ada María. *En la Lucha/In the Struggle: Elaborating a Mujerista Theology*, 2nd ed. Minneapolis: Fortress Press, 2004.

Rodríguez, Jeanette. *Our Lady of Guadalupe: Faith and Empowerment among Mexican-American Women.* Austin: University of Texas Press, 1993.

Villafañe, Eldin. *The Liberating Spirit: Toward an Hispanic American Pentecostal Social Ethic.* Grand Rapids: Eerdmans, 1993.

6

African American Liberative Ethics

Keri Day

AFRICAN AMERICAN ETHICAL PARADIGMS continue to serve as moral resources when discussing issues of liberation, quality of life, and flourishing of all persons within human communities. From the founding of the American democratic republic, African American intellectual thinkers and sociopolitical leaders have articulated ethical and moral tenets that emphasize the importance of human dignity, social equality, justice, and human fulfillment, particularly persons who are oppressed and alienated within society. This chapter will first discuss the history and development of African American liberative ethics. We will next explore three ethical paradigms, or broad tenets, that have shaped and guided African American ethics, which include: (1) human dignity, (2) social justice, and (3) intragroup equality and fairness.

In addition, this chapter will introduce some major black theological and religious figures and thinkers who have contributed to the history and development of these three central tenets. These figures and thinkers have wrestled with questions that have challenged specific oppressive structures such as racism, advanced capitalism, and patriarchy. Finally, this chapter will offer some brief future

trends that African American liberative ethics in religious and theological perspective can anticipate.

History and Development of African American Liberative Ethics

African American ethics must be understood against the historical backdrop of racial apartheid in America. Within what social contexts have African American thinkers and leaders cultivated moral and ethical paradigms? And how have these paradigms positively influenced these same social contexts? These questions guide an investigation into the history of African American liberative ethics. The first social context out of which African American ethics emerged was slavery in early colonial America.

Black historian Albert Raboteau's book *Slave Religion: The Invisible Institution in the Antebellum South* offers a seminal analysis of the inhumane institution of slavery in America as well as African slaves' desires to make meaning despite the cruelty they experienced. The system of

American slavery developed and became codified beginning in the mid-seventeenth century. By 1680 it was fully established. Under this system, slaves were treated as chattel and as articles of property that could be bought, punished, sold, loaned, used as collateral, or willed to another at an owner's whim. Slaves were not recognized as persons in the eyes of the law. Consequently, they had no legal rights. Slaves could not legally marry, own property, vote, serve as witnesses, serve on juries, or make contracts. The offspring of female slaves also belonged to their owners, regardless of who were their fathers.

In particular Raboteau charts how white Christianity in America fueled, reinforced, and justified such racist ideologies and practices against African slaves. The attempt to legitimate slavery in America through Christian faith was a powerful contributing factor to this institution's potency and practical force.

One argument, widespread at a time when most people were prepared to accept the literal truth of the Bible, took the Africans to be the descendants of Canaan. In the biblical account of the "peopling" of the world by the sons of Noah after the flood, Canaan was condemned to be "a servant of servants unto his brethren," because his father, Ham, had seen "the nakedness of his father." Canaan was believed to have settled in Africa. Noah's curse served conveniently to explain the color of Africans' skin and their supposed "natural" indebtedness to the other nations of the world, particularly to the Europeans, who were seen as the alleged descendants of Japheth (whom God had promised to "enlarge").

KEY TERM 6.1

White Christianity. A brand of Christianity articulated and adopted by whites that supported racial inferiority and bigoted practices of slavery and Jim Crow in America.

This reading of the book of Genesis merged easily into a medieval iconographic tradition in which devils were always depicted as black. Later pseudo-scientific theories would be built around African skull shapes, dental structure, and body postures, in an attempt to find an unassailable argument, rooted in whatever the most persuasive contemporary idiom happened to be: law, theology, genealogy, or natural science. Indeed, American slavery was established, regulated, supported, and sanctioned by the Bible. Many white Christian leaders argued that it was a common practice during the time of both the Hebrew Scriptures (Old Testament) and the Christian Scriptures (New Testament). White Christianity used the Bible as a tool to legitimate racist institutions in America.

Moreover, for white slave owners, African slaves needed to adopt Christianity in order to alienate slaves from their own native religious rituals and practices. It proved very hard for slaves to preserve their various religions in North America. As discussed earlier, most of the slaves lived under harsh conditions and high death rates, which reduced their numbers. Although African slaves tried to maintain their religious practices, white owners' efforts to eradicate such practices made the preservation of their religious traditions difficult. Consequently, many African traditional beliefs, rhythms, and isolated songs did not survive well into the nineteenth century.

While white owners forbade African slaves from practicing their own religious traditions and rituals, slaves still escaped to the hush harbors where they mixed freely and practiced parts of their traditional religions. However, African slaves did this in secret. White slave owners believed that giving the slaves the freedom to perform their religious ceremonies would give them a chance to plot a rebellion against them. White slave masters were determined to eradicate the non-Christian customs that Africans slaves possessed. Owners forbade African religious expressions because they did not want slaves to embrace their own humanity. Instead, owners articulated Christian doctrines of racial inequality to inculcate inferiority into slaves.

However, African slaves did not embrace or internalize white Christian doctrines of inequality. Instead, African slaves merged Christian values of love and human equality with their own African religious traditions and expressions. Many Africans had little trouble adopting Christianity because it preached many of the same beliefs that were central to African religions, such as Supreme Being, creation myths, priest-healers, and moral/ethical systems. Christianity's "life after death" was also attractive to slaves because it offered the promise that they would someday regain make contact with their ancestors.

A Baptist missionary to the Yoruba of Nigeria observed in 1853 that they had words for monotheistic god, sin, guilt, sacrifice, intercession, repentance, faith, pardon, adoption, heaven, and hell. Muslim slaves had even more points of identification with Christianity, since they possessed a religion based on a written text, in which some passages, moreover, resembled Christian texts (Old Testament). An American minister reported in 1842 that Muslim Africans called God Allah, and Jesus Mohammed. According to them, "The religion is the same, but different countries have different names." Due to their own religious traditions, African slaves were able to fashion a new brand of Christianity that promoted ethical and moral paradigms of dignity and equality in response to the oppression and injustices of white Christianity and its practices of slaveocracy.

Almost a century later, slavery and its racist ideologies would lay the groundwork for legalized racial segregation in America known as Jim Crow laws. In 1896, with the case *Plessy v. Ferguson*, racial segregation in America became legal and throughout the southern United States became standard and represented the institutionalization of the Jim Crow period. Jim Crow operated primarily, but not exclusively, in southern and border states, between 1877 and the mid-1960s. Jim

KEY TERM 6.2

Jim Crow. A legal system of racial apartheid in America in which black and whites were mandated to have separate but "equal" public services. However, in practice, the services and facilities reserved for African Americans were almost always of lower quality than those reserved for whites. This legal system operated primarily, but not exclusively, in southern and border states, between 1877 and the mid-1960s.

Crow was more than a series of rigid antiblack laws. It was a way of life.

Under Jim Crow, African Americans were relegated to the status of second-class citizens. Everyone, theoretically, would receive the same public services (schools, hospitals, prisons, etc.), but there would be separate, distinct facilities for each race. In practice, the services and facilities reserved for African Americans were almost always of lower quality than those reserved for whites. For example, most African American schools received less public funding per student than nearby white schools. Law in the northern states never mandated segregation, but a de facto system grew up for schools, in which nearly all black students attended schools that were nearly all-black.

Through laws, Jim Crow legitimized and institutionalized white racism. Many Christian ministers and theologians taught that whites were the "chosen people," blacks were cursed to be servants, and God supported racial segregation. Craniologists, eugenicists, phrenologists, and social Darwinists, at every educational level, buttressed the belief that blacks were innately intellectually and culturally inferior to whites. Prosegregation politicians gave eloquent speeches on the great danger of integration: the "mongrelization" of the white race. Newspaper and magazine writers routinely

Fig. 6.1. An African American, in 1939, at a "Colored" drinking fountain located in streetcar terminal, in Oklahoma City, Oklahoma.

referred to blacks as niggers, coons, and darkies. Even worse, these articles reinforced antiblack stereotypes. Even children's games portrayed blacks as inferior beings. All major societal institutions reflected and supported the oppression of blacks.

It is against this historical backdrop of American slavery and racial segregation that African American ethical and moral paradigms first developed. The three broad tenets or ethical and moral paradigms include human dignity, social justice, and intragroup equality. In the following section, we briefly explore these three tenets.

Basic Tenets of African American Liberative Ethics

The first tenet or moral paradigm within African American ethics is human dignity. As discussed,

white supremacy and racial apartheid in America sought to dehumanize African Americans. Human dignity is a term used to describe the intrinsic worth of a person, which, as a matter of principle, should be equal in all people. When one is humiliated, their self-worth is harmed, and because of this, their human dignity is violated. Human dignity is about being treated as a person, regardless of any distinction of race, sex, or religion. In the eras of American slavery and racial segregation, there are many examples of human dignity violations, which are the main reasons

KEY TERM 6.3

Human dignity. The intrinsic worth of a person, which, as a matter of principle, should be equal in all people.

African American people fought so long and hard against these inhumane institutions. For instance, under slavery, whites did not recognize slave marriages, so families were often split up at sales, with no regard as to what that would mean for enslaved people.

Enslaved women were often the victims of sexual exploitation by their white male owners, and it was tolerated because they were considered less than human. To inculcate fear in their slaves and to make them behave the way they wished, white slave owners frequently used brutal punishments such as whippings or brandings. Under slavery, a slave counted as three-quarters of a person for population purposes and could have no vote. African Americans were treated not as people but as property. However, African Americans under slavery and legal racial segregation always knew they had been created in the image of the divine and innately possessed human dignity and worth.

In response to inferiorization and dehumanization, black thinkers and leaders have articulated ethical and moral paradigms that recovered and affirmed the innate human worth and dignity of African Americans. For example, slave spirituals were songs that covertly proclaimed the innate human dignity and worth blacks possessed despite the inhumanities of slavery and racial oppression. Slave spirituals were protest songs, which decried the practices of white slave masters who purported to be "Christian." For obvious reasons, direct expressions of protest during slavery were dangerous. Yet, it is very clear that some of the songs created by enslaved people served to do just this.

Creators of the songs went to considerable lengths to disguise the true meaning of the lyrics. For those within the enslaved community, however, the meanings were very clear. The best example of a protest spiritual is the song commonly called "I Got Shoes" but also known as "Heav'n, Heav'n." When it is performed in concert settings, the lyrics of this song are rarely understood fully. In its original context, the song is a bold protest against slavery. Basic necessities like shoes were rare in slave quarters. However, the creators and original singers of this song insisted that "all God's children got shoes" (and robes, and harps, and crowns, and any number of items that were considered to be luxurious). However, the song lyrics go even further. The lyricist continues, exclaiming that "everybody talkin' 'bout Heav'n

CASE STUDY 6.1

James Byrd was an African American who was murdered by three white men in Jasper, Texas, on June 7, 1998. Shawn Allen Berry, Lawrence Russell Brewer, and John William King dragged Byrd behind a pickup truck along an asphalt pavement after they wrapped a heavy logging chain around his ankles. Byrd was pulled along for about two miles as the truck swerved from side to side. Byrd, who remained conscious throughout most of the ordeal, was killed when his body hit the edge of a culvert, severing his right arm and head. The murderers drove on for another mile before dumping his torso in front of an African American cemetery in Jasper. The African American tenet of human dignity and social justice would be applied to such a heinous act, in which Byrd was attacked due to his race. In fact, the Hate Crimes Prevention Act was passed, in part, due to Byrd's murder in order to acknowledge that this inhumane act was not merely an isolated killing but a racially motivated murder. Might hate-crime legislation be effective in improving the racial attitudes and ideologies in America? How might you address hate crimes here in America?

ain't goin' there." Here, the emphasis is on hypocrisy. The slave master, claiming to be Christian, goes to church every Sunday morning, where he and other congregants talk and sing about Jesus and heaven. But when he returns to the plantation on Sunday afternoon, he presides over a decidedly unheavenly, immoral enterprise (slavery) and participates actively in the unheavenly and immoral physical, emotional, and frequently sexual abuse of other human beings.

Through the veiled lyrics of the song, the creator of this spiritual (whose name has long been lost) is expressing (on behalf of the whole community) a sense of outrage at the hypocritical behavior of white slave masters who have no God-given right to promote racially oppressive ideologies and practices. And through the simple yet almost regal musical appeal of the song's melody, the singer turns the tables on the oppressor, reversing the power hierarchy. God's children (so-called slaves) have a place in heaven, while the oppressor "ain't goin' there." These slave spirituals not only decry the hypocrisy and immorality of the slave system but also affirm and encourage the human dignity of slaves, who are *God's* children.

A second tenet or moral paradigm that has guided African American ethics is social justice. Social justice generally refers to the idea of creating a society or societal institution that is based on the principles of equality and solidarity, that understands and values human rights, and that recognizes the dignity of every human being. Social justice is also based on concepts of human rights and equality and involves a greater degree of economic egalitarianism through progressive taxation, income redistribution, or even property redistribution. At the very least, social justice includes equal rights under the law, such as security, voting rights, freedom of speech and assembly, and property rights. However, it also includes concepts of economic equity (i.e., access to education, health care, and other social securities). It includes equal opportunities and obligations, which involves the whole of society.

Social justice has always been a tenet of African American liberative ethics, as blacks have a long

---

BOX 6.1

Slave Spirituals

Although numerous rhythmical and sonic elements of Negro (slave) spirituals can be traced to African sources, Negro spirituals are an indigenous musical form, specific to the religious experience of Africans and their descendants in the United States. They are a result of the interaction of music and religion from Africa with music and religion of European origin. Further, this interaction occurred only in the United States. Negro spirituals were primarily expressions of religious faith. Some may also have served as sociopolitical protests veiled as assimilation to white American culture. For instance, many popular books claim that songs such as "Wade in the Water" contained explicit instructions to fugitive slaves on how to avoid capture, and on which routes to take to successfully make their way to freedom. "Wade in the Water" allegedly recommends leaving dry land and taking to the water as a strategy to throw pursuing bloodhounds off one's trail.

KEY TERM 6.4

Social Justice. The creation of a society or societal institution that is based on the principles of equality and solidarity, that understands and values human rights, and that recognizes the dignity of every human being.

history of experiencing racial, political, and socio-economic injustice. For instance, Frederick Douglass was first and foremost an abolitionist and civil rights activist. Fighting against his own slavery from his earliest youth, he continued to fight against the institution of slavery until its abolition. He spoke and lectured widely for the abolitionist cause throughout the 1840s and 1850s. In 1851, he organized his own series of lectures in Rochester, which focused on social justice for blacks in America. In addition to advocating abolition in his lectures and in his publications, Douglass became active in the Underground Railroad, and was instrumental in shepherding many fugitive slaves to Canada.

Douglass continued to fight tirelessly for African American rights to full legal equality, backed by the power of the ballot. He supported passage of the Fourteenth and Fifteenth Amendments, and lectured widely for their adoption. In later years, he even spoke out against the increased lynchings of African Americans. For Douglass, social justice for blacks was essential to America making good on its promise as a land of equality and opportunity for *all*. Social justice not only includes political equality but also economic equity. Social justice for African Americans was essential and remains essential to their equal participation and flourishing within our American democratic context.

A third and final broad tenet or moral paradigm that guides African American ethics is intragroup equality and fairness. Intragroup equality refers to the type of parity that exists among members within a particular community or group. Although African American thinkers have advocated for social equality among ethnic groups, other thinkers have advocated for social equality among members *within* a particular ethnic community or group. For instance, Maria Stewart was the first-known African American woman to publicly lecture to audiences that included both women and men. Stewart wrote for the *Liberator*, a paper that was

very influential in changing attitudes about slavery in the United States. However, she wrote about the overt sexism that existed not only in American society but also within black communities. In response to the repressive sexism that women—and in particular, black women—endured within black communities, she poses a particular question in one of her writings. She asks, "How long shall the fair daughters of Africa be compelled to bury their minds and talents beneath a load of iron pots and kettles?" This question affirms the need for black women to experience social equality and equity within black communities who are also oppressed by racial inequality.

Stewart encouraged women not to be dependent on men, and to start their own businesses. She thought women should rely only on themselves to change things in society. Unfortunately, black woman writing at that time were scorned, and she was forced to leave the city due to the violent reaction to her writings, which even came from black men. Stewart emphasized a moral paradigm that promoted equality among members within the same community—namely, equality between men and women.

Major Black Figures: Visions of Liberation

Being guided by these three aforementioned broad tenets or moral paradigms, African American theological and religious figures and scholars have articulated visions of liberation that address oppressive structures such as racism, advanced capitalism, and patriarchy. Although a number of figures have been important to black liberation, two black religious figures are come to the forefront: Martin Luther King Jr. and Malcolm X. More recent black theological and religious thinkers have also offered visions of black liberation. Three primary African American religious scholars that are explored include James Cone, Delores Williams, and Cornel West. Ideas of black liberation are certainly not reduced to these particular figures and thinkers. However, the aforementioned scholars and figures illuminate the major issues and questions that African American liberative ethics wrestles with.

Deeply influenced by Howard Thurman and Benjamin Mays, Dr. Martin Luther King Jr. is one of the primary major black religious figure who confronted racism in America. From 1960 until his death in 1968, he was co-pastor with his father at Ebenezer Baptist Church and president of the Southern Christian Leadership Conference (which he also helped found). King was a pivotal figure in the civil rights movement. He was elected president of the Montgomery Improvement Association, the organization that was responsible for the successful Montgomery Bus Boycott from 1955 to 1956 (381 days). He was arrested thirty times for his participation in civil rights activities.

King was a vital personality of the modern era and one of the greatest African American figures to challenge racist and capitalist structures. King's commitment to nonviolence in the face of racist hatred and capitalist exploitation gave black people and poor people a new sense of worth and dignity. His lectures and questions on the inequality and irrationality of racist hatred stirred the concern and sparked the conscience of a generation. His philosophy of nonviolent direct action against racial segregation in America reflects his wrestling with the rationalization of racial hatred. For King, racial hatred legitimated and codified in laws not only reflected social inequality but also undermined the innate human dignity all persons possessed, dictating that all be treated as equal.

King's commitment to addressing the legality and irrationality of American racism was central to the strategies that would be employed within the civil rights movement during the 1960s. His nonviolent strategies for rational and nondestructive social change galvanized the conscience of the United States and reordered its priorities. The Voting Rights Act of 1965, for example, went to Congress as a result of the Selma to Montgomery march. His wisdom, his words, his actions, his commitment, and his dreams for equal opportunity and racial integration helped America make good on its promise as a land of liberty for all. However, while legislation was being passed in order to dismantle racial segregation in the 1960s, King knew all too well that racist ideologies and practices continued to guide and inform America's political, economic, and social institutions. Consequently, near the end of King's life, he continued to maintain that America had still not fully addressed its own racist demons and racial bigotry.

King wrestled with questions concerning methods of challenging and eradicating racial hostility and bigotry within American institutions. He pondered two specific questions. How do we, as a society, define an unjust law, and what kinds of strategies and tactics have proven most effective in changing such laws? If we are able to abolish legal injustice, will it necessarily result in social justice? These questions reject arguments that see racial injustice being achieved merely through laws. While laws were needed to end

---

KEY TERM 6.6

Black Liberation. Social, political, economic, and psychological liberation for black communities from oppressive institutions and ideologies within a context of hegemony and domination.

racial segregation, King knew all too well that racism is also about the bigoted attitudes and ideologies that white people possessed. Visions of racial justice also entailed changing minds and hearts. And this task proved far more insurmountable than legal solutions to racial injustice. Even up to his death, King felt that America still had a long way to go in ridding itself of its racist inclinations and predispositions. However, King felt that only nonviolence and love coupled with justice could win the day and usher in visions of liberation for blacks that could be sustainable.

Another black religious figure that also proffered visions of black liberation was Malcolm X. Intelligent and articulate, Malcolm was appointed a minister and national spokesman for the Nation of Islam by the group's leader, the Honorable Elijah Muhammad. He was appointed to establish new mosques in cities such as Detroit, Michigan,

Fig. 6.2. Martin Luther King Jr. and Malcolm X meet before a press conference. Both men had come to hear the Senate debate on the Civil Rights Act of 1964. This was the only time the two men ever met; their meeting lasted only one minute.

and Harlem, New York. Malcolm utilized newspaper columns, radio, and television to communicate the Nation of Islam's message across the United States. His charisma, drive, and conviction attracted an astounding number of new members. In fact, Malcolm was largely credited with increasing membership in the Nation of Islam from five hundred in 1952 to thirty thousand in 1963.

A contemporary of Martin Luther King, Malcolm X vehemently spoke against American racist institutions and structures as well. However, Malcolm discussed racism in different terms than King. For King, nonviolence and love were the primary means and methods toward the ends of racial justice. For Malcolm, black liberation was not about blacks trying to integrate with whites in the name of "community" or "brotherly love." For Malcolm, violent resistance through continued segregation was the primary means toward black self-love and self-determination. Black liberation, in other words, could only be achieved through Black Nationalism—the reinvigoration of black self-love and pride in their history and way of life. As a self-determined community and people, then, they could demand equal rights and liberties.

Malcolm did not think that black self-determination could be achieved through integratiion with whites (which for him was more about seeking white approval). He possessed a vision of black liberation that was controversial because it wrestled with a key question: Could America ever be a land of equality and opportunity when racism was stitched into the fabric of America's way of life? For Malcolm, American racism was not merely an aberration or anomaly within American life. Racism was a part of America's very identity, an identity it possessed when it built itself upon the backs of African slaves. Consequently, Malcolm believed that whites could never partner with blacks to achieve liberation.

Inevitably, many white people (and many blacks) were alarmed by Malcolm X's segregationist

BOX 6.2

Black Nationalism

Black Nationalism was a political and social movement prominent among some African Americans in the 1960s and early 1970s. The movement, which can be traced back to Marcus Garvey's Universal Negro Improvement Association of the 1920s, sought to acquire economic power and to infuse among blacks a sense of community and group feeling. Many adherents to Black Nationalism assumed the eventual creation of a separate black nation by African Americans. As an alternative to being assimilated by the American nation, which is predominantly white, Black Nationalists sought to maintain and promote their separate identity as a proud, self-sufficient black nation.

perspective on black liberation. He and the Nation of Islam were described as hatemongers, black segregationists, violence-seekers, and a threat to improved race relations. Civil rights organizations denounced Malcolm X and the Nation of Islam as irresponsible extremists whose views were not representative of African Americans. Malcolm X was equally critical of the civil rights movement. He described its leaders as "stooges" for the white establishment, and said that Martin Luther King Jr. was a "chump." He criticized the 1963 March on Washington, calling it "the farce on Washington." He said he did not know why black people were excited over a demonstration "run by whites in front of a statue of a president who has been dead for a hundred years and who didn't like us when he was alive."

However, as King's views evolved near the end of his life, Malcolm also went through a transformation of his perspective on how to achieve

black liberation in America. This shift from "white man as devil" began to occur when he took a pilgrimage to Mecca, where he began to reappraise the "white man." In the Muslim world, Malcolm observed that men with white complexions were more genuinely brotherly than many of his black brothers from the Nation of Islam. White men in Mecca embraced other men of dark hues as brothers and not as inferior beings. Malcolm said there were tens of thousands of pilgrims, from all over the world, of all colors, from blue-eyed blondes to black-skinned Africans. But all were participating in the same ritual, displaying a spirit of unity and brotherhood that his experiences in America had led him to believe could never exist between the white and the nonwhite person.

He maintained that America needed to understand Islam, because it is the one religion that erases the race problem from its society. Throughout his travels in the Muslim world, he met, talked to, and even ate with people who in America would have been considered white, but the "white" attitude was removed from their minds by the religion of Islam. Malcolm commented that he had never before seen sincere and true brotherhood practiced by all, regardless of their color.

This experience in Mecca started a radical transformation of Malcolm's entire perspective on "white men" in relation to black liberation. He learned that the "white man" in America was less about complexion and more about racist attitudes and actions toward the black man and all other nonwhite people. Consequently, Malcolm no longer saw all white people as intrinsically evil. Rather, he saw white people in America as socially conditioned by the insidious practice of racism. Before his assassination, Malcolm saw whites as partners in the struggle for black liberation and black self-determination (although whites could not be leaders within this struggle).

Although they both primarily focused on challenging racist institutions and structures, Martin Luther King and Malcolm X also critiqued

Fig. 6.3. March on Washington, DC, 1963.

American capitalist exploitation that poor blacks and other nonwhites experienced in America and around the world. They both castigated economic militarism, which continues to be promoted by America around the globe. Although major African American figures are not to be reduced to Martin and Malcolm, both leaders illuminate the central questions black people have wrestled with in relation to black liberation and determination.

Black Scholars: Visions of Liberation

Black scholars use a multitude of methods in describing ideas of black liberation: theological, philosophical, ethnographic, and social-scientific, among others. This chapter highlights theological and philosophical methods, as scholarly discourses on black liberation primarily emerged out of the humanities and social sciences.

African American theological and religious thinkers have challenged racist ideologies and structures in America. Black theologian James Cone is a religious scholar who has written

KEY TERM 6.7

Racism. The belief that there are inherent differences in people's traits and capacities, which are entirely due to their race or ethnicity, however defined, and which consequently justify those people's being treated differently and unequally at both personal and institutional levels.

voluminously on Christianity's contributed to racism here in America. As a Protestant minister who grew up in Arkansas under the heavy hand of segregation, Cone observed firsthand the way white Christians treated blacks, even after desegregation was ordered by the federal government. The Christian messages of peace and brotherly love contrasted sharply with white Christians' bigoted behavior, and this left a lasting mark on Cone's thinking.

In response to the ways in which white Christianity fueled American racism, Cone developed a "Black Theology" of liberation from oppression, racism, and poverty. Cone argued that the white church and white theologians had all failed in their duties to uphold biblical principles of helping the poor and marginalized of society. Indeed, white Christians had become actively complicit in making the lives of others worse. Because of this, Cone contended that it was no longer safe or acceptable to leave the interpretation of the Bible to white Christians. Blacks must take responsibility for their own religion and their own relationship with God.

For Cone, White Christians throughout American history might have preached a message of love and peace, but at every turn they have failed to live up to their own words. The existence of segregated denominations and segregated churches prove this. Cone could also point to the long history of Christian theologians using religious arguments to defend both slavery and segregation. Although Cone's most obvious target is racism, his message is actually much broader. He also criticizes middle-class black churches and argues that racism is only part of the problem. The much larger issue is the failure of Christianity to properly motivate people to care for others. Instead of acting on Christian principles of love and charity, they remain isolated in social or cultural groups.

Although Cone is suspicious of European thinkers and theologians, he can at times find some good things to say about them. He points

BOX 6.3

Black Theology

Black liberation theology, also known as Black Theology, is a relatively new theological perspective found in some Christian churches in the United States. It maintains that African Americans must be liberated from multiple forms of bondage—political, social, economic, and religious. This formulation views Christian theology as a theology of liberation—a rational study of the being of God in the world in light of the existential situation of an oppressed community, relating the forces of liberation to the essence of the gospel, which is Jesus Christ. Black Theology deals primarily with the African American community in terms of how to make Christianity real for blacks. It explains Christianity as a matter of liberation here and now, rather than in an afterlife. The goal of Black Theology is not for special treatment. Instead, black theologians are asking for freedom and justice. In asking for this, black theologians turn to Scripture as the sanction for their demand, arguing that the gospel message is a message of justice and freedom for oppressed people such as blacks.

to white theologians such as Karl Barth and Dietrich Bonheoffer who, at great risk to themselves, used their theological writings to aid resistance to Hitler. Cone contrasts Barth and Bonhoeffer to the passivity of American theologians in the face of oppression of blacks and other minorities. Most of the time, however, Cone is critical of the ideas of European theologians who are part of the American experience. He notes, for example, that many white Christians emphasize ideas like justification by faith and grace as central Christian themes. From the perspective of black Christians, however, the idea of liberation from oppression is much more important and has a much more immediate relevancy to their lives.

The story of the Jews' liberation in the book of Exodus naturally figures prominently in Cone's arguments. Cone also cites the prophets, many of whom were frequent critics of the status quo and of Israel's failure to properly fulfill their duties to the poor in society. Cone identifies the establishment of justice for all, rich and poor alike, as the key principle that God has been trying to get humanity to understand in both the Old and New Testaments.

While the project of racial justice has been central to the quest for black liberation, patriarchy (sexist hegemony) has also been an important theme highlighted by black religious scholars. Mirroring Maria Stewart's commitment to challenging sexist domination from within and without black communities, Delores Williams emphasizes the ways in which patriarchy inhibits black liberation, particularly black women's sense of flourishing. In *Sisters in the Wilderness*, Williams finds in the biblical figure of Hagar (mother of Ishmael, who was cast into the desert by Abraham and Sarah, but protected by God) a prototype for the struggle of African American women. African slave, homeless exile, surrogate mother, Hagar's story provides an image of survival and defiance appropriate to black women today.

Exploring themes inherent in Hagar's story such as poverty and slavery, ethnicity and sexual exploitation, exile and encounters with God, Williams traces parallels in the history of African American

women from slavery to the present. She employs womanist theology, which is a theology that emerges from the shared experience of poor black women. Specifically, womanist theology exposes the ways in which multiple oppressions such as

KEY TERM 6.8

Patriarchy. Institutional ideologies and practices of sexism in which women are oppressed socially, politically, economically, and sexually.

BOX 6.4

Womanist Theology

Womanist theology is a religious conceptual framework that reconsiders and revises the traditions, practices, Scriptures, and biblical interpretation with a special lens to empower and liberate African American women in America. Womanist theology associates with and departs from feminist theology and Black Theology specifically because it integrates the perspectives and experiences of African American and other women of color. Feminist theology's lack of attention to the everyday realities of women of color and Black Theology's lack of understanding of the full dimension of liberation from the unique oppressions of black women require bringing them together in womanist theology. The goals of womanist theology include interrogating the social construction of black womanhood in relation to the black community and to assume a liberative perspective so that African American women can live emboldened lives within the African American community and within the larger society. Some of its tasks are excavating the life stories of poor women of African descent in the church and understanding the "languages" of black women. It is strongly associated with black feminism. Womanist theology is not only for African women; it attempts to embrace women of color all over the world.

race, sex, and class repress black women. For Williams, despite the patriarchy black women experience (as Hagar experienced), God's liberating presence remains a possibility for these women.

A model of freedom and liberation within black churches as well as black communities must involve eradicating sexist ideologies and practices. For example, Williams challenges the traditional notion of atonement within black churches, which promotes surrogacy experiences among already oppressed black women. Williams explains how, throughout American history, black women have been forced into the role of surrogate. Slave women were often forced to take the place of white mothers by caring for the children, the place of white men by working in the plantation fields, and even the place of white wives by being forced into sexual relations with white slave owners. This history of black women's role as surrogate causes Williams to critique the Christian depiction of Christ on the cross, suffering in the place of humanity.

Williams argues that in his death on the cross, "Jesus represents the ultimate surrogate figure standing in the place of someone else: sinful humankind." Surrogacy, attached to this divine personage, thus takes on an aura of the sacred. Williams examines how this image is problematic for black women because it "reinforces the exploitation that has accompanied their experience with surrogacy." She wonders whether the acceptance of this glorification of Christ's role as surrogate will encourage black women to passively accept or yield to similar surrogacy roles.

Williams highlights that African American liberative ethics must include not only the promotion of racial justice but also the promotion of gender equality and equity. She encourages American and black communities to abandon both ideologies and practices that reinforce patriarchal hegemony. Black women experience both racial and gender injustice, which means that liberation must address the ways in which interlocking oppressions affect black people (racism, sexism, classism, etc.). Williams's work reflects the central tenet of intragroup equality, as she promotes gender justice within black communities, black churches, and broader society.

Similar to addressing racial and gender injustices, other African American thinkers have

CASE STUDY 6.2

Many would argue that the images of women in hip-hop have become progressively and destructively more negative than at any other time in history. Lyrics that were at one time provocative and merely suggestive are now blatant and overtly obscene. Music videos have become machismo fairy tales that have more "ogre and ass" scenes than the Shrek trilogy. These images attempt to pass off the objectification of black women specifically as "true beauty" in the name of entertainment. These images and lyrics, while acceptable for adults, are targeted to a demographic made up of young people ages twelve to sixteen. Studies have shown that these images, and more importantly these lyrics, play a role in how young black people view themselves and process sex and relationships. In part, opponents of hip-hop believe that the problem of patriarchy can be seen in hip-hop: black men treat and view black women as objects instead of human agents worthy of human dignity. Is hip-hop culture and music "salvageable" given its patriarchal bent? How might youth think critically about hip-hop culture?

addressed the problem of advanced capitalism and the ways capitalist exploitation affects black people. Liberation includes challenging exploitative capitalist institutions and structures. Black philosopher Cornel West argues that black liberation depends on black leaders' challenging capitalist exploitation as well as the class injustices such systems perpetuate. West challenges exploitative capitalist practices by turning to the manner in which free-market structures intensify poverty for disenfranchised communities around the world. West invites readers to consider how our current capitalist modes of production are connected to a grossly unequal distribution of wealth.

For West, while emphasizing how racist practices affect black communities remains critical, these racist practices must be linked to the current modes of production. Such practices play a role in buttressing advanced-capitalist processes and ensuring the unequal distribution of wealth in different societies. West further notes that elite wealth, power, and the monopolized influence of multinational corporations often leads to the lack of access to wealth for more deprived communities.

West drawn on Marxist thought in linking racism with capitalist exploitation. He argues that Marxism is indispensable because it highlights the

---

KEY TERM 6.9

Advanced capitalism. A capitalist mode of production that is not only connected to a grossly unequal distribution of wealth but also treats human beings as commodities.

---

relation of racist practices to the capitalist mode of production and recognizes the crucial role racism plays within the capitalist economy. Yet, he maintains that Marxism is inadequate because it fails to probe other spheres of American society where racism plays an integral role, especially the psychological and cultural spheres. Furthermore, Marxist views tend to assume that racism has its roots only in the rise of modern capitalism.

West also illuminates American capitalism's influence not only black communities in America but also people of color around the world. For instance, a poor black woman named Katrina has two children. Katrina experiences poverty due to a number of factors. First, she continues to seek employment but cannot secure a job making a living wage, which reflects a broader problem of cheap, exploited labor within the global economy. Second, these jobs (that do not offer living

---

CASE STUDY 6.3

The absence of a living wage is an example of capitalist exploitation of working-class laborers in America. Working-class Americans receive a minimum-wage pay rate, but these wages due not keep up with inflation, which devalues their earnings and creates experiences of deprivation. There are living-wage campaigns presently taking place in over seventy-five cities. However, opponents of the living-wage movement note that demanding a living wage has more weaknesses than strengths. For example, they argue that promoting a living wage will cause poor people to lose out on benefits, as their salaries will be higher (and they will consequently have to pay for such health benefits). However, these arguments among critics of the living-wage campaign have not been conclusively proven. Can you make a case against a living wage? If so, how might one respond to critics of the living-wage movement?

wages) do not provide child care or health care for Katrina and her family. As she is unable to care for her two children with meager wages, Katrina may feel forced to depend on government assistance. She also realizes that she does not have access to specialized education needed to compete in a postindustrial political economy. Even when attempting to transition from welfare to work under the 1996 TANF welfare reform policy, she is met with fear that she will be unable to care for herself and her children due to minimum wages and an absence of benefits. The vicious cycle of poverty for Katrina and her children continues. Broader processes of the global political economy victimize poor African American women in the United States. Advanced capitalist structures continue to affects black communities, perpetuating cycles of deprivation.

Possible Future Trends

While African American liberative ethics has addressed issues of racism, patriarchy, and advanced capitalism, other issues related to black liberation have developed over the last two decades and continue to develop. In particular, religious tolerance and greater sexual inclusivity have been explicitly addressed in relation to black liberation. For example, womanist scholars such as Melanie Harris and Monica Coleman argue that achieving black liberation and flourishing includes honoring the range of religious diversity represented within black communities. Because persons within black communities may employ different religious perspectives to make meaning and to thrive, visions of black liberation must include the celebration of religious diversity. Black religion should not be reduced to black Christianity. Although black Christianity has been central to the religious life of many African Americans, blacks in America also practice other religious expressions. African Americans have practiced Islam in America, even before the emergence of the Nation of Islam in the middle of the twentieth century. Many blacks also practice African traditional religions and Buddhism as a way to make meaning and experience transcendence.

Similar to emphasizing greater religious diversity, African American religious scholars such as Victor Anderson and Kelly Brown Douglas challenge black communities to include the

LIBERATIVE ETHICS IN ACTION 6.1

Liberative Ethics in Action: The Issue of Capitalist Exploitation

During the early stages of the apartheid era in South Africa, financial support came from American banks such as City Bank of New York and Chase Manhattan Bank. Although these financial institutions helped initiate activities in South Africa, they often concealed their lending operations by coalescing with other bank branches. For instance, Chase merged its financial enterprises with British Standard Bank. In fact, American direct investments doubled by 1966, and by 1984, US monopoly capitalist corporations held 60 percent of all foreign holdings on the Johannesburg Stock Exchange. The United States became the apartheid state's leading trade partner for both exports and imports. Despite opposition from other countries and outcries by South African citizens themselves, the United States continued to invest in an international outlaw country due to the enormous rates of profit return, cheap and abundant labor, low taxes, and favorable economic climate.

KEY TERM 6.10

Black Christianity. A brand of Christianity that blacks developed out of the crucible of slavery and racial apartheid in America in which human dignity, equality, and social justice are privileged.

celebration of sexual diversity as part of the task of black liberation and flourishing. Homophobia and heterosexism continue to be present within black communities, which hinder African American same-gender loving persons from experiencing liberation. In response to such heterosexist hegemony, these scholars call on black communities to include within concepts of black liberation the full inclusion of gays, lesbians, transgendered, and bisexuals. These two issues will gain greater momentum and more attention as black communities begin addressing the importance of intergroup parity and justice.

While this chapter has not exhausted African American liberative ethics, it has highlighted the major figures, thinkers, arguments, themes, and future trends related to concepts of black liberation in America. African American liberative ethics emerges from the lived experiences of slavery and segregation in America, inspiring black figures and thinkers to fashion visions of liberation. Such figures and thinkers were guided by normative commitments. These commitments are captured in three broad tenets or moral paradigms required for flourishing: human dignity, social justice, and intragroup equality.

Black leaders and thinkers who have critiqued systems of racism, patriarchy, and capitalism in America have articulated these tenets. Moreover, issues of religious and sexual diversity are gaining increased attention by black scholars. Visions of liberation must include the celebration of religious diversity and diverse sexual identities. Visions of black liberation will continue to sit at the forefront of black communities as they respond to persisting discrimination and inequality.

Study Questions

1. What two racist systems explain the history and development of African American liberative ethics?

2. What are the three major tenets/moral paradigms that inform African American ethics, and what oppressive experiences were these tenets responding to?

3. What are some similarities and differences between Martin Luther King's and Malcolm X's visions of black liberation?

4. Is racial justice the only oppressive structure African American figures and thinkers are responding to? If not, what other oppressive structures do black leaders and thinkers challenge, and why do they challenge these structures?

5. This chapter names future trends in African American liberative ethics such as celebrating religious and sexual diversity. What other future trends might emerge within the field of African American liberative ethics?

Suggested Readings

Cone, James. *God of the Oppressed.* Maryknoll, NY: Orbis, 1997.

Douglass, Fredrick. *Narrative of Life of Fredrick Douglass: An American Slave.* 2nd ed. New York: Bedford/St. Martin's, 2002.

King, Martin Luther. *Where Do we Go From Here: Chaos or Community?* Boston: Beacon, 1968.

Raboteau, Albert. *Slave Religion: The "Invisible Institution" in the Antebellum South.* Oxford: Oxford University Press, 1978.

Stewart, Maria. *America's First Black Woman Political Writer: Essays and Speeches.* Edited by Marilyn Richardson. Bloomington: Indiana University Press, 1987.

West, Cornel. *Prophesy Deliverance!* Louisville: Westminster John Knox, 1982.

Williams, Delores. *Sisters in the Wilderness: The Challenge of Womanist God-Talk.* Maryknoll, NY: Orbis, 1993.

Malcolm X. *The Autobiography of Malcolm X: As Told to Alex Haley.* New York: Penguin, 2010.

7

Asian American Liberative Ethics

Sharon M. Tan

In *A Free Life*, Chinese American novelist Ha Jin describes the life of a Chinese immigrant to the United States and his evolving sense of self in relationship to his family. Nan Wu is a promising doctoral student in political science who is stranded in the United States in the aftermath of the Tiananmen Square massacre in 1989. His wife, Pingping, is with him; but his son, Taotao, is living with his grandparents in China. Blacklisted by the Chinese government because of his involvement in an inchoate plan to kidnap government officials and needing to bring his son over while supporting his family, Nan drops out of graduate school with an MA and goes to work.

The novel chronicles Nan's internal struggle in several ways: his struggle to maintain his self-image as a scholar, intellectual, and poet while working menial jobs and eventually running a Chinese restaurant; his struggle to be content with his wife while maintaining an infatuation with a former girlfriend; and his struggle to raise a son who is now growing up in a culture different from the one in which he was raised. *A Free Life* is about Nan's struggle to finally accept the life he is able to carve out in the United States, intertwining his struggle to make a living in an alien land and culture with his ability to achieve the American Dream.

A Free Life's recurrent themes and stories are ubiquitous in the Asian American experience. By and large, these themes are told in stories of hardship and exclusion, and how the American Dream was achieved. In many instances, these themes are told side by side, juxtaposed and intertwining in the same story. They are inseparable from the notion of "Asian American."

Basic Tenets of Asian American Liberative Ethics

The term *Asian American* was first used in the 1960s and 1970s to describe and unify Americans of Asian origin, for example, Chinese, Japanese, and Korean Americans. The presence of pan-Asian immigrants in the United States, however, predates the term. In addition, a variety of ethnicities represent the term *Asian Americans*. They are from South, East, and Southeast Asia; hence the term Asian Americans, as used in this chapter, includes residents in North America who can trace their origins to all these places.

One of the earliest Asian American liberation theologians was Roy Sano, a Japanese American influenced by black liberation theology. Subsequently, Asian American theology was developed in the 1980s and 1990s as Asian theologians who worked or taught in US seminaries hammered out Asian and Asian American theologies of liberation. The basic premise of these liberation theologies is that God is on the side of the economically and socially downtrodden. God's work in this world is to liberate them from poverty and captivity—personal, institutional, structural, and theological.

Asian American liberation theologies adapted this message to Asian American experience and cultural backgrounds by using Asian and Asian American theological symbols and images. They focused on particularly Asian and Asian American concerns, such as pluralism, immigration, and Asian religious influences, drawing from Asian religious and cultural terms to articulate their theology.

History and Development of Asian American Ethics

The first Asians to enter the Americas were Filipinos who came in galleons to Acapulco. Some of the earliest Asians to enter the territories of the United States were Chinese traders and agricultural workers who came to Hawaii in the early nineteenth century. The history of Asian Americans has since been marked by exclusion, discrimination, and the struggle to make a living. What follows are a few highlights that are illustrative (but by no means comprehensive) of the more recent Asian American experience.

BOX 7.1

Asian American Womanist/Feminist Liberative Ethics

The first generation of womanist/feminist liberation theologians writing within an Asian and Asian American context included Chung Hyun Kyung, Rita Nakashima Brock, and Kwok Pui-Lan. These are women who were born in either Asia or in the United States who addressed the Asian American context. More recent feminist liberation scholars writing for the Asian American context include Wonhee Anne Joh, Greer Anne Wenh-In Ng, and Young Lee Hertig.

Asian American womanist/feminist theologians write with several themes in common. One is their recovery of images and terms from Asian language and culture to describe their experiences and theology; examples of this include bamboo for flexibility in a state of cultural hybridity (Ng), the terms *jeong* for revolutionary love and *han* for suffering (Joh), cooking "off the menu" to describe creating a hybridized identity (Brock), and Jesus as mother and woman, *minjung within the minjung* (Chung). Another is the emphasis on multicultural and multifaith hermeneutics and dialogue. Kwok Pui Lan argues for dialogue and imagination in biblical interpretation, reflecting Asian American cultural hybridity, which brings together multiple influences but does not fuse them.

Chinese Immigration and the Chinese Exclusion Act

Attracted to the discovery of gold in California, as well as pushed out by civil war and natural disasters in China, Chinese immigrants came primarily to the United States in the mid-nineteenth century to perform menial tasks and to work in the mines. When mining work ran out, they turned to farm labor, and then to work on the Central Pacific Railroad, completed in 1869. They faced immense prejudice when they arrived, on both the national and local levels. Local inhabitants saw them as inferior, dirty, unhygienic, and heathen; consequently, they passed laws restricting their residency and freedom of movement. Strict immigration laws limiting the entry of Chinese women as well as antimiscegenation laws led to a preponderance of single men, which curtailed the Chinese American population.

Such anti-Chinese laws and sentiment culminated in the Chinese Exclusion Act of 1882, which suspended Chinese immigration to the United States until 1943. These exclusive actions and laws were not restricted to the Chinese: immigrants from other nations were also restricted by the Asiatic Barred Zone Act of 1917, the Johnson-Reed Act of 1924, and the Tydings-McDuffie Act of 1934 (excluding immigration from the Philippines).

Internment of Japanese Americans during World War II

On February 19, 1942, President Franklin Roosevelt ordered the internment of 120,000 Japanese

CASE STUDY 7.1

Slavery exists in the twenty-first century. Human trafficking is reported to be the second-largest illegal profit industry after drug trafficking. Asians in particular experience human trafficking in the form of economic and sexual slavery. Women, often wives and mothers, from the Philippines and Indonesia go all over the world to work as domestic help. They send back the money to their families, whom they do not see for years. While in some cases they are treated reasonably well, in many instances they are abused by their employers. Their passports and money are often withheld so they cannot leave or complain. Often the governments of their native countries are unable to help. Even though these conditions are often known to women who enter the domestic worker global labor market, they are compelled to do so because of the poverty in their home countries.

Poverty also forces young girls and women to leave their homes and travel to cities and other regions in search of work. Sometimes they are kidnapped. They often end up in brothels, to serve the sex trade in cities. Some young women, on the promise of jobs to pay for their passage, enter the United States, legally and illegally. They are held hostage in brothels until their debts are paid, and they are severely punished or murdered if they attempt to escape. They suffer untreated diseases and, if they get pregnant, undergo forced abortions so they can continue working. They have multiple clients in the course of a single day or evening, yet only a fraction of their earnings is applied to their debts.

What should the response of Asian Americans be to economic slavery of Asian women as domestic workers in the world? In North America? What should the response of Asian Americans be to the sex trade in Asian women, both globally and in North America? Should forced labor and sex be legalized, so that this illegal activity can be taxed and regulated? If not, what are some concrete actions that can be taken?

residents of the United States, 77,000 of whom were US citizens, because their loyalty to the United States during World War II could not be assumed. In fact, many of these people had been Americans for generations, and had even fought in the US war. German Americans, however, whose nation of origin was also at war with the United States, were not interned.

Japanese Americans, forced to leave their homes with as little as six days' notice, had to abandon or sell their possessions at fire-sale prices. What was left behind was looted or raided. They lived in concentration camps across the United States for three years. During this time, American-born Japanese, or Nisei, fought for the United States in Europe, even while their families were in internment camps. In fact, the 442nd Regimental Combat Team, a significant percentage of which were Nisei from both Hawaii and the mainland, fought with such distinction that they became the most highly decorated regiment in World War II.

After the war, Japanese Americans had difficulty returning to their former lives and rein-

Fig. 7.1. A large sign reading "I am an American" placed in store window, at 13th and Franklin streets in Oakland, California, on December 8, 1941, the day after the attack on Pearl Harbor. The store was closed following orders to persons of Japanese descent to evacuate from certain West Coast areas. The owner, a University of California graduate, was interned with thousands of other evacuees in concentration camps throughout the United States for the duration of the Second World War.

tegrating into society, politically and economically. Although the United States instituted a claims procedure for property lost, it only paid a fraction of those claims. It was not until 1988, sixty years and a lawsuit later, that the US government acknowledged this wrongdoing against its own citizens, and awarded symbolic restitution to the few living survivors of the concentration camps.

Vincent Chin

Vincent Chin was a twenty-seven-year-old Chinese American man living and working in Detroit. In 1982, a few days before his wedding, he was out with friends at a nightclub for his bachelor party. At the same club were Ronald Ebens and his stepson, Michael Nitz. Ebens was a foreman at an automobile factory, and Nitz had been laid off from the factory a few days prior to this incident. Ebens mistook Chin for Japanese and accused him of taking away American jobs. A fight ensued. After the club evicted them, the fight continued outside, where Ebens and Nitz beat Chin with a baseball bat. Chin died of his injuries four days later.

Ebens and Nitz were charged with second-degree murder. Ebens pleaded guilty to manslaughter, and Nitz did not contest the charge. The judge, Charles Kaufman, a World War II veteran who had spent time in a Japanese prisoner of war camp, sentenced both to three years of probation and a fine of three thousand dollars. After a public outcry from Asian Americans, the judge justified the light sentence by saying that he had cast the sentence to fit the criminals and not the crime: Ebens and Nitz were first-time offenders, and the judge did not think they would repeat the crime.

Los Angeles Riots

On April 29, 1992, Rodney King, an African American man, was arrested and beaten by several Caucasian American police officers. The incident, recorded on video, was played extensively by the media. A jury comprising ten white jurors,

one Hispanic juror, and one Asian juror acquitted the police officers of assault and excessive use of force. In response to the verdicts of acquittal, riots broke out throughout South Central Los Angeles and raged for several days. The police force proved ineffective and was advised to withdraw for its own safety. It was days before other peacekeeping forces could be deployed. Fifty-three people were killed, thousands were injured, and property damage was estimated at over a billion dollars.

When the rioters realized that there was no police presence, they looted with impunity. Stores in Koreatown were particularly targeted. Korean storekeepers used guns in an attempt to defend their stores, shooting above and into the crowd. The riots continued for four days, until federal troops arrived. The riots highlighted the racial tension and unrest existing between the African American and the Korean American communities of Los Angeles. African Americans accused Korean storekeepers of discriminating against them by refusing to hire them while taking money out of the local community. Tension had been running high since the prior year, when a Korean storekeeper had mistakenly thought an African American teenage girl was attempting to shoplift and, after an argument, shot and killed her from behind. The storekeeper received only five years' probation for this crime. Korean Americans, however, saw this as an instance in which the police protected property owned by Euro-Americans, but not property owned by them. This left them feeling extremely vulnerable and unprotected, and their social and citizenship contract violated.

Need for Liberation

Asian American theology has focused on marginalization as the primary social experience of oppression for Asian Americans. The primary manner in which marginalization comes about is

CASE STUDY 7.2

Some Asian Americans come from nations such as Pakistan and Indonesia, which are predominantly Muslim. These Muslim Asian Americans, or even non-Muslim Asian Americans of South Asian ethnicity—for example, Sikhs—have been the target of religious and ethnic prejudice in the wake of September 11, 2001, when al-Qaeda terrorists flew airplanes into the World Trade Towers in New York, the Pentagon in Washington, DC, and an empty field in Pennsylvania. Al-Qaeda is a multinational Islamic group, but its members predominantly hail from the Middle East. Its leader, Osama bin Laden, was from Saudi Arabia, but purported to travel throughout the Middle East, Afghanistan, and was ultimately found in Pakistan.

In the wake of the September 11 attacks, there has been heightened and violent anti-Muslim sentiment in the United States. This has also included non-Muslims that are believed to be Muslim because of their ethnicity, physical features, or clothing. Consider the rash of hate crimes and violence against Sikh-Americans

Fig. 7.2. On August 22, 2010, hundreds of protesters gathered in downtown New York City both in support of and against the construction of an Islamic community center and mosque near Ground Zero, called "Cordoba House." Many opponents of the project argued that it was located too close to the site of the 9/11 terrorist attack. Many supporters believed that the center would set an example of tolerance of American difference.

because they wore turbans and were thus mistaken for Muslims. Sikhs wear turbans for religious reasons, and because they originate mostly from the Punjabi region of northern India, they can bear similar physical features to people from the Middle East. In fact, some Sikhs came to the United States to escape religious discrimination and violence in Punjab.

Proposed construction of an Islamic cultural center near Ground Zero, the site of the former World Trade Towers, met with tremendous controversy. Those in favor of allowing the construction to proceed cite issues of religious freedom and tolerance, as well as the opportunity for interfaith dialogue. Those against it cite issues of sensitivity to the victims of the attacks, public opinion opposing the project, and question sources of funding for the construction. Anti-Muslim sentiment has also been encouraged in politics and government. Racial profiling is found during police and border functions, and anti-Muslim rhetoric in state and federal politics has not only targeted Asian Americans but also other nonwhite Americans. Although the death of Osama bin Laden has given Americans a sense of justice, it is not clear what the long-range effect of this event will be on the "war against terror."

How do issues of race and religion interact in the accounts given? How should the church respond to anti-Muslim sentiment? Is the violence against Sikhs religious or racial? What would be liberation for Sikh Americans, who came to the United States to pursue religious freedom and became instead subjects of religious and racial violence? What should the response of Asian American Christians be to violence against Americans of Middle Eastern descent or origin? If they are Muslims? If they are not Muslims?

through cultural alienation, racialization, and racism; and for those who are Christians, Western theological imperialism. Marginalization of Asian Americans manifests itself in three ways: through their roles as middleman minority, model minority, and in their globalized and transnational experiences and relationships.

From Marginalization

Asians experience the role of "middleman minority" in the different societies they have migrated to and settled in. Middleman minority groups function as economic intermediaries between the culturally, politically, or economically dominant and subordinate groups. This is accomplished when Asian Americans fill certain professional or specialty roles in the economy, usually prescribed by the dominant culture.

In a variation of the middleman minority status, Asian Americans in the United States have also been categorized as model minorities. This term refers to a group that is economically self-sufficient and relatively crime-free, with values synchronistic with the dominant culture. This designation is actually a form of racism, as it implies that Asian Americans are the "model" immigrant group while other groups are inferior. The appearance of economic success, however, masks the higher percentage of Asian American household members participating in the labor market to offset lower per capita income. The term acts as a glass ceiling, veiling discrimination and other serious problems, carrying the implication that Asian Americans are not assimilable.

Asian Americans have global family ties. Immigration patterns in the twenty-first century entail

CASE STUDY 7.3

Chai Vang emigrated from Laos when he was twelve years old. He and his family initially settled in California, where he served in the California National Guard and earned a good conduct badge and a sharpshooting certificate. The family moved to St. Paul, Minnesota, in 2000, where there is a significant Hmong population.

In 2004, he went hunting in Wisconsin. He began his hunt on public property, but moved at some point to privately owned property. The owner of the property approached Vang and asked him to leave. As he was leaving, other friends of the owner arrived, and an altercation ensued. It is not clear who started the altercation, but Vang claims that racial insults were hurled at him, and he started shooting. By the end, he had fired approximately twenty rounds of ammunition, killed six people, and wounded two.

The Hmong leadership in St. Paul made statements to the media and the public emphasizing that this incident was the action of a lone person, possibly mentally ill, and pleaded that the public not view it as representative of the Hmong community. Vang was tried for and convicted of six counts of first degree murder and two counts of attempted murder, and sentenced to six consecutive life sentences and an additional seventy years in prison.

What entails liberation from marginalization for the Hmong community? Might liberation mean integration? What might be the difference between liberation and integration? Why did the Hmong community plead with the public not to view Vang as typical? What would be liberation for an individual like Vang? His family?

multiple types of relationships between one's country of origin and one's resident country, facilitated by a technology that enables communication with extended family across continents. This has led to a hybridized and multidimensional transnational identity, where Asian Americans experience cultural and family loyalties simultaneously in the United States and in Asia. In such cases, Asian Americans are doubly marginalized: they are considered American, or "too American," by their Asian families, while North American society views them as Asian and therefore not American.

Peter Phan, in *Christianity with an Asian Face: Asian American Theology in the Making*, calls these experiences of marginality "betwixt and between," or sites of intercultural encounters where premodernity, modernity, and postmodernity intersect. It comes at a cost. Fumitaka Matsuoka, in *Out of Silence: Emerging Themes in Asian American Churches*, describes a "deep spiritual pain" that arises from the unresolvable conflict between the impossibility of letting go of one's own ethnic, cultural, and ancestral belonging and at the same time realizing that the assertion of one's own particularity is perceived as deviance by society at large.

From Racism

The primary form of marginalization Asian Americans as a group experience is that of racial discrimination. When an Asian living in the United States, either in the first generation or often in the transition to the second generation, starts to identify as "Asian American," the transition that takes place is a form of *racialization*. In the transition to being "Asian American," one's prior ethnic and sociopolitical identity is transformed into a racial identity. Thus, in addition to the conflict between the cultures of the old and new world, the Asian American also experiences an identification with other Asians in North American society who are dissimilar in ethnicity, culture, religion, and/or national origin. The Asian American must now negotiate cultural identity both as an American and as a person of a particular national and ethnic origin, and must do so according to the racial identity "Asian" and/or a "person of color." If the Asian-living-in-America is marginalized by culture, religion, and/or national origin, the Asian American is also marginalized by race. In other words, a person's adoption of Asian American identity is an implicit recognition *and acceptance* of the way race shapes US society.

From Imperialism

San Francisco's Chinatown was squalid and overcrowded in the nineteenth century. Its inhabitants, with a high proportion of single men, were perceived as heathen, superstitious, immoral, and unhygienic—and thus "un-American." A public health campaign ensued to teach them the norms or morals of American middle-class family life; for example, nuclear families living in apartments, infant nutrition, and American notions of hygiene. This would "Americanize" them, consequently making them less of a threat.

Today, Asian American Christians also suffer under cultural and theological imperialism in the church. Many Asian Americans who become Christians have been taught that they must set aside their Asian religious heritage and embrace Western norms in order to embrace Christianity. Arguably, liberation for Asian Americans would include recovering Asian sources of knowledge, Asian cultural norms, and Asian methods of conflict resolution for the Asian American church.

BOX 7.2

Marginality

The most influential factor in Asian American theology is that Asian Americans are part of a minority group in North America due to race and culture. An influential book in Asian American liberation theology by Jung Young Lee is *Marginality: The Key to Multicultural Theology*, in which Lee plumbs the term *marginality* and the condition it describes for theological meaning and its potential for liberative and redemptive work. Asian American identity and experience—middleman minority, model minority, and transnationalism—are all experiences of marginality. Asian Americans find themselves marginalized by being in between worlds—ethnic or racial, and national—thus belonging to neither. Their ethnic and cultural identities differentiate from larger society. In fact, Asian Americans are doubly marginalized: from the dominantly European culture for being Asian but also from Asian society by being American. In addition, if they are Christian, they are marginalized from the dominant church because of their race and from traditional Asian culture because of their religion.

KEY TERM 7.1

Minjung (Korean). Meaning "common people," it indicates suffering humanity, or the oppressed masses.

Issues and Questions: On Partial Privilege

American-born Michelle Kwan, of Chinese origins, is a five-time world champion and the most decorated ice skater in US history. When she won the silver medal in the 1998 Winter Olympics and a Euro-American won the gold, a Seattle news agency announced: "American beats Kwan." The news agency later withdrew the headline and apologized for the error implying Kwan was not American.

This incident describes the common dilemma for Asian Americans. They are educationally and economically successful, but they remain perpetually marginalized and excluded. This mixture of privilege and oppression is perplexing. Asian Americans cannot claim to be oppressed because of their educational and economic advances, yet they are excluded from the dominant culture and political power because of their ethnicity. They remain on the margins among the dominant and the marginalized. Because of this double marginalization, Asian Americans often lack the ability to understand and formulate the options, decisions, and goals necessary to develop their own sense of identity and agency.

Asian Americans have some privilege and power, and hence the responsibility to use that privilege and power for the common good. Yet they find themselves without the models and resources to do so. They lack a model for agency that takes into account their partial privilege and partial oppression.

Current Themes and Methodologies

Asian American theology has predominantly focused on liberation theology. Peter Phan, a Vietnamese Catholic theologian, articulates a method for Asian American liberation theology. First, liberation theology is in conversation with the social sciences. It pays attention to history and how other disciplines understand what is occurring. Second, because a fundamental influence on Asians and Asian culture is religious, liberation theology must be linked to interreligious dialogue. Third, liberation theology must engage the deep stories of human beings, paying attention to the underside of history—the poor, the unwelcome, the not-listened-to.

Phan argues that that the primary metaphor for Asian liberation theology is the reign of God. The church has a unique message of justice and equality, with an emphasis on the preferential option for the poor, context, the historical reality of the people of God, and the transformation of their lives. Still, to the extent that Asians equate obedience to authority as obedience to God, political concern and action can be understood as disobedience or rebellion. It is thus necessary to disentangle notions of patriarchy from the church's message of justice and the equality of all persons.

From Marginality to Liminality

Liberative ethics for Asian Americans is first liberation *from* marginalization. It is not only personal liberation but also liberation from the social structures and institutions that cause or perpetuate the marginalization. Asian American theologians have explored liberty from cultural marginalization in terms of multiculturalism and postcolonialism. For example, Wonhee Anne Joh argues that freedom from marginality means rejecting the dichotomization of dominant/marginalized identity and redefining Asian American identity as one of *hybridity*. Asian Americans have complex notions of identity due to their globalized and transcultural experiences and relationships. Freedom from marginalization means accepting their identity as encompassing their multiple worlds. In other words, Asian Americans are neither inferior Asians nor inferior Americans, but are both Asian *and* American. Rita Nakashima Brock terms this existence "interstitial integrity," or the ability to live simultaneously and fluidly in different cultures, honoring them all appropriately.

Although the terms *liminality* and *marginality* are often used interchangeably, Sang Hyun Lee proposes that liminality is marginality that is open to creative possibilities. It is marginality with an eye toward the reign of God. Lee utilizes Victor Turner's work in liminality to describe its creative potential and its openness to the new. It can lead to the creation of a new identity, genuine community, and an alternative reality, challenging a community with prophetic and subversive knowledge to re-create new allegiances.

To be liberated from marginality means to affirm *both* the Asian *and* the American characteristics of a person. It is to be both in-between and in-both, and thus in-beyond. Jung Young Lee suggests that Jesus exemplifies this by overcoming marginality without ceasing to be a marginal person. Paul Nagano relates marginalization to the incarnation. Marginalization helps us to identify with the oppressed while at the same time recognizing the image of God in us and them. As a Japanese American, he suggests that Japanese Americans should first affirm their Japanese American identity and marginality, and then develop relationships of solidarity and action with other marginalized groups, working toward the reign of God in the world.

From Racism to Solidarity

Liberty from racism would mean to be free from racist social structures that cause marginalization. Asian American liberation theologians have focused on this issue in a variety of ways. Andrew Sung Park describes the racial woes of Asian Americans with the Korean word *han*, the pain and resentment that comes through experiencing injustice on a personal, social, and structural level. For example, Koreans experienced *han* in the way the United States played Japan and Korea against each other after World War II. *Han* is also experienced because of the racism toward Asians and Asian Americans within the white church, and in the negative manner the media portrays Asians. Park argues that freedom from *han* must come from transmutation, which means change within economic and structural injustice, and liberation from patriarchy and racism. Racial *han* can be healed through seeing one another truthfully.

Freedom from a state of racialization would recognize liminality or creative possibilities while working to benefit Asian Americans and other groups of people. For example, Anselm Min proposes that as citizens of the United States, Asian Americans are responsible for the laws and policies of the United States. To withdraw into apoliticism would be to abdicate this responsibility to more powerful and oppressive groups. Min urges Asian Americans to live and act in a *solidarity of others*. He advocates a solidarity in which each

---

KEY TERM 7.2

Hybridity. New and blended cultural concepts and ways of being formed in response to the introduction of different cultures to each other.

KEY TERM 7.3

Liminality. The condition of openness and possibility that accompanies being on the margins of society.

KEY TERM 7.4

Han (Korean). Resentment toward injustices, helplessness or a sense of abandonment, and pain.

group can only exist in relationship and in need of each other. No group can claim universality, but each group does have particular contributions to make to the whole. Liberation occurs in relationship with others. He also argues that we must look at the solidarity of *others* in their particularity and otherness. All voices must be heard. Min also distinguishes solidarity *of* others from solidarity *with* others. The latter implies, on the one hand, the privilege of being able to make oneself the center and select others to support one's own interests. The former, solidarity *of* others, on the other hand, implies a solidarity among those who are other, and who actively cooperate toward a mutually desired future. It implies activity, cooperation, and agency on behalf of each other.

From Imperialism to Story

For Asian American Christians, liberation from theological and cultural oppression would be to recognize that Western theology has automatic normativity and orthodoxy in Christianity. Asian Americans, however, must develop a theology that is indigenous to Asian Americans, incorporating the best of both their Western and Asian heritage.

"Story theology" is a way of doing theology that focuses on telling the stories of people's religious experience and deriving meaning from the stories. Story theology is also known as "autobiographical theology," storytelling from the perspective of faith, relating life's events to divine meaning. Articulating and promulgating doctrine is secondary. The hermeneutical theme of theological reflection on stories, according to Phan's book *Journeys at the Margin: Toward an Autobiographical Theology in Asian American Perspective* is, "How can the message of the Bible, especially as it is incarnated in Jesus, become the good news for those who are poor, oppressed, and marginalized?" (1999: xvi).

C. S. Song calls this the "theological one-stroke," by which he means seeing culture and history through a theological eye. For Song, the

---

BOX 7.3

Story Theology

Story theology is the telling of one's story, personal or societal, with the inquiries, Where is God? and, What is God doing here? In other words, story theology involves doing theology inductively by attending to narrative and context rather than by deducing from abstract principles. Western theology was formed in Western contexts, while Asian American theology must be formed with attention to Asian American contexts. Story theology pays attention to deep stories of pain and oppression, good news, and liberation. It draws from all the sources that shape one's culture and theology. It pays attention to the particular, relating the particular to universal themes. It recognizes that persons and ideas are historically located and shaped by their experience of the world. Story theology draws inspiration from liberation theology to describe liberation from imperialistic and colonizing universalist tendencies in Western theology. For example, one of the weaknesses of Western-style liberation theology is the dichotomization it makes between oppressed and oppressor, poor and rich. Asian Americans, however, are both, with partial privilege (economic and educational) and partial disempowerment (political and social).

---

one-stroke is God's saving love for the world. Through this lens, we can imagine and further God's work in history, religion, and culture. Because story is ongoing, and only in the end will it all be told, story theology will not be complete until the end of the world. Song argues that Asian

KEY TERM 7.5

Third eye. The metaphor for the insight and perception needed to understand deep meanings in human experience.

theologians must possess the ability to listen to the depths of human experience and suffering and be able to discern the theological meaning of these experiences.

For Asian Americans, doing story theology can be liberation from the universalizing norms, constructs, and models of understanding the world from a Eurocentric perspective. By paying attention to Asian American experiences and narratives, story theology liberates Asian Americans from Eurocentric expectations of what is "normal," "healthy," and "acceptable" in society. It liberates them from the binary dichotomies in western constructs, which fail to describe them fully: Oriental versus Occidental, Eastern versus Western, foreign versus American, white versus brown, acculturated versus inassimilable, dominant versus marginalized. It liberates them from mindless acceptance and pursuit of the American dream through the realization that the American dream can only be purchased by non-whites and immigrants at great cost to themselves.

Inasmuch as story theology differs from the norms and methods of the dominant Eurocentric ways of doing theology, doing story theology itself liberates from the colonizing and universalizing tendencies of abstract and doctrinal theology. It

KEY TERM 7.6

Jeong (Korean). The capacity to embody love, vulnerability, and difference in a relationship without resorting to binary divisions.

is active engagement in liberative ethics because it is a close examination of one's life and story, with a theological one-stroke to perceiving the work of God in one's past, present, and future.

Story theology liberates us theologically, and it can also provide guidance for ethics that is free from the domination of Euro-American cultural norms. "Story ethics" could then be a way of living and doing ethics that takes account of a particular context and culture; it tells the deep story of a person or people, from the past, from within, and moving forward. Story ethics incarnates the gospel in society and in personal life. When one does story ethics, one finds the incarnation of the gospel in one's life, and in one's context, and takes the gospel into the future of one's life.

Story ethics as the ethical dimension of story theology is incarnational and contextual; it is the good news of God's love and liberation expressed in the totality of all life, society, and culture. This is an ethics that is culturally and historically located, global, and public. Story ethics acculturates the good news of the reign of God to ordinary people. It is deeply particular; thus, it is neither utilitarian, seeking the greatest good of society, nor is it utopian, seeking a beatific society for all. Neither is it deontological in approach, governed only by abstract, generalized rules; rather, it pays attention to the work of God in the present. As H. Richard Niebuhr asks, "What is God doing in the world?" In the liberative tradition, story ethics might ask: Where and how is God acting to liberate the world?

Story ethics is ecumenical and open-minded; it serves truth wherever it is found. It engages in a multifaith hermeneutics and interfaith dialogue, respecting the knowledge and wisdom of other cultures. Because at times this can lead to a confusing cacophony of moral claims, the Asian American Christian must develop a method of prioritizing these moral claims. Moral norms of most religions are usually not dissimilar. For example, the "Golden Rule" has equivalents in

Christianity, Confucianism, Islam, and Hinduism. When cultural norms or mores clash, Asian American Christians must discern which norms more adequately express the reign of God, and if none do, they would be *free* to imagine and fashion new norms and mores that accomplish this. Thus story ethics is imaginative and forward looking, making the future a present reality. God is not only acting to liberate the world in the present, but God is also acting to liberate human beings and the world in the future. God acts to liberate human beings through dismantling oppressive personal, institutional, and social structures.

Intercultural and Interreligious Dialogue

Judeo-Christianity drew from the cultures and religions of the ancient Near East and the Babylonians. Western Christianity has drawn from Western non-Christian sources; for example, the ancient Greeks and Romans. Asia is the cradle for all the world religions; thus Asian Christianity likewise must draw from the traditions, religions, and wisdoms of the cultures in which it grows. Asian American Christianity has inherited both Eastern and Western traditions (in all their diversities).

For Asian Americans, then, liberative ethics must be intercultural and interreligious. The consensus of Asian American liberation theologians is that Asian American liberative theology must attend to the multiple cultures and religions that form the worlds out of which Asian Americans live. There are Asian traditions of introspective wisdom and psychology that Asian Americans can inherit. Struggle for political and economic justice must be integrated with the religious dimension. Kwok Pui Lan argues for a multifaith hermeneutics that relates Christianity to other texts and traditions. This calls for imagination in biblical tradition and liberation from Western notions of orthodoxy in doctrine and method. An Asian American approach brings together these traditions but also recognizes their separateness.

Possible Future Trends

Fumitaka Matsuoka argues that Asian American churches are politically and culturally silent because they are marginalized. This marginalization continues at various levels in culture and society. Liberative ethics for Asian Americans must therefore involve a model for developing agency and voice.

There are two dimensions to the notion of liberty: negative and positive. Negative liberty is the notion of "freedom from" restraint, or constraint by another. this involves not only freedom from physical constraint but also the threat of physical constraint (e.g., jail), as this reduces one's overall options. Thus negative liberty would involve freedom from oppression—political, economic, social, and even theological. The Western liberal tradition focuses on negative rights. Much of the focus in liberation theology is also on negative liberties (e.g., freedom from poverty and freedom from oppression).

While negative liberty focuses on freedom from personal, institutional, and structural oppression, positive liberty focuses on the freedom to free oneself and others from oppression. Positive liberty is the idea that one has the "freedom to" act toward realizing one's goals and purposes in life, and in fact one can and does do so. This involves having the abilities and capabilities to pursue one's goals—in other words, having agency and empowerment. The attention to positive liberative ethics is vitally important—hence, liberative *ethics*, and not simply liberation theology. The *ethical* dimension suggests the agency, freedom to act, and practical wisdom needed to make liberty a reality for the oppressed.

Western-style liberation theology tends to dichotomize into oppressed and oppressor, powerful and powerless. However, Asian Americans—as middleman minorities and model minorities—have both partial power and partial privilege. Inasmuch as liberation realizes Asian

Americans' complex notions of identity, it needs to recognize that Asian Americans have both partial power and partial oppression.

The experience of marginality can provide a creative opportunity to develop a moral agency that attends and responds to the particularities of Asian Americans in both the experiences and interpretations of partial power and of partial oppression. Asian Americans have different interpretations and different *responsibilities* from both the dominant and other subordinate groups. In particular, Asian Americans have a responsibility to connect their partial privilege to their partial oppression. This is the task of liberative ethics: to use partial privilege to ameliorate the oppression of others. The particular pain of oppression Asian Americans feel is a call to work for justice for others who suffer similar pain, or worse.

Liminality is the pivotal point between negative and positive liberty; the point where freedom from marginalization can also be the beginning of freedom to act against marginalization, and the freedom to act against oppression on behalf of oneself and others. At the point of liminality, liberation is freedom to act out of oppression, both against the oppression and toward one's goals and purposes. Liberation is freedom to act toward one's conception of the good and

LIBERATIVE ETHICS IN ACTION 7.1

Liberative Ethics in Action: Apologies Accompanied by Reparations

In 1993, the president of the United Church of Christ, the Rev. Paul Sherry, apologized to native Hawaiians for the denomination's support of the overthrow of Queen Lili'uokalani and the Hawaiian nation by the United States. This apology spurred some Asian American churches in the Hawaiian conference to propose a resolution for a further apology along with an offer of reparations for participating in the cultural and economic oppression of Hawaiians after the overthrow of their nation. The Asian American representatives of churches in the conference admitted that while they were outsiders like the Hawaiians in white-controlled Hawaii, they had benefited from the overthrow of the Hawaiian nation.

This apology and the resolution offering reparations led into a yearlong debate surrounded by controversy. Asian churches were divided from Asian churches, some acknowledging responsibility and others denying it. Finally, at a polity conference, a Hawaiian-Chinese pastor, the Rev. Kekapa Lee, stood up and spoke about the apology from a Hawaiian perspective. As he spoke of the pain of the Hawaiians, he was slowly joined by almost all the rest of the Hawaiians in the polity. White and Asian Americans finally grasped the depth of the pain that their refusal to acknowledge the past injustice had perpetuated. The conference adopted a variation of the initial resolution, proposing apology and reparations that included monetary reparations and the creation of a trust fund for the general community.

The Rev. Lee is an example of an Asian American doing liberative ethics. He took the courage to articulate the pain he and other Hawaiians felt. He exercised his own partial privilege as an Asian American pastor and member of the conference to articulate the pain that he and others experienced, to call for repentance, and so to create "solidarity of the others." These words, however, were also accompanied by the prospect of monetary reparations, or concrete expressions of the apology, incarnating the notion of repentance.

common good, by starting with particular and concrete actions. It is to find one's sense of moral agency, by attending to the particularities of experience and suffering and the details of one's own story, and then finding the creative potential in that story and acting on it in specific ways. In other words, liberation from marginality is to see its potential as liminality: it is to give marginality a direction and purpose for one's personal good and the common good.

Study Questions

1. In what specific ways have the particular contexts of Asian Americans shaped their liberation theology and their liberative ethics?

2. What are some of the issues that Asian Americans have in common with other immigrant or minority groups?

3. What are some of the primary issues that Asian Americans need to grapple with further in regard to liberation?

4. What are some of the primary ways Asian Americans can contribute to the liberation of others?

5. What are some barriers to the "solidarity of others" that Anselm Min advocates?

Suggested Readings

Brock, Rita Nakashima, Jung Ha Kim, Kwok Pui-lan, Seung Ai Yang, eds. *Off the Menu: Asian and Asian North American Women's Religion and Theology.* Louisville: Westminster John Knox, 2007.

Chung, Hyun Kyung. *Struggle to be the Sun Again: Introducing Asian Women's Theology.* Maryknoll, NY: Orbis, 1990.

De La Torre, Miguel A., ed. *Handbook of U.S. Theologies of Liberation.* St. Louis: Chalice, 2004.

Fernandez, Eleazar S., and Fernando F. Segovia, eds. *A Dream Unfinished: Theological Reflections on America from the Margins.* Maryknoll, NY: Orbis, 2001.

Floyd-Thomas, Stacey M., and Anthony B. Pinn, eds. *Liberation Theologies in the United States: An Introduction.* New York: New York University Press, 2010.

Joh, Wonhee Anne. *Heart of the Cross: Postcolonial Theology.* Louisville: Westminster John Knox, 2006.

Lee, Jung Young. *Marginality: The Key to Multicultural Theology.* Minneapolis: Fortress Press, 1995.

Lee, Sang Hyun. *From a Liminal Place: An Asian American Theology.* Minneapolis: Fortress Press, 2010.

Matsuoka, Fumitaka. *Out of Silence: Emerging Themes in Asian American Churches.* Cleveland: United Church Press, 1995.

Matsuoka, Fumitaka, and Eleazar Fernandez, eds. *Realizing the America of Our Hearts: Theological Voices of Asian Americans.* St. Louis: Chalice, 2003.

Min, Anselm Kyongsuk. *The Solidarity of Others in a Divided World: A Postmodern Theology after Postmodernism.* New York: T&T Clark, 2004.

Park, Andrew Sung. *Racial Conflict and Healing: An Asian American Theological Perspective.* Maryknoll, NY: Orbis, 1996.

Phan, Peter C. *Christianity with an Asian Face: Asian American Theology in the Making.* Maryknoll, NY: Orbis, 2003.

Phan, Peter C., and Jung Young Lee, eds. *Journeys at the Margin: Toward an Autobiographical Theology in Asian American Perspective.* Collegeville, MN: Liturgical, 1999.

Song, C. S. *The Believing Heart: An Invitation to Story Theology.* Minneapolis: Fortress Press, 1999.

Tan, Jonathan. *Introducing Asian American Theologies.* Maryknoll, NY: Orbis, 2008.

American Indian Liberative Ethics

Mark Freeland

TEACHING AND WRITING ABOUT American Indian liberative ethics is a challenging task. To give an honest picture of what ethics means for American Indians, several preliminary comments are required to build a framework that better grasps ethics as liberative within an American Indian context. First, for the purpose of distinguishing the deep cultural differences between American Indian culture and Euro-Western culture (namely, American), it is important to note that this chapter is a demonstration of traditional American Indian ethical perspectives. Although there have been numerous colonial influences imposed on Indians for the past three hundred to five hundred years, intact traditional beliefs and practices still exist and are significantly different from the colonizing cultures with which Native people interact. While many American Indian people are now Christian, I will not be describing those ethical influences, because Christian and other Euro-Western ethical systems have fundamentally different starting places. And while Indian ethical systems might appear as romanticizing some past existence, it is a forthright description of the

contemporary ethical systems that still exists, and will continue to exist.

History and Development of American Indian Liberative Ethics

To best understand the development of American Indian ethical systems, we begin with origin narratives. Some non-Indian peoples call these "creation stories," even though it is a poor translation. To call them creation stories assumes nothing preexisted, as in the Judeo-Christian model of God's creating the universe from nothing. Indians believe humans were placed into an already existing world. Although origin narratives are too diverse to reiterate within this limited space, suffice to say that a consistent theme exists: Indians were placed on the preexisting land complete with all of its surroundings.

Vine Deloria Jr. elaborates on this point in his book *God Is Red*. According to Deloria, there exists no narrative of any Native North America people that traces its origins back to Asia. American

BOX 8.1

Indianized Christianity

There is debate among American Indian people about the assumed universality of Euro-Western thought and ethical systems. The starting places for developing ethical systems is very different between Euro-Western and American Indian thought; as a result, many Native people have turned away from Christian forms of ethics, decolonizing their categories of thought with their own languages. Other Native people, like Richard Twiss and Casey Church, have become Christian ministers and have attempted to syncretize or "indianize" the Christian modes of thought to make them more relevant to American Indian people. This can be interpreted as a nuanced form of a colonized mind because the basic Christian categories of sin, salvation, hierarchy, and God are almost always present in their "indianized" practices. More and more, Native people are turning away from that type of colonization of Indian thought and are digging deeper into their own languages and cultures to find ethical systems more congruent with the communities in which they live.

Indian people reject the notion of a Bering Strait land crossing, most of whom consider it to be an attempt to place Indian origins outside of the Western Hemisphere. This "intellectual" move creates a convenient settler myth that identifies all Indian people as immigrants rather than as proprietors of the land. American Indians instead claim an autochthonous origin on the lands of the Western Hemisphere.

KEY TERM 8.1

Origin Narrative. This term is used to designate what is often discussed as American Indian creation stories. However, rarely are Indians created in the Euro-Christian sense, and more often than not they came out of the ground (usually from caves) or fell from the sky.

KEY TERM 8.2

Bering Straight Land Crossing. This is an archaeological theory that suggests the first humans emigrated to the Americas from Asia across a land bridge between what is now Siberia and Alaska, some sixteen thousand years ago. This theory contradicts other archaeological evidence that places humans in the Americas twenty to sixty thousand years ago. No indigenous peoples in the Americas trace themselves to Asia in their origin stories; hence, many consider the theory political rhetoric thinly veiled as science.

KEY TERM 8.3

Authochthonous. Having spontaneous creation. In the context of this chapter, it is meant to demonstrate that we were placed here in this land, as derived from our origin narratives. This is important, as Native Americans have no memory as American Indian people of coming across the Bering Strait "land bridge."

BOX 8.2

What Is an American Indian?

For the purposes of this essay, the term *American Indian* is used to describe the original human inhabitants of what is called North America, which many of us call Turtle Island. *Native American* is a term imposed on us as a means of political correctness by people who are not originally of this land. Furthermore, there is no such a thing as a monolithic, universal, or common American Indian culture. The term *Indian* itself was imposed on us by European colonizing forces, and we have co-opted it ourselves for political expediency. When a people experiences a reduction in population of about 90 to 95 percent due to the vicious cycle of disease, colonial war, and cultural dislocation, and they are forced to participate in a system of American-style free-market democracy, there are some benefits to alliance building under that banner of American Indian so as to boost numbers, visibility, and agency. Nevertheless, this chapter will demonstrate that there are some common themes and practices that can be used to describe an American Indian liberative ethics. To accomplish that task, a number of examples from particular places in Native North America to demonstrate some of the ethical perspectives and actions from the indigenous peoples of Turtle Island will be utilized. This is not to be taken as a definitive description of ethical perspectives, but a starting point.

The best way to demonstrate a traditional American Indian ethical system is to start with a particular origin narrative of a people that exemplifies the lessons taught by this type of narrative. Employing this approach can illustrate how Native American ethical systems flow from origin narratives, developing particular customs and norms that in turn influence Indian behavior and thought. To this end, we will examine a basic version of the Sky Woman story, demonstrating some of the ethical lessons that narrative teaches. The following excerpts of the Sky Woman narrative appear in Barbara Mann's *Iroquoian Women: The Gantowisas*.

> Eagle cried, "Look! A woman is falling from the sky!" Loon and Heron looked up and they too saw her. It did not take much thinking for Heron and Loon to understand that if they let her fall to the watery world below that she would no doubt drown, so they decided to help her. Up they flew and they caught Sky Woman with their wings. Not knowing what to do next they flew with her for a while until Eagle sought the help from Grandfather Turtle, who was swimming in the water below. The animals decided they needed to have a council to decide what should be done with her. If they let her drown, her death may injure the earth. So Grandfather Turtle decided that he would provide a place for her to live on his back with dirt that was fetched from the bottom of the ocean, while Bass volunteered to provide sustenance for her. After two failed attempts to get dirt from the ocean floor by muskrat and otter, beaver finally succeeded, and the dirt he brought up would become Turtle Island on the back of the Great Turtle. Then Heron and Loon could set Sky Woman down on her new home.

By using this origin narrative from the northeast, we can elucidate some of the major themes of American Indian ethical systems.

An Ethic of Place

This brief origin narrative begins to build an ethical framework, revealing the deep cultural foundations that serve as the basis of Indian ethical systems. The Sky Woman narrative reveals that most of the world preexisted the appearance of humans, and that the origin of the earth and the land on which American Indians live is of primary importance. Noticeably absent from this and other American Indian narratives are references to linear time. This is a primary difference between Indian culture and the imposed Euro-Western culture. According to Vine Deloria Jr in *God Is Red*, "American Indians hold their lands—places—as having the highest possible meaning and all their statements are made with this reference point in mind" (1992: 62). In contrast, Euro-Western cultures emphasize the progression of a people through linear time, with place having secondary importance. For example, the Judeo-Christian Bible begins with, "In the beginning," obviously giving preference to a linear conceptualization of time; furthermore, the Euro-Western world counts each successive year in a linear progression from the time of the birth of Jesus. Where these events take place is of little importance. American Indians, in contrast, begin with their particular places, the lands upon which they live and interact. The brief outline of this origin narrative demonstrates the importance of place, and the role humans occupy as a young member of the earth community in relationship to their elders, the other animals who were already occupying the land. Humans share this land with other life forces, which guides their ethical actions.

Ethics of Community

The Sky Woman narrative also teaches the importance and scope of community within Native North American culture. First, we notice the beginnings of a communal system of interdependence. Even though Sky Woman is a foreigner to the water world into which she falls, the elder animals help care for her because *if they let her drown, her death may injure the earth*. Indian people are taught to help maintain all life by their elders, even the life of a stranger. Additionally, community is understood a widely inclusive concept. Community is not limited to a small group of people, like a church or even a village. The community of life encompasses all with whom the world is shared, including all of our four-legged relatives, the two leggeds (which includes birds), the plant relatives, all of the little critters in and on the ground, and even the rocks that are built on Grandfather Turtle's back. This entire community has its own sense of dignity and deserves respect in all interactions. Therefore, wanton killing and destruction of animals and places causes injury, which should never be allowed.

Second, the nature of this community of life is intimately interrelated. To live, we must eat, and much of that eating comes at the expense of others. The deer eats grass and tree buds; the bear eats insects, berries, fish, and other animals; birds eat berries and worms; and we as humans eat all of these animals, along with some of the foods they eat. We are all tied together and are utterly dependent on one another for our very sustenance. All of life (including the rocks) is included in our community. No order of importance is implied; no hierarchy or chain of being exists. We

---

KEY TERM 8.4

Anthropocentrism. A Euro-Western system of thought that places all of humanity on top of a socially constructed hierarchy of being, often synonymous with the Aristotelian "chain of being." In this system of thought, humans (read white, male, heterosexual humans in particular) are the center of the cosmos, and the rest of creation is subsidiary to their desires.

rely on the deer for food, and the deer rely on the forest to provide food. What we do to the forest and the water, in turn, affects us as humans. This is why deforestation is such a destructive act. Clearing forests for profit deprives the entire community without thought of or care for its effects upon all life dependent on this area. To take from life without reciprocating is an affront to the entire community, creating dangerous consequences for all. This is the lesson that Heron and Loon already knew, a lesson all of us have a responsibility to learn.

Ethics of Balance

Even though as humans we must kill other members of our large community for sustenance, each

---

LIBERATIVE ETHICS IN ACTION 8.1

Liberative Ethics in Action: Reclaiming Land

In an attempt to directly address the ongoing problem of land and forest loss on their homeland, Anishinabeg elders started the White Earth Land Recovery Program (WELRP), on the White Earth reservation in what is now known as northern Minnesota. The land set aside for them after their 1867 treaty was illegally auctioned off to white landowners, and much of the forest was quickly cleared. As a method of comparing what it means to have a forest clear cut, Winona Laduke has quipped, in *All Our Relations*, that after high winds flattened over 100,000 acres of trees on the White Earth reservation, it was called a "natural disaster." However, "when lumber companies similarly vanquish the trees, it is commonly called 'progress'" (1999: 127).

While the return of the land is helpful for a number of reasons, the concept of land ownership does not really translate into Native languages, for it is indicative of a relationship of land domination. Hence, WELRP focuses on teaching both the adults and children of the area how to develop an appropriate relationship to the land, which includes the ability to produce food with cultural integrity. The issue of food production was more directly addressed in 2001 with the *Mino Miijim*, or good food program. With the onset of colonialism and the original destruction of the northern forests, the Anishinabeg's diet dramatically changed from traditional foods to processed wheat flour, sugar, and beef. This change in diet created a significant epidemic in diabetes among American Indian people. Fortunately, studies have shown that a return to a more traditional indigenous diet can lead to diabetics' being able to better control their disease without insulin. By acquiring traditional maple sugarbush forests and actively harvesting traditional foods like maple sugar, wild rice, natural meats like deer and buffalo, and growing hominy corn on available farmland, *Mino Miijim* is able to help the Anishinabeg improve their health, simultaneously improving their relationship to the land, and regenerating their traditional culture along the way. To date, WERLP has purchased over 1,700 acres from willing sellers and put that land in trust for the Anishinabeg people to use. In addition to the *Mino Miijim* project and the reacquisition of land, WELRP also helps teach Anishinabeg people how to cultivate food in traditional ways, works on a wide range of language projects, and provides legal help to protect their relationship to the land. All of these actions taken together help show liberative ethics in action.

of those acts places us out of balance with that community of life surrounding us. A system of reciprocity helps us restore balance after killing an animal or taking plant life. This most often takes shape through the offering of tobacco or some other gift for the offended community. It also includes the recitation of a song or a few words of thanks, and possibly the observance of some customs associated with that particular type of plant or animal. For example, if a beaver was to be killed for food, some tobacco with a few words of thanksgiving might be offered. Care would be taken that no dogs would be allowed to chew on the beaver's bones and that these bones were returned to the water, based on some of our narratives, which teach that this is the way beavers want us to behave and honor our relationships with them. For following these directions, the beavers will allow some of their numbers to be killed for food, and the community of beavers will continue to live on as a whole. Hence, the introduction of the fur trade and other developments like it were not compatible with the Indian culture of balance. Wanton killing of beavers for their fur, void of reciprocity, depleted the beavers to almost extinction.

Ethics of Gifting

When an ethical system takes as its starting point the place (land) upon which one lives, the entire community that resides in that place, and a sense of balance that needs to be maintained via systems of reciprocity, it follows that a system of action which maintains balance within these communities and places becomes the bases for liberative ethics. The system of Indian acquisition and distribution (i.e., their economic system) is best thought of as a system of gifting. All the actions of Native people are permeated with the belief that they receive gifts from the community of life, and as Barbara Mann explains, they do not take lives without purpose. Gifting is how material goods were distributed throughout American

Indian communities, including food and ceremonial items.

As Indians negotiate their lives in this world, they must maintain their relationships with the world, relationships between humans and human groups, on the one hand, and nonhuman inhabitants of the land, on the other. Gifting not only distributes goods but also maintains a balance in relationships between people and between communities. Political relationships are annually remembered and acted on within the seasonal gifting rounds. These acts of gifting usually occur during summer gatherings, providing communal strengthening within and between communities.

Gifting also provides for healthy relationships of mutual interdependence. Two parties learn to rely on and trust each other as they give what they have to offer and receive gifts from each other. As you can tell, this system of relationship only works when the Euro-Western notions of capital accumulation and self-centeredness are not in play. Capitalism and individualism destroys gifting systems.

In conclusion, the Sky Woman origin narrative, along with other origin stories, provides a basis for an American Indian ethical system that teaches to give place primary importance, offers an inclusive understanding of community, demands that balance be kept through actions of reciprocity, and that material wealth be distributed through gifting. An important distinction is that American Indian ethical systems are wholly derived as a responsibility to one's surroundings and the community with which one's surroundings are shared. There exists no divine mandate for any of these actions.

Discussing history from an American Indian perspective provides an interesting comparison of thought as well as a good transition into a discussion concerning the need for liberation. History as a concept is primarily thought of as a linear understanding of time. As discussed earlier, place is of primary importance to American Indians, not time. Therefore, rather than focus on history, it would be more appropriate to think of memory as the way past events are understood. Native traditional cultures, languages, and lifeways are not some past primitive existence, but a memory based on balance and beauty. Communities are remembered as intact and relationships as balanced. Cycles of seasonal hunting, farming, and living are also remembered as seasonal communal celebrations, not as something once done. These cycles continue to exist, even if they are transformed in new ways. The history of American Indian ethical systems is in the memory of their lives on their lands, as continued and practiced today.

The concept of history is problematic when applied to American Indian cultures. History is primarily a Euro-Western category of thought, based on linear progress, a progression from primitive to advanced, from sin to salvation to eschaton, from ignorance to advancement to the future promise of technological utopia. When applied to American Indian cultures, they are invariably placed on the primitive past-tense state of that linear trajectory. Linear historical thinking is so pervasive that more often than not people talk about American Indian culture and people with past tense verbs! However, just like Native

ancestors, they are still here, on their lands. History as a Euro-Western concept is one of the specific structures that American Indians need liberation from.

Need for Liberation

The American Indian need for liberation from specific structures stems from the very onset and presence of Euro-Western colonialism in the Western Hemisphere. Prior to the colonization of their lands by Europeans, Native people were able

KEY TERM 8.5

Memory. This term is used to differentiate American Indian thinking from the Euro-Western reliance on history, which is based on assumptions concerning linear progression. Memory helps to designate indigenous understandings of the passing of time as different from Euro-Western perspectives. For Indians, time is best understood in its cyclical function as they follow the seasons and different cycles of time.

BOX 8.3

Colonialism

Two main types of colonialism have been manifested since Europeans began to impose themselves on the rest of the world: classic colonialism and settler-state colonialism. The most common form was classic colonialism, where Europeans set up political and economic power within the respective colonies and, with very few settlers, ruled them with the help of a created ruling class of indigenous people. With exploited indigenous labor, resources were extracted and the wealth was sent to investors in the home country. Settler-state colonialism was less common; in these cases, early colonists eradicated the indigenous populations in wars of genocide and conquest and set themselves up as the ruling population, importing the labor, such as the chattel slavery of Africans to the United States, or as other immigrant groups such as the Irish or Italians in urban ghettos. This has also been the case in Canada, Australia, and New Zealand.

In an attempt to educate people about the racist and genocidal legacy implicit in the celebration of a state and national holiday devoted to Christopher Columbus, numerous groups around the country began to protest this display of colonial domination. One of the largest and longest lasting Columbus Day protests started in Denver, Colorado, by the Colorado American Indian Movement. Since 1989, in a lead up to the 1992 Columbus Quincentenary, a large demonstration was mobilized every year to educate the public on the realities of what the Columbian landfall, or "discovery," has meant for indigenous people. When Columbus got lost and ended up in the Caribbean, he set off a chain reaction that resulted in the genocide of the Taino people on the Island of Española. The results on Española, of course, were repeated everywhere Europeans landed in the Western Hemisphere, with a vicious cycle of disease transmission, colonial war, and cultural dislocation.

Columbus's legacy of genocide is both masked and subversively celebrated every October. The Transform Columbus Day Alliance, the resulting coalition of seventy-five organizations who have worked to end the Columbus holiday in Colorado, have used numerous tactics over the years to bring this reality to light. There have been massive street arrests, picketing, and lobbying at the state level. Simultaneously, presentations have been made in the schools and numerous churches and civic locations to raise consciousness concerning the reality of the Columbian legacy. While today Columbus Day is still a recognized holiday in the state of Colorado, numerous other states have abolished the holiday. It is through the combination of these educational and street actions that the liberative ethical message of creating a more balanced world can occur. What do you think is at stake for Euro-Western Americans who maintain that celebrating the Columbus holiday is a good idea? What does Columbus represent to Americans? What is the opinion of Christopher Columbus in your area, and does he deserve a national holiday?

to live good lives, free from present-day oppression. With colonization came numerous interlocking difficulties with which American Indians are forced to struggle to this day. An entirely different way of viewing and interacting with the world, the land and the community has been imposed on a broad scale.

The systemic oppression and violence that American Indian people experience is due to particular Euro-Western thought systems; a worldview based, as previously discussed, on the notion of linear progression of time and the concept of the individual being the primary social unit in regard to political and economic rights.

In addition to these two components, there exists an anthropocentric (human-centered) conceptualization of the world and an ordering system that imposes a hierarchy of value, with God on top with Jesus, then men (specifically during colonialism, white, heterosexual, land-owning men). This system of Euro-Western thought was imposed on people and land with the full force of violence that colonizers could muster. While limited space prevents describing this vicious cycle of colonial violence in full detail, nevertheless, a brief sketch is provided. The colonial invasion of the Western Hemisphere is understood as a vicious cycle of disease, war, and cultural dislocation

BOX 8.4

Worldview

The concept of worldview can be helpful in developing a framework for understanding traditional American Indian cultures. It is important to remember that the fundamental starting points for the organization of American Indian and Euro-Western cultures are very different. One culture cannot simply be translated into another. To do so creates misunderstanding. A worldview, as defined here, refers to a fundamental orientation to space and time, a method of seeking and organizing knowledge, and a prescription for an ordering of the world shared by a particular group of people. In the American Indian worldview, an orientation to space, a cyclical understanding of time, an organization of balance, and an ordering of relatedness as community are primary. The Euro-Western worldview, by contrast, emphasizes linear time, the domination of space, the dualistic organization of reality into good versus evil, and the ordering of creation as a hierarchy.

to subdue and bring under colonial control. The Eurocentric colonial venture has been, and continues to be, a deadly imposition upon American Indian people, and is made worse by those Native people who have accepted the dominant colonial narrative, including Euroforming their own languages and cultures to fit dominant so-called universal cultural categories. Obviously, the predominant Euro-Western worldview is neither the most advanced form of human thought nor does it contain universally applicable categories of cognition. The Euro-Western worldview is simply one of many ways of thinking about and interacting with the world. It is neither the only way nor necessarily the best way.

Still, a thought system in and of itself does not cause the violence experienced by bodies and land. Eurocentric worldviews become manifested in specific institutions and actions that allow for and promote acts of violence. For example, when the base cultural organizations of the West are founded on anthropocentric separation from nature and the hierarchical ordering of life, then no deep cultural restraints exist to prevent the potential violence that the Euro-Western thought system can produce. Early in the colonial period, the European invaders continually plundered more and more land in search of more and more

KEY TERM 8.6

Euroforming. A term used by Barbara Mann that describes the process of imposing Euro-Western modes of thought onto American Indian lifeways. For example, there is no traditional understanding of good and evil in American Indian cultures, but those categories have been imposed on us and have been used as methods of describing Indians (evil) as compared to the European colonialist (good).

that was and continues to impose various forms of political, economic, social, and military domination and violence upon Native people. With no regard for life, the early colonists both intentionally and unintentionally spread numerous diseases among the Native populations. Decimation through diseases of Native people provided colonists, once they were able to muster sufficient military strength, the opportunity to wage brutal wars of extermination.

Diseases and war wreaked havoc on the Native populations, causing significant cultural discord in their communities, thus making them easier profit. For example, tobacco farming in Virginia failed to be a sustainable enterprise because of European monocropping agricultural techniques, which quickly exhausted the land of its resources. As each parcel of land became depleted, new land was cleared and also quickly destroyed in the name of progress. Similarly, the fur trade wreaked havoc on the landscape and people. Manifest Destiny and the constant move west was more than an ideological mandate; it was an economic necessity. As each river valley and watershed was depleted of fur-bearing animals, the economics of the fur trade demanded that new resources be exploited. So the fur-trading companies and their trappers and forts moved further and further west into the American Indian land, perpetrating the vicious cycle of colonial disease, war, and cultural discord on more and more peoples.

This vicious cycle also played out in industries like lumber and mining. Easy-to-obtain resources would be extracted without regard for its effects on the overall environment. The only consideration was profit. Euro-Western worldview and ideology are merged with the economic and political manifestations of these systems of thought. A worldview of the white European men and women on top of a hierarchy of being, separate from and superior to the rest of life, lacks the necessary cultural constraints needed to stop the destruction of

its surroundings. As the European elite competed with each to create economic empires, the American Indian and much of the rest of our larger community became collateral damage in the quest for more wealth. To facilitate the creation and expansion of wealth at the expense of Native people, a legal system, created by these same colonizers, was constructed to protect their narcissistic interests. Thus, not surprisingly, American Indians are in need of liberation from this type of Euro-Western worldview and its particular economic and political manifestations.

Issues and Questions

Several hundred years of continual oppression as witnessed in today's reservations, caused by significant changes imposed upon this land, has created a number of issues and questions with which American Indians wrestle. Four questions in particular garner of the attention of Native people: (1) dealing with trauma, (2) issues concerning land, (3) questions about identity, and (4) concerns about living with integrity within the community.

Numerous issues surround overcoming the trauma of historical and contemporary forms of genocide. American Indian people as a group still suffer with some of the worst poverty and highest rates of alcoholism in the Western Hemisphere. These conditions contribute both to other curable diseases and to high rates of incarceration. The Native population has internalized the violence perpetrated against them by the colonizing population to the point that they now participate in their own domination.

Remedies to these social ills have included a return to traditional Native culture. Studies show that diseases like diabetes can be controlled and sometimes eradicated by returning to traditional foods like corn, wild rice, fish, and venison. Also, traditional ceremonies, like purification lodges

KEY TERM 8.7

Manifest Destiny. A term coined in the mid-nineteenth century justifying the westward expansion of the United States. This "inevitable" expansion had religious undertones, as the process of expansion into American Indian territory was consistently justified as expansion into the "New Israel," America being the "promised land" for the "promised people."

(poorly translated as "sweat lodges"), have been instrumental in helping people overcome their alcoholism and other physical, emotional, and social problems. The resurgence of traditional practices, ceremonies, and languages has significantly helped in addressing historical and contemporary concerns; nevertheless, more work and research is needed.

Although many are returning to their traditional ways, they still face issues concerning land, for example, the continual assault experienced by Earth Mother. Areas once considered wasteland were set aside to serve as reservations for Indian people. Ironically, it was discovered that some of these lands contained significant natural resources like coal, natural gas, and uranium. Nevertheless, the American colonial population has manipulated the legal structures to continue extraction of these and other natural resources at the expense of American Indian communities. Indian communities are normally paid about 10 percent of the royalties that would be paid on non-Indian people had these resources been extracted from their land.

The identities of American Indian peoples, and their ceremonies, are dependent on their relationships to that land, to Earth Mother. Wherever Native people live, numerous relationships exist between humans and other animals, other than human energies that live in the land. These relationships are necessary to both ceremonies and to the general well-being of the people. When coal is strip mined, forests are clear cut, or dams built, those lands and the other-than-human energies are destroyed or significantly altered. We are part of the land and must be able to live with it for us to continually exist. Although greater involvement by American Indian people in both traditional ceremonies and its associated land use is occurring, when their cultural integrity conflicts with timber, mining, and energy companies, Indians consistently lose in court, and those lands under question are either taken away, inappropriately occupied, or outright destroyed.

Considering the significant trauma that has been created with the long-standing European invasion of the Western Hemisphere, Indians now face difficult questions concerning themselves about their identity. Since the US government instituted the racist policy of blood quantum, essentially measuring culture with genetics, to measure Indians out of existence, many people, including some American Indian people, have bought into that method. This has caused difficulty and discord within Native communities, as a desperately poor population fights over extremely limited resources. Additionally, the daily lives of Indians revolve around actions and behaviors associated with free-market democracy, and most predominantly use the English language, raising a set of questions that are just beginning to be asked. For example, what does it mean to be a member of an American Indian nation? How are boundaries effectively drawn around who Indians are as peoples? What are the best criteria to use to begin to answer these questions? These questions have arisen in the last couple of decades as it becomes increasingly more desirous to claim some sort of Indian heritage, especially in the nations who have been able to open up casinos.

Different nations presently use different criteria for determining their status; for example, the Bahweting Anishinaabe Nation (or Sault Saint Marie Tribe of Chippewa Indians), to which this author belongs, does not use blood quantum per se, but they do have to demonstrate a lineage to some specific census rolls. Other nations still use blood quantum as an identity marker. Some communities of people are using their own definitions and understandings outside of the official rules of the national registrars, such as cultural knowledge, practices, language, and ceremonies, as boundary markers of community members, for better or worse.

The question of whether or not American Indians are or can even live with integrity in their communities, sharing this Turtle Island, is also an

CASE STUDY 8.2

In 2004, the National Forest Service began the process of approving a plan to increase the development of the Arizona Snowbowl, a popular ski resort destination in northern Arizona. This ski resort has been under local American Indian and environmental groups' scrutiny for more than twenty years because of its importance as place for Hopi, Navajo, and other American Indian people in the region. The resort is located on the San Francisco Peaks, a place where many American Indian people of the region are originally from, their autochthonous origins. The place holds the utmost value and is where medicinal herbs and plants are collected for ceremony. It is also a place where traditional leaders and elders go to communicate with their ancestors and the life embedded in the land.

There are two primary issues at hand. First, the Snowbowl is planning to expand its already existing land base and add more chairlifts. Additionally, they plan to pipe treated wastewater from Flagstaff, Arizona, to use for snowmaking. To spray reclaimed wastewater as snow on what you consider to be your place of origin is beyond an affront to decency. To have an intimate relationship similar to the one between the American Indian people and the San Francisco Peaks is to have a responsibility to the land. The landscape was already adulterated when it was altered with a ski resort; but to also spray reclaimed wastewater as a means of making snow significantly damages the indigenous people's relationship with the mountain.

In response to the potential harm that could be caused by the actions of the Snowbowl and the Forest Service, a coalition of activists and concerned citizens, called Save the Peaks Coalition, was created to oppose that expansion. This coalition is made up of the Navajo and Hopi Nations, other American Indian nations, as well as environmental groups like the Sierra Club, the Center for Biological Diversity, the Flagstaff Activist Network, and many others. They have used multiple tactics to bring this issue to light, including legal challenges, marches, rallies, and a significant use of social media. These multipronged educational efforts have helped bring awareness to this issue in the area and throughout the United States and Canada. Their court challenges were decided in favor of the Save the Peaks Coalition at the Ninth Circuit Court; however, other courts have overruled that decision. As of June 2011, the US Supreme Court had refused to hear their case, letting the lower court decision stand, which allows for the spraying of waste water on the San Francisco Peaks. The concept of religious freedom of the American Indian people has failed to protect their relationship to the land. Considering that the legal tactics in this case are not effectively protecting the peaks from ongoing destruction from "development" and the building of a pipeline that will deliver wastewater to be sprayed on a location of significant importance, what other tactics can and should be employed to protect the land? If this was your place of origin, what would you be willing to do to protect the land?

ongoing question. Some American Indian people are so disconnected from their own traditional ways that this is not even a salient question. Others are attempting to find methods of acting with reciprocity in their daily activities as they negotiate their lives in the midst of transformed places. These are difficult tasks, considering that Indian people currently experience a lack of relationships

BOX 8.5

Blood Quantum

This is a racist method of measuring the quantum of "full blood" status among American Indians. The amounts are usually rated in fractions, so a half blood quantum person would have one Indian and one non-Indian parent. These measurements were used to measure Indians out of existence, and are still in use to mark American Indian identity today. They are recorded on an individual identification card, or CDIB (Certificate Degree of Indian Blood). In order to receive tuition waivers and other governmental benefits, Indian people must be at least one-fourth blood quantum.

with other living beings, especially those relationships who give their lives for human consumption. How do we foster a relationship with the animals that give us meat to eat or the plants like blueberries that give us sustenance when they are imported from faraway places? Furthermore, how do Indians have a relationship with other community members in and around their living spaces? Turtle Island has been so altered that it has caused significant difficulty in living lives in continuity with the original people of Turtle Island. American Indians will continue to ask these and other questions as they learn to negotiate and decolonize their traditional homelands.

Leading Scholars and Figures

Far more scholars and activists than can be covered in this limited space have been influential in helping American Indian communities attain a greater degree of freedom and understanding of themselves. Still, a few scholars and activists have pushed the envelope of ethical thought and action, helping untold numbers of people begin the process of decolonizing their minds. This list is not designed to be exhaustive but to orient someone new to the field to some of the best-known American Indian authors who have dealt with ethics. It is important to note that the work of these and other scholars do not come from the thoughts and ideas of one person; they are the culmination of years of work, not only writing in the academy and other places but also of consistent and vigilant social and political action within their particular communities.

Anyone interested in American Indian liberative ethics should begin with Vine Deloria Jr. As both an author and an activist in the 1960s wave of American Indian regeneration of cultural traditions, Deloria set the bar high for other authors and activists who came after him. His writings—for example, *God Is Red*—expose some of the deep cultural differences between American Indian culture of spatiality and Euro-Western cultures of temporality. Even though he wrote on numerous topics, including law, religion, anthropology, and metaphysics, all his writings demonstrate the deep cultural differences between American Indian cultures and Euro-Western traditions.

Paula Gunn Allen provided a better understanding of some of the matrilineal and matrifocal realities of Indian cultures in her book *The Sacred Hoop*. This book helped pave the way for

KEY TERM 8.8

Turtle Island. The name often given to what is now called North America. Most often used in the American Northeast, it recognizes that from a water world, land was created for Sky Woman and the other animals to live on, literally on grandfather turtle's back.

other thinkers to decolonize some of their own thought by remembering their nonpatriarchal societies and how gender balance was maintained within them. These acts of remembering, similar to Deloria's remembering of spatiality as a fundamental component of culture, have been essential to the development of better ethical decolonizing thought and action.

Another author engaged in ethical remembering is Barbara Alice Mann. Her historiographical method of using oral tradition as a basis for writing about Haudenosaunee (Iroquois) culture and their interactions with the European colonizers has helped define what it means to write about one's own culture with integrity. Her book *Iroquoian Women: The Gantowisas* combines an exposition of an American Indian culture with, in her own words, "an urgent need to revive ancient knowledge, not to retreat from the present into a romance of the past, but to shore up the present with the strength of memory, the agility of cultural wisdom" (2004: 4). As previously discussed, this revival of cultural memory and wisdom is the basis of ethical thinking and action.

George "Tink" Tinker has also added to the realm of liberative ethics. Several centuries of Christian colonization in the Americas has led to the internalization of much of the colonizers' categories of thought, in particular Christian thinking about the world and Natives place within the world. In his book *Missionary Conquest*, he dispels the myth of the honorable missionary helping to bring the "light of civilization" to the "new world." For Tinker, missionaries were part of a larger colonizing project, often acting as the tip of the colonial spear, negotiating treaties that stole land and brought the natives into submission to the dominant European order. In his latest book, *American Indian Liberation*, he outlines some of the cultural differences between American Indian cultures and Christian thought, again reiterating that for American Indian people, liberation can

only come from our own cultural ceremonies and traditions, not from the colonizer.

Possible Future Trends

While colonizing forces have been attempting to dominate and/or erase American Indians from existence from the time of European landfall in the Western Hemisphere, there simultaneously also existed resistance to these genocidal acts. When Native people were chased down by military forces, some fled while others agreed to live on reservations in order to survive. When Native ceremonies were outlawed, they were continued out of sight of the colonial authorities or dances were held on "official" holidays like Independence Day, on July 4, even though American Indians have nothing to celebrate on that day. When US government officials came to take Indian children away from their communities and relocate them in residential schools, some parents hid their children in remote areas with relatives.

Indians continue to resist genocide today. This ongoing resistance culminated in a much larger 1960s movement, when much of the world's colonized people revolted against Euro-Western colonial control. Numerous land-rights struggles and movements came to the fore in the late 1960s and early 1970s as young people, with the

BOX 8.6

Residential Schools

Starting in the late nineteenth century and continuing into the mid-twentieth century, the US government and Christian churches began a process of cultural genocide and the eradication of American Indian people in the form of forcibly taking their children and placing them

BOX 8.6 (continued)

in "boarding schools." At these "schools," they were supposed to be taught Western education. Instead, what occurred was that they had their own cultural traditions and languages physically beaten out of them. Children were often physically, emotionally, and far too often sexually abused by their white, usually churchgoing, "caretakers." Boys were taught manual labor like farmwork and girls were instructed in menial cleaning chores. Usually, they received basic school instruction for about an hour per day. As Ward Churchill notes in *Kill the Indian, Save the Man*, approximately one-half of Indian children, over a fifty-year-plus period from 1893 to 1933, were incarcerated in these "schools." It has also been documented that as many as one-third of the children died during their stay from malnourishment and disease caused by living in substandard housing with little to no access to medicine. For them, these schools were literal death camps. This is one of the primary forms of trauma from which American Indians are still recovering. Several generations of Indian children were subjected to significant abuse with almost no contact with their home communities. The alleged superiority of the white culture and related "inferiority" of traditional Indian culture was internalized among many of the survivors, who had no parenting examples to follow except violent white people at the "schools." That violence was then transferred into their own communities. These cycles of abuse stemming from the trauma of boarding schools are still present among American Indians.

help of their elders, began to openly assert their treaty and land rights. This period of resistance led many American Indian people back to their home communities and to their traditional ways. As Tink Tinker has noted in *American Indian Liberation*, "I want to argue that Indian people who are serious about liberation—about freedom and independence—must commit themselves to the renewal and revival of their tribal ceremonial life, bringing their ancient ceremonies back to the center of their community's political existence" (2008: 139). Native people are now forty years into the reclaiming of their culture and have had a number of victories and setbacks along the way. They have consistently discovered that the intergenerational trauma of the last several hundred years will more than likely take a few more generations to heal, a healing that can best occur by regenerating traditional indigenous ceremonies, languages, and communities.

The last several decades of the regeneration of Indian cultural traditions has exposed some of the internalization of colonial categories of thought and action. As Taiaiake Alfred states in *Wasáse*, "The *resurrection* of a reality experienced by our ancestors is obviously impossible: thus, a *regeneration* is the way to think about the challenge we face" (2005: 254). The future trends for American Indian people have to do with a cycle of action and reflection that revolves around four areas: (1) a deeper understanding of their languages for those communities where that is still an option, (2) a deeper understanding of communities as distinct social units, not only as humans but as wider networks of life, (3) a greater understanding of and active participation in traditional land use as much as that is possible in Native communities, and finally, (4) a deep reflection on how these processes interact with each other.

Native languages are essential to the development of a deeper decolonizing process, of appropriate community involvement, and of proper

Fig. 8.1. Group of Omaha boys in cadet uniforms, Carlisle Indian School, Pennsylvania, 1880.

interactions with the land. For example, in anishi-naabemowin (anishinaabe language), *manidoo* is a concept that is hard to define but has been most often been translated as "spirit." This is an unfortunate translation because spirit under-stood as nonmaterial does not work well for Indi-ans. Manidoo connotes the underlying life and energy that is in all things, and it is manifested in and around us in multiple ways. Some people can see different manidoo, and others have mani-doo that travel with them. Manidoo are part of Indian community and are also in relationship with them. Manidoo also reside powerfully in the land; therefore, as Indians go about their way upon the land, they need to take manidoo into consideration as land-use policies and actions are implemented. Additionally, Indians need to con-sistently reflect on what it means to live in rela-tionship with manidoo.

This cycle of ongoing participation in Indian languages, communities, land use, and commu-nity reflection is an ongoing process. It is what Native ancestors did before the arrival of the European colonists. As American Indians engage in this process of action and reflection, they must be conscious that while they have struggled with settler-state colonialism on their homelands, they have thrived as communities for a much longer period. Consequently, they will thrive again as they regenerate their traditional communities.

As American Indians participate in this cycle of regeneration, they can once again become healthy communities. As they become healthier, they will be able to engage in international relations with a much greater sense of agency. They will be able to defend their lands better and regenerate cycles of gifting between communities and between nations. They will then be able to renew their

CASE STUDY 8.3

Rainbow Bridge is a geological formation in what is now southern Utah. It is a natural bridge over a narrow canyon, one of the largest such structures in the world. It has been a place of great significance for Navajo, Hopi, and many other American Indian peoples in that region. At this site, traditional "medicine people," or interpreters, go to communicate with the Thunderbeings, the beings in the sky that bring rain to that dry place. This relationship between the Thunderbeings and the American Indian people of the area is very old, and as long as that relationship has held, the rain has come.

However, Euro-Western "development" has once again threatened this relationship. In 1956, the Glenn Canyon Dam was authorized, and in 1963 the water levels began to rise on that stretch of the Colorado River, endangering the area with water inundation. In 1974, the Navajo Nation filed suit against the Secretary of the Interior and the National Parks Service as a means of protecting this site, but the courts, once again, ruled against the American Indian people and their relationship to the land. But what is poignant to an understanding of liberative ethics is what has happened since.

During the court proceedings, a Navajo traditional healer, or "medicine man," was called in to testify to the significance of Rainbow Bridge as a place. Through an interpreter, he described at length what it is that he and others do at that site and why it is important. According to Glenn Morris, a Shawnee lawyer working for the Navajo Nation on this case, this traditional healer explained very clearly what would happen if the waters continue to rise. When it became clear he was not being heard in the courtroom, he pointed to the judge and said, "And you tell this man that if the rain doesn't come for us, it's not coming for him either!" After the arrogant laughter of the courtroom subsided, most of the people assembled forgot these words. Meanwhile, the waters continued to rise, and in the early 1990s the water depth under Rainbow Bridge reached forty-two feet. Also during this time, the region has undergone a severe and sustained drought. So much so that the water level of Lake Powell behind the Glen Canyon Dam significantly receded. Today, there is no water under Rainbow Bridge, and once again Navajo traditional people are communicating with the Thunderbeings. How would you describe the methods employed by the Navajo and other peoples, including the interpreters, protecting Rainbow Bridge? Are there any other situations and actions where the people called on other-than-human beings for help?

---

process of treaty making as their ancestors once did. For example, the five Anishinabee Nations in what is now called the state of Michigan renegotiated a treaty from 1836 that had been selectively forgotten by both state and federal agencies. This renegotiation, titled the 2007 Inland Consent Decree, effectively reestablished treaty rights to traditional hunting, fishing, trapping, and gathering activities within the boundaries set forth by the 1836 treaty. This is one of many examples of treaty rights being asserted by American Indian people and demonstrates some of the potential direction for American Indian liberative ethics and action.

BOX 8.7

Warrior

This term is often used to describe American Indians as people possessing an ethic of action. Anthropologists and others have mistakenly used this term to describe Indians as a "warlike" people, often giving detailed descriptions of their political systems as necessitating war and war acts so that young men can achieve status in the culture. However, that cultural tradition of achieving "war honors" as a means of political advancement is a Euro-Western projection onto the indigenous culture, so as to define them as primitive. While there were occasionally battles between groups, rarely did these actions ever

BOX 8.7 (continued)

result in death, and they were often treated as athletic games between competing peoples. When we look at our American Indian languages and the words that have been translated as "warrior," we notice a different connotation. As Taiaiake Alfred explains concerning his traditional Mohawk language, *rotiskenhrakete*, which is usually translated as "warrior," literally means "to carry the burden of peace." To have peace as your mandate for your actions provides a very different understanding for being a warrior. More often than not, when traditional people think of going into battle, the translation used is that of defender.

Fig. 8.2. This image depicts an 1851 Sioux treaty signing ceremony in Minnesota. While not illustrative of the 1836 Anishinaabe treaty signing, the depiction is representative of how such signing ceremonies were conducted.

Study Questions

1. Considering the long-standing settler-state colonialism that Indians have had to negotiate, including the imposition of identity categories like blood quantum and federal recognition, what are the ways in which American Indian people have begun to establish and live into particular traditional identities? What is the significance of the relationships among indigenous peoples, land, and ceremony in regenerating these traditional identities?

2. With a number of American Indian communities entering into gaming enterprises like casinos, how does an indigenous nation balance traditional ethical responsibilities to other people and land with the necessity to participate in a capitalist system to help provide services like health care for its people? How have American Indian communities helped their own communities with the proceeds from casino properties? What have been some of the problems associated with casinos?

3. While the First Amendment to the Constitution has "guaranteed" the rights to the freedom of religion for all US citizens, and American Indian ceremonies have been considered "religious" by the government, how has that "guarantee" played out for American Indian people? How has the land-based nature of Indian ceremonies affected their ability to practice their ceremonies?

4. Considering the inability of the US Constitution to protect the land and Native cultural traditions, what would be some guiding ethical considerations for activist responses by American Indian people and others who have a responsibility to protect the land? In particular, when violence is happening to the land and to the community on the land, what would be an ethical response to the ongoing destruction? What ethical moorings could be used to guide a process of action and reflection along this path of defending the land and one's community?

5. With all of these preceding questions in mind, what would be an ethical response from the colonial population who now resides on the land that was and still is called Turtle Island? What would be an appropriate ethical response from people who now live with privileges that several centuries of violence and genocide made possible? How do people who have electricity as a result of violent copper-mining techniques, coal, and nuclear power generated with resources taken primarily from American Indian communities, and live in homes built with the forests that were destroyed on indigenous land, identify with and participate in an ethical response to both the historical and the ongoing genocide of American Indian people? What are you willing to give up? What are you willing to live without? Are there ways in which living with less material goods can help to create a greater sense of beauty, health, and well-being for you and others around you? Where else and in what other ways can we find beauty to live into/within this land?

Suggested Readings

Alfred, Taiaiake. *Wasáse: Indigenous Pathways of Actions and Freedom*. Peterborough, ON: Broadview, 2005.

Allen, Paula Gunn. *The Sacred Hoop: Recovering the Feminine in American Indian Traditions*. Boston: Beacon, 1992.

Churchill, Ward. *Kill the Indian Save the Man: The Genocidal Impact of Residential Schools.* San Francisco: City Lights, 2004.

———. *A Little Matter of Genocide: Holocaust and Denial in the Americas 1492 to the Present.* San Francisco: City Lights, 1997.

Deloria, Vine, Jr. *God Is Red: A Native View of Religion.* Golden, CO: Fulcrum, 1992.

———. *Custer Died For Your Sins: An Indian Manifesto.* Norman: University of Oklahoma Press, 1988.

———. *Red Earth, White Lies: Native Americans and the Myth of Scientific Fact.* Golden, CO: Fulcrum, 1997.

Laduke, Winona. *Recovering the Sacred: The Power of Naming and Claiming.* Cambridge, MA: South End, 2005.

———. *All Our Relations: Native Struggles for Land and Life.* Cambridge, MA: South End, 1999.

Mann, Barbara Alice. *Iroquoian Women: The Gantowisas.* New York: Peter Lang, 2004.

———. *George Washington's War on Native America.* Lincoln: University of Nebraska Press, 2008.

———. *Tainted Gift: The Disease Method of Frontier Expansion.* Denver: Praeger, 2009.

Smith, Andrea. *Conquest: Sexual Violence and American Indian Genocide.* Cambridge, MA: South End, 2005.

Tinker, George "Tink." *Missionary Conquest: The Gospel and Native American Cultural Genocide.* Minneapolis: Fortress Press, 1993.

———. *American Indian Liberation: A Theology of Sovereignty.* Maryknoll, NY: Orbis, 2008.

Weaver, Jace. *That the People Might Live: Native American Literatures and Native American Communities.* New York: Oxford University Press, 1996.

Williams, Robert, Jr. *The American Indian in Western Legal Thought: The Discourses of Conquest.* New York: Oxford University Press, 1990.

PART THREE

The US Gender, Sexual Identity, and Disability Context

9

Feminist Liberative Ethics

Michelle Tooley

PEOPLE DEFINE FEMINISTS WITH a variety of observations. There's a great disparity in these definitions, many of which rely heavily on emotion. A Republican vice-presidential candidate stated publicly that she is a feminist; she is against abortion. A history major said that early feminists worked for equality in the 1960s. We all benefit, she said. An economics major added that feminists advocate women's equal pay for equal work. A student involved in campus ministry said that her rabbi is a feminist. One sociology major declared that feminists have been a part of all important social movements in the United States, including suffrage, civil rights, abolition of slavery, peace, welfare rights, labor, reproductive rights, and more. A student athlete assumed they are pro-lesbian. One religion major reported that they raised awareness about the roles women hold in her church: secretary, pastor, deacon, children's minister, janitor, and youth minister. Another student said that a man can't be one and that most hate men. A radio talk show host called them feminazis. A communications major announced that they don't shave their legs and they are reactionary. A gender studies major explained that feminists struggle for social, political, and economic equality and they believe that men are privileged. Do any of the responses resonate with what you believe about feminism? How have you heard *feminists* or *religious feminists* used? In what ways is feminism linked to liberative ethics? Who does it give a voice to, and how has feminism been helpful to those who live on the margins? At its core, what does feminism stand for?

Feminism draws attention to the exclusion and oppression of women and works for a world where women's contributions are valued. Ideally, those in the struggle recognize and identify with the struggles of other marginalized persons, but this does not necessarily hold true. While feminists have gained ground in the struggle for equal rights and have won increased opportunities for women and girls, it is important to ask who benefits and

KEY TERM 9.1

Sex. Inherited, biological differences between male and female.

165

to always remember that feminism responds to patriarchy, a system of oppression that feeds other oppressive systems, and not just to one individual's attitudes or circumstances. How do feminists participate in the system of patriarchy? One historical example of feminism polluted by patriarchy is nineteenth-century, white, middle-class women who advocated for women's rights but were blind to daily encounters with slave women and immigrant women in the service economy. The lesson for feminists is to become aware of their exclusion and oppression and to be aware of others' struggles.

As with other important expressions of liberative ethics, feminists share common commitments, but they are not limited to one narrow definition or expression. Although scholars and activists may claim to possess the last word on feminism, in reality feminists have multiple understandings of the priorities and norms of feminist ethics. It is true that feminists are found in almost all political and social positions. They may be religious and nonreligious, Republican and Democrat, upper class and working class, liberal and conservative, heterosexual and homosexual, pro-life and pro-choice. Although diverse, feminists articulate shared commitments that convey deeply held loyalties, convictions, and perceptions of threat. For example, most feminists resist violence against women and sexism in policies and practices. Likewise, feminists advocate for a history that recovers women's voices, respects women's bodies and sexuality, believes in the human dignity of women and other marginalized persons, and works for gender justice in a world that welcomes the participation of women.

As a working definition, cultural critic bell hooks's understanding of feminism fits the concerns and commitments of feminist religious liberative ethics. In *Feminist Theory: From Margin to Center*, hooks writes that feminism is the struggle to end sexist oppression. Feminism does not intend to benefit only one particular race, class, or group of women. It does not privilege women over men. It has the power to meaningfully transform all persons' lives.

BOX 9.1

bell hooks

Cultural critic, writer, and social activist bell hooks has shaped feminism through her books, articles, and conversations with other scholars. From a working-class African American family in Kentucky, hooks journeyed to Stanford University after high school for an undergraduate degree in English and then on to the University of Wisconsin and University of California, Santa Cruz, for her MA and PhD. The author of more than thirty books, hooks writes for children and adults. Her adult books deal with feminism, masculinity, social class, race and racism, engaged pedagogy, love, and community. As a second-wave feminist, she has criticized feminism for its exclusivity, pushing at the de facto boundaries of white, middle-class feminism with ever-present reminders of the interconnected injustices of race, class, and gender. Although not a religious ethicist, hooks's emphasis on class, race, and gender provides an analytical framework for feminists and persons of faith and conscience. hooks shares a priority on conscientization with liberative educator Paulo Freire. Like Freire, hooks emphasizes critical consciousness and action for justice. hooks uses the phrase "imperialist white-supremacist capitalist patriarchy" to describe the connected systems of domination in the Western world.

Gender. Culturally constructed ideas about sex differences.

hooks's definition allows for the centrality of awareness, analysis, resistance, and transformative action against sexism. With the inclusion of transformation, hooks affirms the potential of feminists to be change agents, to transform structures and systems, policies and practices, while also transforming individuals and groups who participate in the struggle for justice as they stand in solidarity with marginalized individuals and groups. She does not limit participation or membership to only women, nor does she replace male domination and privilege with female domination and privilege. By imagining men as possible partners in the struggle for gender justice, hooks does not agree with the student who claims that feminists are man-haters. Instead, although they benefit from patriarchy, men may be allies in the feminist struggle since they, like women, are captive to the system of patriarchy.

Although hooks does not include religion or spirituality explicitly in her definition, the definition is large enough to include religion and spirituality as one possible tool of analysis and transformation in the work of eliminating sexism and other injustices. Although institutional religion has a long history of oppression against women, healthy religion, whatever form it takes, does not rely on harming or exploiting others.

Her-Story: Feminist Religious Liberative Ethics

At its best, religion gives women and men, girls and boys, a sense of being loved, valued, empowered, and connected with others. Persons of faith are called to act for justice for self and neighbor. Women have been inspired and empowered by their religious beliefs and practices, not simply to live in hope for the future but also to strive for better things here and now, such as antislavery campaigner Sojourner Truth, Catholic Worker movement founder Dorothy Day and newspaper editor and antilynching activist Ida B. Wells. Empowered by their faith to confront injustice whatever the risks, they practiced a feminist religious liberative ethic.

In its oppressive forms, religion feeds shame and guilt and limits human imagination and

Solidarity

True solidarity often comes as a result of conscientization. Activists speak of solidarity as relational action because a conscientized person decides to do something about the injustice she has seen. In response to the observed or discovered injustice, a person may research the issue or injustice, feel rage or anger at the source of the injustice, or engage in one or numerous actions for social change. Most important, solidarity begins when a conscientized person stands for herself or with others who suffer as a result of injustice and then acts in community with them to change the injustice. Solidarity is not an act of charity bestowed on a victim; instead, solidarity is a shared experience with mutual responsibility born out of mutual interests. Although solidarity takes many shapes and forms, it always involves accompaniment. Solidarity helps people move beyond us-and-them paternalism to an ever-expanding circle of inclusion that crosses borders and barriers.

potential. Institutional religion has often been an impediment to women and girls through stained-glass ceilings, restrictive gender roles, and poisonous portrayals of women's bodies and sexuality. From the perspective of a feminist religious liberative ethic, bad religion replaces agency with blind obedience to rules and dogma.

Islam, Christianity, and Judaism, the three Abrahamic religions, do have good news for women and girls. Each tradition teaches that God created humans, female and male, in God's image. Like men, women are a good creation responsible to God; as such, they are tasked with moral agency and moral responsibility. These three religious traditions affirm the value and human dignity of women as well as men. Sacred texts in all three traditions recount stories of strong, powerful women of faith who serve as role models and sources of inspiration, yet the story of religion has largely been told by men for men as the public actors, with women relegated to the private sphere.

Religious studies scholar Karen Armstrong observes that in spite of positive teaching about women, the three Abrahamic religions have excluded women from full participation and limited women's roles in the political, cultural, and religious life of their community. Within the Judeo-Christian tradition, some texts are particularly problematic. Hebrew Scripture texts in Deuteronomy and Judges reflect male domination in marriage, a patriarchal family structure, patrilinear inheritance, unequal standards on adultery, and the sexual abuse of women. The rape of Dinah, the exile of Hagar, the leprosy of Miriam, the sacrifice of Jephthah's unnamed daughter, and the death and mutilation of the Levite's unnamed concubine—all occur with no criticism toward the perpetrator of the violence.

Judeo-Christian readers are left wondering how to find meaning and value in texts about women. In the Christian tradition, biblical scholar Phyllis Trible identifies three feminist approaches

to reading and interpreting scriptural texts about women. The first approach is to document the misogyny in sacred texts. From the days that women are considered ritually unclean to the double standards of adultery and divorce to the rape of Tamar by her half-brother Amnon, a plethora of evidence exists to justify this approach, but to what end? Entangled as the texts are with marginalization and vilification, how should contemporary women respond to troublesome texts? If the reader has a high view of scripture, she may ignore the oppression and find a different and more unquestioning interpretation of troublesome passages, or she may decide that sinful women deserve their treatment. Other feminists cease to identify with any religious tradition.

Trible's second feminist approach builds on the painful conclusions of the first approach, while at the same time persistently searching for texts, patterns, and traditions that challenge the exclusion and marginalization of women. Within Islam, feminists speak of the Prophet Muhammad's openness to women and how he learned from women. Aisha, one of Mohammad's wives, wrote more than two thousand Hadith, a collection of the words and actions of Muhammad. Jewish feminists tell stories of Susanna, Jael, and Judith, and they emphasize feminine names for God in the Torah. Feminists with this approach carefully examine the two creation narratives and realize that Genesis 1 refers to humanity, both female and male, created in God's image. In Christianity, feminists notice women disciples' courageous actions after Jesus' crucifixion and their prominence in the early Christian movement.

Trible's third feminist approach acknowledges the embedded violence and oppression in the texts, but then uses the learned lessons as teachable moments so that readers do not repeat what Trible calls "texts of terror." Instead of ignoring the Judges 11 account of Jephthah and the sacrifice of his daughter, feminists using this approach ask tough questions like, Why did Jepthah promise

God that he would sacrifice someone in exchange for his victory? Why does the author of Hebrews praise Jephthah as a stellar example of a man of faith? and Why didn't God miraculously save Jephthah's daughter like God saved Isaac? In addition to interrogating the text, a feminist asks how Jephthah's story might be understood by a marginalized community as a tool with which to overcome oppression. In the same way that the Catholic Church recorded narratives from war-related violence in Guatemala, then published the stories of torture, killing, and massacres in a report titled *Nunca Mas* ("never again"), the third approach tells the terrible stories to remember the victims and as a caution against future violence against women.

The stories and cultural interpretations that emerge from them form an ideology that keeps women in their place and, at least from the silence, allows for violence against women. Without critical readings, all are translated in some form to contemporary settings and serve to marginalize and discriminate against women as individuals and as a social group. Because the Christian Gospels record names of twelve male apostles, some Christian groups forbid female clergy. Do these groups mention the role of Mary Magdalene in the early church or talk about Martha's confession in the Gospel of John? Should we assume that because these twelve men were from the Middle East and were Jewish that all clergy should be Middle Eastern Jews? The Pastoral Epistles and 1 Corinthians include the Greco-Roman household codes, a common source of moral order: slaves, obey your owners; children, obey your parents; wives, obey your husbands. More than one pastor has translated the household codes across two thousand years and a different culture to the twenty-first century United States when counseling a battered wife to return to her husband. Why? Because the Bible instructs wives to obey husbands and, of course, to love them sacrificially.

> ## KEY TERM 9.3
>
> *Ideology.* A system of beliefs, symbols, myths, rituals, and values that expresses itself in concrete attitudes and that influences and guides the action of a particular class or social group in its own interest.

> ## KEY TERM 9.4
>
> *Hermeneutics.* The process of interpretation. For texts like the Christian Scriptures, where women are not authors and rarely have a voice, feminists often use tools like archaeology, history, linguistics, anthropology, as well as literary, cultural, and historical criticism to increase information about women.

For feminist religious liberative ethicists, religious traditions may also have a recoverable past with alternate readings and lessons learned to renounce the harmful actions in these stories and others. In addition to renouncing texts used to oppress, religious feminists teach stories from sacred texts and history, stories about Khadijah, the first wife of the Prophet; or the Jewish heroine Judith. In the Judeo-Christian context, some place the beginning of feminist liberative ethics with the story of Shiprah and Puah in the Hebrew Scriptures of Exodus. In the midst of the slavery and oppression of the Hebrew people by Egyptians, the Egyptian ruler orders two midwives to kill all Hebrew baby boys at birth. The two women, without the power and privilege of gender, ethnicity, or class, act against the orders of the ruler and instead engage in a radical act of human liberation and let the baby boys live. For their revolutionary action, God rewards them with a family.

The mixed message about women's roles in Scripture and religious history raises questions about whether a positive portrayal of women is recoverable and if teaching about women is empowering or even useful for persons of faith.

History of Feminism

Most people begin the history of feminism in Britain and the United States with Mary Wollstonecraft. Like ethicists before her, Wollstonecraft prized reasoning more highly than feelings. Animals have feelings, but humans' added capacity for reasoning sets them apart from animals. In *A Vindication of the Rights of Women* (1792), Wollstonecraft concluded that if women are to be regarded as ethical, they should also display the psychological traits associated with men of virtue.

The nineteenth century marks the beginning of first-wave feminism, as early foremothers marched for the vote, used axes to demolish bars, and joined husbands in the work of the Underground Railroad. The struggle for a woman's full participation in society found expression in the social movements protesting slavery and war, and advocating women's right to vote and Prohibition. Although not explicitly Christian, movements were organized by leaders who recognized the centrality of religion for the analysis of the injustice and the empowerment of participants. At the first women's rights convention in Seneca Falls, New York, Elizabeth Cady Stanton attacked Christianity because it limited women to second-class citizenry. Later, because she connected the Bible with women's disempowerment and empowerment, Stanton and a revising committee extracted offensive parts of the Bible and emphasized stories of foremothers like Esther, the judge Deborah, and Mary Magdalene, the first witness of Jesus' resurrection. Their work was published it in 1898 as *The Woman's Bible*.

The women's movement made significant advances in several sectors of US religious and political life in the nineteenth century. On the religious front, both the United Church of Christ and the Presbyterian Church ordained women as ministers, and a major Jewish seminary opened its doors to women. On the political and social front, women organized into social groups, like the National Association of Colored Women and antialcohol groups, like the Woman's Christian Temperance Union, groups that organized for race relations and prohibition but that also participated in the suffragette movement. Although first introduced on the Senate floor in 1878, the right to vote proved elusive but was eventually granted in 1920.

The story behind the elusive vote illustrates the identity and influence of stakeholders. On the eve of World War I, Woodrow Wilson's administration negotiated a hiatus to the suffragettes' almost daily protests in front of the White House. The president agreed to support the right to vote after the war if the suffragettes stopped protesting during the war. The suffragette movement stopped during the war and lost credibility with the masses. For the largely white, middle-class activists, delaying their voice and vote was no inconvenience, but had their group been more conscious of race and class or had they considered the situation of other women, like African American women in the South, immigrant factory workers, or poor, working-class women, they might have come to a different conclusion.

In addition to the Nineteenth Amendment to the United States Constitution, which guarantees women the right to vote, the twentieth century brought advances in human rights and labor rights. With protests and strikes, women and their allies courageously drew attention to abysmal working conditions and inadequate pay in factories. After dramatic demonstrations like the Uprising of the Twenty Thousand, factory owners signed labor union contracts. Fifty years later,

Fig. 9.1. On May 6, 1912, suffragettes marched on the streets of New York City for the right to vote.

Congress passed the Equal Pay Act, and at least on paper, most women received equal pay for equal work.

In 1973, the landmark case of *Roe v. Wade* focused the attention of religious and nonreligious women on reproductive rights, a public debate that continues today.

In the last half of the twentieth century, Vatican II and the increasing number of Protestant and Jewish women clergy generated discourse and disagreement about women's roles in religion and society. Women gave homilies and sermons, they worked as hospital and prison chaplains, they taught as seminary professors and university religion faculty; they served as pastors, rabbis, and campus ministers; and they led Islamic and Christian education. Shortly after the Supreme Court decision for abortion rights, a small group of evangelical Christian feminists began a journal,

Daughters of Sarah, announcing, "We are Christians; we are also feminists. Some say we cannot be both, but Christianity and feminism for us are inseparable."

Even as the number of women in professional positions grew, opposition to women clergy and feminist theology grew rapidly. Feminist theologians and church leaders drew the ire of conservative wings of their denominations after the 1993 Re-Imagining Conference that invited participants to reflect on God and their faith through the lens of women's experience. After the Re-Imagining Conference ended, several organizers who worked in women's divisions were dismissed by their denominations, and feminist theology was marked as dangerous for conservative religious groups.

In the larger feminist movement, the last few years of the twentieth century saw a new expression of feminism. Self-proclaimed third-wave feminists declared a new age in feminism, one that builds on the strengths of the past while correcting deficiencies. Third-wavers value the rights and opportunities earned by early feminists, and they realize they stand on the shoulders of feminists who worked for better working conditions, the right to equal pay, women's vote, reproductive rights, and access to careers that their grandmothers would not have been considered for. Similarly to second-wave feminists, third-wave feminists work on multiple issues through education, advocacy, and direct action. Most important, third wavers criticized second-wave "essentialist" feminism, claiming that second-wavers' definitions overemphasized the experiences of educated, upper-middle-class white women.

Drawing attention to the contributions of women, the United Nations declared the first

Fig. 9.2. In the United Kingdom from 2009 to 2012, Mind the Gap activists worked on human trafficking, violence against women, organizing working-class women, sexism on campus, and better prostitution and lap dancing regulations.

BOX 9.3

Waves of Feminism

Scholars identify three "waves" of feminism in the United States and Great Britain. Although the waves are chronological, each wave builds on the legacies of the previous wave, while addressing deficits and challenges.

1. First-wave feminists worked to reform women's social and legal inequalities, primarily in the nineteenth century. First-wavers worked on education, employment, marriage laws, and concerns of educated, middle-class women. Scholars place the end of first-wave feminism with the ratification of the Nineteenth Amendment of the US Constitution, which guaranteed women's right to vote.

2. Second-wave feminism began in the 1960s, when middle-class white women began to band together to contend against their discrimination. The second wave focused on women as a group having the same social, political, legal, and economic rights that men have. Second-wavers worked on reproductive rights, equal access to sports in schools, civil rights, equal pay for equal work, better legislation to protect women against domestic violence, and peace. Instead of one unified movement, in this period, differences emerged between black feminism, Latina feminism, lesbian feminism, liberal feminism, and social feminism.

3. In 1992, in the aftermath of the Clarence Thomas confirmation hearing for the Supreme Court, Rebecca Walker, the daughter of author Alice Walker and godchild of second-wave activist Gloria Steinem, wrote an article in *Ms*

BOX 9.3 (continued)

titled "I Am the Third Wave." Third-wave feminists intentionally include various groups of women left out of first- and second-wave feminism, including women of color; lesbian, bisexual, and transgendered women; and low-income women. Third-wavers place less emphasis on social movements and collective action than previous feminist movements and value individual expressions of feminist action and identity.

Feminist scholars expect a fourth wave of feminism to emerge in the twenty-first century.

decade of the twentieth century as "the Decade of the Woman." Women have made strides toward greater inclusion and opportunities in public life and politics and in religious life. In 2012, the president of Liberia is a woman, as is the prime minister of Germany. The United States boasts a female secretary of state who was narrowly defeated in the Democratic primary as the presidential nominee.

Need for Liberation: Why a Feminist Religious Liberative Ethics?

While philosophers begin the search for justice with first principles or a definition of perfect justice, feminist religious liberative ethicists begin their work with the concrete experience of sexism and related forms of injustice. When we hold a mirror up to our world, what we see reflected for women and girls is not justice, but the lived reality of injustice. The justice mirror reveals that women form over half of the world's population, yet the earth's resources are not distributed equitably or fairly. A majority of the world's poor are women, two-thirds of the world's illiterate people

TIMELINE: FEMINIST ETHICS

1848	The world's first women's rights convention is held in Seneca Falls, New York. Elizabeth Cady Stanton criticizes Christianity because it relegates women to second-class citizenry. In 1898, Stanton and the revising committee complete the Woman's Bible project.
1853	Antoinette Brown Blackwell is the first woman in the United States ordained by a congregation in a major Christian denomination.
1860	Of 2,225,086 black women, 1,971,135 are held in slavery. In San Francisco, 85 percent of Chinese women are essentially enslaved as prostitutes.
1874	Reformers organize the Woman's Christian Temperance Union, under the leadership of Frances Willard, uniting women across class and race.
1875	Rabbi Isaac Mayer Wise founds Hebrew Union College in Cincinnati and encourages women to attend. However, at this time women cannot be ordained as rabbis.
1878	The Susan B. Anthony Amendment, to grant women the vote, is introduced in US Congress.

1896 The National Association of Colored Women (NACW) forms, bringing together more than one hundred black women's clubs. Leaders in the black women's club movement include Josephine St. Pierre Ruffin, Mary Church Terrell, and Anna Julia Cooper.

1903 The National Women's Trade Union League (WTUL) is established to advocate for improved wages and working conditions for women.

1909 Women garment workers strike in New York for better wages and working conditions in the Uprising of the Twenty Thousand. Over three hundred shops eventually sign labor union contracts.

1913 Alice Paul and Lucy Burns organize the Congressional Union, which later becomes the National Women's Party. Members picket the White House and engage in other forms of civil disobedience, drawing public attention to the suffrage cause.

1920 The Nineteenth Amendment to the Constitution, granting women the right to vote, is signed into law.

1960 Women now earn sixty cents for every dollar earned by men, a decline since 1955. Black women of color earn forty-two cents for every dollar earned by men.

1963 The Equal Pay Act, proposed twenty years earlier, establishes equal pay for men and women performing the same job duties. It does not cover domestics, agricultural workers, executives, administrators, or professionals.

1972 Rabbi Sally J. Priesand, America's first female rabbi, is ordained in June by Hebrew Union College-Jewish Institute of Religion in Cincinnati, Ohio.

1973 The first battered women's shelters open in the United States in Tucson, Arizona, and St. Paul, Minnesota.

1973 In *Roe v. Wade*, the Supreme Court establishes a woman's right to abortion, effectively canceling the antiabortion laws of forty-six states.

1974 A small group of evangelical Christian feminists initiates a journal, *Daughters of Sarah*, in November 1974, announcing "We are Christians; we are also feminists. Some say we cannot be both, but Christianity and feminism for us are inseparable."

1981 Sandra Day O'Connor is the first woman appointed to the US Supreme Court. In 1993, she is joined by Ruth Bader Ginsberg.

1984 Geraldine Ferraro is the first woman vice-presidential candidate of a major political party (Democratic Party).

1990 The number of African American women in elected office increases from 131 in 1970 to 1,950 in 1990.

1992 Republican president George Bush nominates Clarence Thomas, a conservative African American attorney, for the Supreme Court. Anita Hill, a law professor at the University

TIMELINE: FEMINIST ETHICS (continued)

of Oklahoma, testifies at the Senate Judiciary Committee confirmation hearing that Clarence Thomas had sexually harassed her. Thomas and supporters deny Hill's testimony and the incident becomes one person's word against another's. In the end, the Senate votes fifty-two to forty-eight to confirm Clarence Thomas as associate justice of the Supreme Court.

Women are now paid seventy-one cents for every dollar paid to men. The range is from sixty-four cents for working-class women to seventy-seven cents for professional women with doctorates. African American women earned sixty-five cents, Latinas fifty-four cents.

1993 The Re-Imagining Conference brings together two thousand female theologians, clergy, and laypeople to examine ideas about God and the church born out of women's experience. With this conference, feminist theology becomes a part of public conversation and awareness.

2008 The National Organization for Women (NOW) organizes the March for Women's Lives, focusing on reproductive rights and the needs of immigrant women, indigenous women, and women of color. The turnout, 1.4 million, sets a Washington, DC, protest record.

2011 US Representative Michele Bachmann (R-MN) is the first woman presidential candidate for the Republican Party.

are women, and three-fourths of the world's refugees are women and children. The work of women continues to be undervalued, underpaid, or not paid at all. If women's unpaid housework were counted as productive output in national income accounts, global output would increase by at least 20 percent. Even though women do 75 percent of all paid work in the world, they earn only 10 percent of the salaries, and own less than 1 percent of all private property.

Violence against women crosses race, class, and geographical boundaries, observable as rape, assault, harassment, intimidation, trafficking, domestic violence, and child abuse. In some family systems, men and women are educated to believe that a man is allowed to beat a woman; it's one of the rights he insists on in order for them to be a couple. The man beats the woman and she goes back to her mother; but her mother tells her: "No, go back home. He's your husband. He has the right to beat you. That's the cross you must bear."

Less obvious but equally dangerous, women are often invisible or uncounted in research and policy development. Even though women's primary cause of death in the United States is heart disease, until recently research focused on men, not women. Law enforcement officials have not collected rape kits, nor have they done DNA testing on suspects because of the costliness of procedures. Gender dynamics have been ignored in the development of policies or programs for dealing with economic, social, and cultural issues. UNICEF now speaks of "the invisible adjustment," the assumption of policy makers that they could save money because women heads of households automatically sacrifice their resources so that their children would have more.

Discrimination that limits women's and girls' human rights and human dignity is historically

Fig. 9.3. Schoolgirls sit in their school in Bamozai, near Gardez, Paktya Province, Afghanistan. Research shows that an educated girl will marry later and have healthier children. The children she does have will have a longer life expectancy and will be better educated. She will be more productive at home and better paid in the workplace.

ingrained in many cultures and countries. In India, pregnant women regularly ask for sex-determination tests; if the fetus is female, they have sex-selective abortions. The phenomenon is so pervasive in India that activists and scholars refer to it as the disappearing daughter crisis. In one part of India, researchers have found that third-born daughters are half as likely to survive as third-born sons.

Gender discrimination is not limited to India. After the thirty-four-year war ended in Guatemala, most people assumed that violence against women would decrease, but in the almost twenty years after the peace accords, violence against women increased dramatically. During the armed conflict, rural women were the targets of violence,

but today both urban and rural women are victims of violence. Within the United States, the legacy of ingrained discrimination is seen less in laws than in practices. Twenty-five years ago, a husband could not be charged with the rape of his wife in most states. Now it is a crime for a husband to rape his wife in all states, but how often are husbands charged with spousal rape? Moreover, less than half of the states have completely eliminated the spousal rape exemption.

The struggle for women's rights and equality is progressing, although much more progress is needed. The dream of feminism must go further. Equality—equal pay for equal work, equal opportunities for employment, equal protection under the law—is necessary, but it is still equality in a

CASE STUDY 9.1

In her second year of college, Marcy began dating Stephen, a senior active in student government. Flattered by his attention, Marcy soon found herself included in a different clique. Although friendly and caring in public, Stephen often made demeaning remarks about her when they were alone. Phrases like, "If you weren't scatter-brained" or "if you didn't talk so much" or "if you lost a few pounds" bothered her, and she wondered if they were true. Occasionally he flirted with girls at parties, and when she complained about his behavior, Stephen became angry and made more disparaging remarks about her, this time that she might not be "woman enough to keep him." When Marcy began crying, Stephen apologized and told her that he loved her but that he was frustrated because they had not been together. He pressured her to go further than she wanted to, but to keep him satisfied, she kept quiet and went along. The next weekend, Stephen invited Marcy to a party off campus. When they arrived at the party, Marcy could tell that a lot of Stephen's friends had been drinking, and Marcy quickly joined in. After a few hours, Stephen suggested they go to another room to get away from the loud music and talk. Away from the others, Stephen started kissing her, fondling her, and she started pushing him away, crying and saying no. Stephen forced himself on her.

Marcy went home and spent the rest of the weekend in her dorm room, trying to decide what to do. Her roommate asked what was wrong, and Marcy said that she and Stephen had a fight. By Monday, she decided to go to a counselor and tell her what happened. The counselor encouraged Marcy to go to the police or campus security, but Marcy was reluctant to go public. Finally she agreed to talk with the director of student life, but when she told the director that Stephen had raped her, he warned her that it was her word against Stephen's and that Stephen was a campus leader and well liked. He asked Marcy if she had been drinking and she admitted that she had but that she had not agreed to have sex. The director explained her options but advised her that it might be easier on her to just keep it quiet. What advice would you give Marcy? If Marcy came to you for advice after she spoke to the director of student life, what would you tell her? Who might be an advocate for her? What are some reasons Marcy did not tell her roommate what happened with Stephen? What might some of her fears be? What insights does a feminist liberative ethics bring to this case?

male-dominated world. The world must be transformed, not only its religious, social, and political systems, but also the underlying patriarchal structure and spirit.

Patriarchy is an ideology that institutionalizes discrimination, prejudice, and oppression, specifically oppression by white men of women, persons who are poor, persons with less status, persons of color, and persons who are other than heterosexual. Everyone participates in patriarchy, regardless of sex, class, or ethnicity; it is a power over/power under system that gives privileged persons and groups unearned advantage and access to power. Patriarchal arrangements of power and status divide people along the categories of race and ethnicity, sexuality and gender, income and class through what historians of colonialization call "divide and conquer," pitting

CASE STUDY 9.2

In a Women in Religion class, the professor invited three Baha'i women to give a presentation about the Baha'i religion and what it is like to be a woman in Baha'i. After telling the story of Bahaullah and the founding of Baha'i, one woman spoke about the importance of women in Baha'i history and how the importance of women shapes their religious policies and practices. In fact, she said, "In our religion if a family has one girl child and one boy child and can only afford to send one child to school, the family sends the girl child to school." A murmur arose from the students, and a male student spoke up, "That's not fair to the boys." Another student said, "It's not fair that boys are usually sent to schools and not girls." The Baha'i woman replied that they have this practice because in educating the girl, they educate the one who gives birth to the future generation, male and female, and the one who is usually the child's first teacher. In the Baha'i view, the material and spiritual progress of society depends on women's full participation in all human activity.

The nursing student spoke again. "I still don't understand why you prefer the girl over the boy." The Baha'i woman asked the class if any of them had ever played Monopoly, and many hands were raised. She continued, "Imagine if the men in this class played Monopoly for one round and bought houses, hotels, and most of the property, and on the next round, the women were invited to begin playing, but the men had resources from the previous round. The women would be at a distinct disadvantage even though, like the men, they started the second game at the same time. What we are trying to do in a small way is to help make the system more just and fair. It is our hope that all children, male and female, are educated, so we offer financial assistance to poor families who are not able to educate all their children." After reading the chapter on feminist liberative ethics, which person in this case would you identify with and why? If the nursing student continued to talk about the unearned and unfair privilege of educating the girl child first, what responses might you give? How might you use sacred Scripture to give a rationale? Do you think that the Baha'i response on education is good? Why or why not?

mutually oppressed groups against each other. Patriarchy manifests itself as individual acts and institutional patterns that range from sexual innuendo to subordinate in the workplace to brutal dehumanization like human trafficking or the sexual violence of Bosnian war camps and US gang initiation rites.

Although privileged men benefit from the patriarchal power arrangement, women are complicit in the system when they become aware of their exclusion and oppression but are blind to others' struggles. Evidence of this claim is achingly familiar in conversations with female clergy and business leaders who find that women congregants and employees are often their harshest critics.

The biblical text is no stranger to the structures and systems of patriarchy, often experienced in religious exclusion and economic dependence. Consider the stories of Hagar, Rizpah, and Tamar and how the three women negotiate gender and class structures. Sarah, the patriarch Abraham's wife, gives her servant Hagar to her husband Abraham, who has sexual intercourse with her and impregnates her. After the birth of their young son, Hagar and her child, Ishmael, are expelled

LIBERATIVE ETHICS IN ACTION 9.1

Liberative Ethics in Action 1: The Issue of Women and Wal-Mart (or Justice in the Workplace)

In 2001 when Christine Kwapnoski asked for her first promotion, her manager told his twenty-five-year employee to update her makeup. Instead, she joined with five other women for a class-action sex-discrimination lawsuit against the retail giant. Although management claimed that it was unrelated, after the suit was filed, Kwapnoski was promoted. The six women in the suit claimed they had been paid less than men in comparable positions or not promoted in comparable circumstances, in violation of Title VII, the federal law that prohibits sex discrimination.

A district court ruled that other female employees could join the suit. In the district court proceedings, a professor testified that he had collected statistical evidence about gender bias, stereotypes, and the structure and dynamics of gender inequality. Over the next ten years, many women joined the suit, alleging that they too had experienced gender discrimination through their paychecks and promotions. Women held 70 percent of the hourly jobs, but only 33 percent were managers. As the class-action case gained momentum, Wal-Mart dismissed any possibility of sex discrimination. Wal-Mart's attorneys argued that the lower court was wrong to allow the women to join together in their lawsuit because they didn't satisfy the "commonality requirement" required to prove that the women have enough in common to proceed as a class.

The issue now was not whether Kwapnoski and other women have indeed been paid less than their male counterparts or if they have been promoted less often or not at all. The issue facing the Supreme Court in spring 2011 was whether the lower court was correct in allowing the women to band together to file their lawsuit, or whether they must file as individuals.

If the court ruled in favor of the women and granted them "class certification," it could become the largest employment class-action suit in history, involving millions of women and dollars. If the court ruled against the women, they would have to file suits one by one or they would have to approach their managers to ask for promotion or salary equity, like Kwapnoski did. Women's groups and consumer groups argued the side of the women, while the chamber of commerce and the business community supported Wal-Mart.

In June 2011 the Supreme Court ruled in favor of Wal-Mart five to four, with the majority ruling that the women did not have enough in common to qualify for class certification. A judge writing for the majority said that the women could not give a common answer to the question, why was I disfavored? A judge writing for the minority insisted that the statistics presented by the plaintiffs provided definite evidence that "gender bias suffused Wal-Mart's corporate culture."

from the community on Sarah's orders. Not even the father of her child, Abraham, advocates for her or the child. Within Islam, Hagar demonstrates agency and autonomy when deserted in the desert. The Hadith recounts Abraham's prayers for their survival and Hagar's courageous journey to find water so that her son Ishmael could survive.

Rizpah and Tamar represent women who use creativity to negotiate survival in the patriarchal system. Rizpah was the concubine of Saul, the first king of Israel, and after his murder, Rizpah was "inherited" by his heir, Ishbaal. Rizpah's sons, her only protection in the social system, were killed by the army of the new king, David. To draw attention to her plight as a widow and to bury her sons, Rizpah stays with their remains, eliciting a compassionate response from David. The third woman, Tamar, was widowed by two brothers, childless, and was to marry their brother within the patriarchal system of levirate marriage. The gatekeeper, her father-in-law, denies her the right to marry the third son, an act that withdraws any economic or social support. With no other option for economic survival, Tamar uses subterfuge to shock her father-in-law into a compassionate response.

Issues and Questions Feminist Religious Liberative Ethicists Wrestle With

Of the many issues feminists religious liberative ethicists confront, the two primary issues are socially constructed gender ideologies and the prioritization of race, class, and sexual orientation.

Gender Ideology

Differences like chromosomes, genitalia, and hormones lead to the determination of the male or female sex. When the biological determination filters through cultural assumptions, gender comes into play. Gender ideology is culturally constructed, and these constructions shape self and social understanding, vocations, and careers, and influence social position and hierarchy and roles for men and women.

Because of its powerful effect, gender ideology usually remains unquestioned. On the basis of sex

differences, we make assumptions about gender roles that result in a superior-inferior hierarchy. Men, accordingly, have greater or exclusive access to landholdings, inheritance, skills, gendered employment, and the high status that comes with these benefits. Women, on the other hand, receive poor nutrition and medical care, lower pay, and inferior education. In social systems, many women suffer violence, poverty, and deprivation, either because they are dependent on a male provider or because they lack access to a male. In some cultures, women are devalued so much that they are denied life, through practices like China's female infanticide and India's sex-selective abortions.

Since most people are blind to ideology and its effect on us, how can we recognize and understand it? Ideological awareness begins with asking good questions and seeing a situation from different perspectives. Like the child who looks at one side of the elephant and draws a big trunk, a partial view reflects only what one individual sees. A more accurate view results from connections with others who see the elephant from different vantage points. In particular, gender ideology is caught more than taught, caught through women or men we see in particular careers, illustrations we see in books and magazines, and images we view in popular culture.

Race, Class, and Sexual Orientation

Like other liberation movements, feminists have prioritized their struggle for its importance and position. Feminists have been guilty of assuming that other struggles should take second or third

> ### KEY TERM 9.5
>
> *Gender Role Ideology.* Attitudes regarding the appropriate roles, rights, and responsibilities of women and men in society or widespread societal beliefs that legitimate gender inequality.

CASE STUDY 9.3

Disney-animated movies offer lessons in gender ideology through popular culture. Heroines like Snow White, Cinderella, Pocahontas, and the Little Mermaid meet handsome, wealthy, and powerful men, fall in love, go through trials, then live happily ever after with their handsome male partners. In Disney's *The Little Mermaid*, the mermaid Ariel changes her physical appearance to be more attractive to the prince, but the cost is the loss of her beautiful voice. To give the prince credit, he never asks the mermaid to sacrifice what is most valuable, her voice, yet she uncritically assumes that such a sacrifice is necessary for his love and approval. Without her voice, she is literally silenced, and she is powerless to change her circumstances. Her voice had been an instrument of power, pleasure, and beauty. Like many girls and women, Ariel moves from one patriarchal system to another, first her father's kingdom under the sea, then her husband's kingdom on land.

What messages do girls and boys hear in the story of *The Little Mermaid* that influence self-image? If you were limited to what you know about the Little Mermaid story as your guide to gender roles, how would you describe male and female gender roles? What lessons about gender do you learn from the Little Mermaid story? If you do not agree with the gender role representations in *The Little Mermaid*, how would you revise the characters and story to fit your thoughts about better gender roles?

place to gender justice. In the same way that Latin American liberation theologians ask or imply that women must delay their struggle until the economically poor obtain justice, feminists in the United States identify goals, concerns, and priorities of white, educated, middle-class, and heterosexual women.

As a white, middle-class first-year college student, I worked in a low-income housing project. Through my interactions and relationship with the residents there, I learned about myself and started to become aware of the world around me. I noticed that all of the residents were African American in a town where less than 30 percent of the population was African American. I saw that most of the heads of households were women. For the first time in my life, I saw with different eyes my privilege and the interlocking systems of race, gender, and class. I understood that I had the advantage of higher education as a third-generation university student. None of my ancestors had been taken from their homes and forced to work for others. Unlike most of the women in the housing project, I did not buy groceries with food stamps, nor did I have to worry that my bills would be paid. As a white American, I realized that persons with my skin color occupied all of the main positions of power in my town and at my university. I never thought about my race, class, or sexual orientation. My new lens, even filtered through my privilege, helped me begin to see structures and systems and how I fit into the picture.

Third-wavers criticize first-wavers and second-wavers because of their blind spots and cultural captivity with regard to race, class, and normative heterosexuality. Third-wavers have been explicit that feminism must include those marginalized persons as active participants in the movement. A beginning point to bridging the historical gap of cultural captivity is to confess participation in destructive structures and systems of oppression. Like me, other white, middle-class, educated women may not be guilty of conscious acts or attitudes, but all have benefited from historical structures and systems that enhanced our opportunities and limited the potential of low-income women and persons of color. Women not only are affected by the structures of domination, but we also willingly or unwillingly participate in them, sometimes taking advantage of or benefiting from them in return for disadvantaging other women.

Instead of only representing one part of women's concerns, feminists must answer the call of the third-wavers, repenting of past actions and joining women of color, LGBT women, immigrant women, mujeristas, womanists, and low-income women already involved in the struggle for justice. Learning the rich resources of collective histories, social locations, and dangerous memories of suffering will enrich mainstream feminism because

of the collective wisdom, knowledge, and experience of stakeholders who have been present but not included throughout mainstream feminism.

Themes and Methodology

Feminist religious liberative ethics demands strong commitments to social justice, to feminism, and to the humanity of all marginalized people.

Justice

Central to any liberative ethics is justice, though the definition and practice of justice may vary. Justice is the basic norm for all social behaviors. All theories of justice agree that justice regulates our associations with people.

Fig. 9.4. Three women's actions for peacebuilding and women's rights were acknowledged in 2011 when Ellen Johnson Sirleaf, Leymah Gbowee, and Tawakkol Karman were awarded the Nobel Peace Prize.

From a feminist religious liberative perspective, justice acknowledges harmful structures and practices of the past and present as well as the incredible human potential of half the world's population. In the three Abrahamic traditions, justice is much more than making two sides of an equation equal—it is not about men having two dollars so now we must give women two dollars, or men having been in charge so now we must let women be in charge. Equality is important, but it is merely one incremental step toward justice. True gender justice is about a society where all persons are valued and the structures and systems bring life rather than domination. In a world with justice, women and men are not seen as victims of economic injustice but rather as a rich resource for formulating policy and contributing in meaningful ways to decision making, to creating a better world.

We know in our heads and by our religious teachings that persons are not more valuable because of their gender or their stock portfolio or because of their race or ethnicity, but our structures and systems, our politics and our economic practices nationally and locally affirm domination and exclusion.

Bodies and Embodiment

The physical body, body image, sexual orientation, and sexual activity are themes that grow from sacred texts and their interpretation throughout religious history. Through centuries of teachings that physicality and sexuality are at best suspect, feminist religious liberative ethicists yearn for religious recognition that their physical bodies are good and not vessels of temptation, as years of religious teachings imply. The problem may be rooted in religious texts like the purity laws in the Hebrew Bible, where adult women were restricted from religious public life for up to half of their adult lives. Within the Christian tradition, few denominations regularly have drawn on the positive imagery for physicality and sexuality in the Song of Solomon. Instead, those passages were read in whispers by adolescents in pews instead of as texts for homilies and lectionary readings.

Women and girls were and are faced with dualistic representations and conflicting role models and, more dangerously, silence about all matters related to sexuality. Were women created in the image of God? Is her body good and blessed, or is it flawed? Are women only good if they delay sexual intercourse? Is it good if they make reproductive choices that their religious community does not endorse? Is it selfishness to choose what happens with their own bodies? More important, what are effective and healthy ways to talk about body and sexuality in religious contexts?

A Usable Past

Given women's history, religious feminists wonder if the past is usable and the present redeemable. Is there room in institutional religion for women and girls? If there is space, what resources do they draw on in history and religious teachings?

Women and girls are present and active, yet their public presence and participation differs from setting to setting. Women's roles and the type of leadership available to them vary according to their context, culture, and their religious tradition or denomination. Most often, women and girls participate in unpaid, volunteer, or as lay positions: girls attend religious education and serve as altar girls. Women sing in choirs, teach religious education, engage in voluntary social work, and bring food for dinners. Women senior rabbis or ministers are less common.

Religious feminists call on their communities to invite women and girls into conversations about what they value about their religious traditions and what must change. Common concerns include women's leadership roles within their church, mosque, or synagogue; how they are represented in the language of their religious services and ceremonies; and moral teachings about sexuality, mothering and families, the content of religious education for children, and how their congregations teach the history of their religion.

Methodology: *Ver, Pensar, Actuar* (to See, to Think, to Act)

For ethicists, methodology is all-important. Rather than being guided by unconscious and unexamined assumptions and biases, liberative ethicists encourage awareness of assumptions, loyalties, and perceptions of threat. What do most feminist religious liberative ethicists reject or strongly say no to? Generally, feminist religious liberative ethicists criticize traditional ethical theory that privileges objectivity and neutrality. They reject gender-ideology claims that mankind has a certain set of qualities, attitudes, and abilities and womankind has a different, though often complementary set of qualities, attitudes, and abilities. They resist any institutional religion or social structure that rationalizes the unjust treatment of girls and women on religious or moral grounds.

Feminist religious liberative ethicists draw on the mother lode, Latin American feminist theology, for their methodological framework. Latin American theologians and Christian ethicist Beverly Harrison use the framework of the hermeneutic circle. They see injustice not as disinterested bystanders but with both head and heart; then they critically reflect on it; and finally they act in ways that bring about the intended end of social justice.

To See

For liberative ethicists of all kinds, methodology must not begin with abstract principles or disembodied theory but with the lived experience of injustice. Injustice is exploitation or domination, oppression, marginalization, and dehumanization. Bigotry and intolerance are a scourge on humankind. These kinds of attitudes can be indicators

---

BOX 9.4

Beverly Wildung Harrison

The *New York Times* called Beverly Wildung Harrison the "foremother of feminist social ethics." A second-wave feminist, Harrison has made important contributions to feminist religious liberative ethics through her activism, her scholarship, and her teaching at Union Theological Seminary in New York. Her address as full professor in 1979 titled "The Power of Anger in the Work of Love: Christian Ethics for Women and Other Strangers" is a classic essay for feminist social ethics. She was the first woman president of the Society of Christian Ethics and served on the board of the American Academy of Religion. Harrison has published and coauthored a number of books, including *Our Right to Choose: Toward a New Ethic of Abortion* and *Making the Connections: Essays In Feminist Social Ethics.*

---

of injustice and can nurture violence and related forms of oppression.

To Think

A better word for this stage in the hermeneutical circle is analysis, critical thinking, or critical consciousness. (See the textbox on conscientization.) Reflect on the seen injustice in light of your loyalties and ethical commitments. Consider the situation of the injustice and reflect on what you know about it or engage in research to learn more. Liberative ethicists prescribe a hermeneutics of suspicion, asking questions about evidence and if the evidence might lead to different conclusions. Analyze the injustice by raising thoughtful questions about race, class, and gender. Ask who has the power and what kind of power each party or group possesses. For example, what questions would you raise when seeing a man grab a woman's arm? Or when an employer rubs his student worker's arm? Or when a parent pushes a small child into a car? This stage encourages ethical actors (all of us) to develop systemic social analysis skills and to pay attention to social differences within the social system, whether that system is a workplace, a college dormitory, or a synagogue. In particular, a feminist liberative ethic encourages attention to difference among women, girls, and other vulnerable persons.

To Act

A feminist religious liberative ethic invites all, especially the marginalized or voiceless, to participate, to enter into the situation of oppression or injustice and to respond. This participation is often spoken of as praxis, action that grows from the concrete experience of injustice. Actions are filtered through the content of ethical commitments, remembering that liberative commitments are not ivory-tower commitments. Liberative ethics is an on-the-street practice of feminism with ethical commitments that grow from norms like love and justice. (See textbox on solidarity.)

Feminist religious liberative ethicists' foundation is love, but not the love of sentimentality, charity, or sacrifice. For Christian feminists, love is set within biblical framework of justice. Jesus' love is seen in his compassion and hospitality for the stranger and in his solidarity with poor. Jesus prioritized the welfare of human beings over rigid obedience to the law. With his understanding of God's movement, Jesus intensified, radicalized, and applied the law of love—love self, love neighbors, and love enemies.

Avoiding sexist jokes, dating someone who uses inclusive language, boycotting sweatshop-made clothes, and attending a university that pays a living wage to those who clean your building—all these represent incremental steps toward justice. Going along with sexist social structures, functioning in the global economic order as it is, and doing one's job without questioning glass ceilings in institutions is to participate in patriarchy. The challenge of praxis is learning daily how to balance individual actions and institutional involvement that displace injustice and nurture genuine community while living in the midst of what hooks calls the "imperialist white-supremacist capitalist patriarchy."

BOX 9.5

Conscientization

Activists speak of conscientization as waking up to the injustice in the world—or seeing it for the first time. It is not that the injustice is beginning; it is that you encounter oppression, injustice, violence yourself, or you see it in a person or situation. You may have seen the same situation many times before, but for some reason you begin to connect the event with a deeper recognition that the injustice is wrong. As a result of conscientization, the newly aware persons experience touched-to-the-roots transformation as part of their self awareness and social awareness. The conscientized persons may examine part or all of their lives through their new lens and recognize how they participate in the injustice or benefit from it. Realizing their privilege, they begin to understand how they benefit from unjust social and economic structures and systems. Like peeling of layers of an onion, they engage in an ongoing process of conscientization and transformation. As part of their transformation, they choose to act to eradicate the injustice or draw attention to the situation. This action is called "solidarity."

Liberative Ethics in Action 2: The Issue of Justice and Your Jeans

Far away from the four walls of her religion classrooms at Belmont University, Cheryl Smith discovered solidarity, and her life would never again be the same. Cheryl had heard the word *solidarity* from several of her religion professors; she could spell it, define it, and use it in a sentence, but the word became flesh on a Witness for Peace delegation in Managua, Nicaragua. In Nicaragua, Cheryl, studying third-world debt and its effect on the country with the highest per capita debt in the world, had already had her eyes glazed over with the language and policies of international financial institutions and neoliberal economics. She had stayed in the home of a single mother in a farming community and seen the faces of the feminization of poverty. She had walked through the Managua garbage dump, where scores of people and dogs scavenged for food. She had sat in countless meetings with economists at the World Bank and the Nicaragua office of the International Monetary Fund, peasant farmers, women's groups, health care workers, church leaders, antipoverty activists, business leaders, government officials, political analysts, and more.

In one more meeting, not even on the official schedule, Cheryl and the group listened to five women union leaders tell how they had been fired from their jobs in the Free Trade Zone that day. At the end of the question-and-answer period, they offered an invitation for anyone who wanted to accompany them to the factories to see what conditions were like. Five members of the group accepted the invitation, and at seven the next morning, Cheryl and four others climbed out of a van outside the Free Trade Zone, where seventeen thousand workers, 75 percent female, work at twenty factories, sewing blue jeans and other clothing to be sold in the United States.

Marta, one of the fired union leaders, grabbed Cheryl's arm and began escorting her into the Free Trade Zone, along with the seventeen thousand other workers. As they wove through the hoards of workers, Cheryl's new friend pointed out workers looking out through barbed wire, muscled gang members hired to intimidate union members, guards with machine guns, and searches as workers entered the factories.

As they neared the factory where the union leaders worked before their firing, a translator explained the abysmal working conditions and poor salaries that the union was struggling to change, adding that only the week before, the union had staged a peaceful protest and a work slowdown with hundreds of workers participating. As Cheryl and others took pictures, looked at the stream of entering workers, the guards with guns, and their new friends, now unemployed in a country with staggering unemployment and extreme poverty, she noticed the smiling faces of the fired union leaders. As they walked with the group back to the gate of the Free Trade Zone, hugged everyone, and bid the foreigners' farewell, it was clear that the visit had met their hopes and expectations. The union leaders reentered the Free Trade Zone, committed anew to their struggle for just wages and better working conditions.

As Cheryl reflected later on what she had learned from her experience, she realized that the morning in the Free Trade Zone had become a lens with which to see her whole experience in Nicaragua and her life

LIBERATIVE ETHICS IN ACTION 9.2 (continued)

at home. Solidarity meant entering into the experience of the fired union workers, knowing that she could never completely understand their reality, but caring enough to try to understand by putting her body in the place of others and accompanying them in their struggle.

Back home in Nashville, Cheryl wrote letters and gave talks about what she had seen. Even as she protested conditions in the factories, she occasionally bought jeans and other clothing from companies connected to the factories. Troubled as she was with what she saw, Cheryl knew that she was part of the global economic machine.

Possible Future Trends

In addition to remaining open yet critical of new iterations of feminism, feminist religious liberative ethicists call for furthering the feminist vision of radical justice and radical equality for women, girls, and all marginalized persons, especially within expressions of spirituality and religion.

Some feminists dream of a single, united version of feminism, while others, especially excluded voices, encourage multilingualism and the strengthening of multiple iterations of feminisms. Given the hegemony of feminisms of the past and present, is a single, united feminism even positive or possible? At the very least, will feminists work collaboratively on justice issues and learn to listen to other women's painful histories? Will

white, middle-class, heterosexual women become good listeners and pay attention to who is and is not included in the feminist movement? Will we have enough communication and collaboration to design programs and protests in ways that do not perpetuate systems of oppression? Will religious feminists in the twenty-first century acknowledge the captivity of "imperialist white-supremacist capitalist patriarchy" and build authentic relationships with others, especially the marginalized?

At its core, religious liberative feminism is an audacious vision of hope, hope that the potential of women and girls will be realized, hope that new structures and systems will be imagined and created, hope that persons of faith and conscience will exercise critical consciousness and will not rest until justice reigns. Will you join the movement?

Study Questions

1. In what ways does bell hooks's definition of feminism fit or not fit with what you have read, heard, or know about feminism?

2. Thinking with the lens of a feminist religious liberative ethicist, describe concrete experiences of injustice faced by women and girls today.

3. Name two current events or events in history that are advances in opportunities and advancement for women and girls. In what

ways have you or a woman you know benefited from the events?

4. How is religion gendered? What is gender ideology, and what roles do religions play in creating, preserving, enforcing, or interpreting it?

5. From the Liberative Ethics in Action case on women employees at Wal-Mart, write a paragraph response to the majority opinion that women did not have enough in common to qualify for class certification.

Suggested Reading

Harrison, Beverly. "Theological Reflection in the Struggle for Liberation." In *Making the Connections: Essays in Feminist Social Ethics*, edited by Carol S. Robb. Boston: Beacon, 1985.

hooks, bell. *Feminism Is for Everybody: Passionate Politics*. Cambridge, MA: South End, 2000.

———. *The Will to Change: Men, Masculinity and Love*. New York: Washington Square Press, 2004.

Kelly, Annie, Laura Turquet, Stephanie Ross, and Anchita Chatak, eds. "Disappearing Daughters—Sex Selection in India." Action Aid and the International Development Research Centre (IDRC). http://www.actionaid.org.uk/doc_lib/disappearing_daughters_0608.pdf.

Snyder, Claire. "What Is Third Wave Feminism: A New Directions Essay." *Signs Journal* 34, no. 1 (2008): 175–96.

10

Women of Color Liberative Ethics

Thelathia "Nikki" Young and Robyn Henderson-Espinoza

AT THE FOUNDATION FOR women of color (WoC) liberative ethics is the consistent acknowledgment that people of color, particularly women, exist at the intersection of many social, cultural, economic, political, and religious categories. This intersectional existence helps to orient many women of color toward an ethics that is guided by the dismantling of oppressive regimes, the resistance to oppressive politics, the reclamation of ignored or silenced culture and values, and the creation of new moral norms. Because ethics derived from identity categories simultaneously attends to diverse human experiences and the distinctive lenses through which those experiences might be understood, WoC ethics provides and prescribes a worldview that regularly calls attention to difference, oppression, and injustice.

The phrase *women of color* represents a complicated historical argument about whether the term is actually an identity category or a political designation. On one hand, because whiteness is often situated as an invisible norm, the term *women of color* calls attention to the distinctive appearance and set of experiences that some women in the world have. It makes it known that there are people in the world who are colored, who live in contexts dissimilar from white people, and who have sets of experiences that are racialized. While the modifying phrase *of color* forces a recognition that certain people are raced, *women of color* emphasizes the important possibility of coalition building, as the phrase draws attention to how people make connections between the ways different women of color are raced and gendered. In this way, *women of color* simultaneously unites disparate racial and

---

KEY TERM 10.1

Intersectionality. Introduced by Kimberle Crenshaw, intersectionality has become a term that is used within the humanities and social sciences to show the interdependence and relationships of categories. This term was popularized by sociologist Patricia Hill Collins. Particularly, this term highlights a type of socioanalytic mediation that works at the intersections of race, class, gender, sexuality, age, and ability, among others.

ethnic groups into a larger collective and points to the distinctive realities of people and groups within the category. On the other hand, *women of color* is not simply an identity category; the phrase also serves a more political function. It is a term used to point to the oppositional standpoint and perspective that many women have taken in relation to sexist, racist, and classist politics, religion, and social practices.

These two meanings infuse WoC ethics, simultaneously designating it as a categorical lens through which moral trajectories have been shaped and a set of political agendas primarily derived outside of the framework of normative white womanhood. Our use of the term in this chapter most often employs it as an identity category that signifies an "umbrella" under which diverse races and experiences are housed. We suggest that women of color, broadly understood, represent something different than normative whiteness and that these experiences have informed the creation of a distinctive ethics.

This chapter has the propensity to tokenize various women of color and particular racialized

CASE STUDY 10.1

Loretta Ross, in her deliniation of the history of the term *women of color*, illustrates its complicated origins. Longtime activist on women's and human rights, and founder of SisterSong, a reproductive justice collective, Ross offers a candid explanation of the term and its historical significance. Below is a transcript of her brief discussion:

Y'all know where the term "women of color" came from? Who can say that? See, we're bad at transmitting history. In 1977, a group of Black women from Washington, DC, went to the National Women's Conference, that [former president] Jimmy Carter gave $5 million to have as part of the World Decade for Women. There was a conference in Houston, TX. This group of Black women carried into that conference something called "The Black Women's Agenda" because the organizers of the conference—Bella Abzug, Ellie Smeal, and what have you—had put together a three-page "Minority Women's Plank" in a 200-page document that these Black women thought was somewhat inadequate.

So they actually formed a group called Black Women's Agenda to come [*sic*] to Houston with a Black women's plan of action that they wanted the delegates to vote to substitute for the "Minority Women's Plank" that was in the proposed plan of action. Well, a funny thing happened in Houston: when they took the Black Women's Agenda to Houston, then all the rest of the "minority" women of color wanted to be included in the "Black Women's Agenda." Well, [the Black women] agreed . . . but you could no longer call it the "Black Women's Agenda." And it was in those negotiations in Houston [that] the term "women of color" was created.

And they didn't see it as a biological designation—you're born Asian, you're born Black, you're born African American, whatever—but it is a solidarity definition, a commitment to work in collaboration with other oppressed women of color who have been "minoritized." Now, what's happened in the 30 years since then is that people see it as biology now. . . . And people are saying they don't want to be defined

CASE STUDY 10.1 *(continued)*

as a woman of color: "I am Black," "I am Asian American" . . . and that's fine. But why are you reducing a political designation to a biological destiny?

That's what white supremacy wants you to do. And I think it's a setback when we disintegrate as people of color around primitive ethnic claiming. Yes, we are Asian American, Native American, whatever, but the point is, when you choose to work with other people who are minoritized by oppression, you've lifted yourself out of that basic identity into another political being and another political space. And, unfortunately, so many times, people of color hear the term "people of color" from other white people that [we] think white people created it instead of understanding that we named ourselves.

This is a term that has a lot of power for us. But we've done a poor-ass job of communicating that history so that people understand that power.

Why is it important to recall the history of the phrase *women of color*? How does Ross's explanation help you understand the phrase *women of color* and WoC ethics? What do you understand as the difference between "women of color" as a biological destiny or a political designation? Is one more useful than the other?

categories. To minimize the degree to which that is done, we will introduce WoC ethics in two ways. First, rather than focus on specific groups, races, or representative women from "diverse" categories under the umbrella of "women of color," we will explain key concepts and methods that distinguish WoC ethics from other ethical categories. Second, this chapter purposefully references some people who are not necessarily trained as ethicists (or works that are not in the field of theological ethics) but who are doing ethics, setting ethical frameworks, and/or drawing on WoC ethicists' materials.

History and Development of WoC Liberative Ethics

The 1980s saw many shifts in theological and ethical discourse as a result of women of color contributing scholarship and teaching to the academy. These paradigm shifts were due largely to changes in the social, political, and economic rhetoric emerging from marginalized communities and resistance movements. In addition, these shifts emerged as womanist, *mujerista*/Latina, Asian and Asian American women began to chart new territories in theological ethics by inserting their own language, experiences, and methods into a larger theological conversation. During this exciting time, women of color began to engage ethics from the perspective of multiple identities and with a focus on various forms of oppression. Their analysis incorporated strong attention to race, gender, and class and sometimes sexuality. Propelled by texts like *In Search of Our Mother's Gardens* (1983) and *This Bridge Called Our Back* (1981), women of color began to analyze and articulate moral frameworks that reflected their own lives.

Analytic ethics, like analytic philosophy, uses strict parameters of logic to achieve its disciplinary goal. Most prominent in WoC ethics is the specific language and methods developed within certain raced groups. Key concepts on which

BOX 10.1

Womanist

The term *womanist* was coined by novelist and poet Alice Walker. In her novel, *In Search of Our Mother's Gardens*, Walker outlines a four-part definition of womanist to describe the behavior, desire, commitment, appreciation, and depth of "black feminists" and/or "feminists of color." She describes a womanist as someone "being grown" with "courageous or willful behavior" who loves women and what women love—not to the exclusion of men, but with the purpose of loving the entire community.

Despite its nonreligious etymology, religious thinkers appropriated Walker's conception and definition of *womanist*. As one of the premier academic disciplines publishing womanist thought, religious studies—particularly theology and ethics—is the locus of the most numerous and the most prevalent womanist work. Womanists theologians and ethicists expanded their fields by adding sources, analyzing the social circumstances of black woman's experiences over time, and utilizing a hermeneutics of suspicion to critique theological and ethical texts. Employing intersectional analysis of race, class, and gender, womanists have used a variety of disciplinary methods—including storytelling and narrative—to ground their work in black women's realities. As a result, womanist work highlights the social reality of the past for black women, critically engages their experiences of oppression and marginalization, tells their stories of religious struggle and triumph, and works to revision a set of theological ethics that

BOX 10.1 (continued)

acknowledges and validates black women and women of color as persons who have valuable moral agency. Womanist theologians and ethicists have moved from a participation in normative, white, male-centered theological conversations to an engagement of more liberating and liberal perspectives. Thus the trajectory of womanism in theology and ethics has moved in the direction of freedom and advocacy of social justice by advancing nuanced conversations about the intersection of race, class, and gender.

WoC ethics is built includes, but is certainly not limited to, praxis, experience as a source, embodiment, mutuality, interdependence, struggle (as opposed to suffering), and resistance. For the most part, we see evidence/employment of these concepts and methods in mujerista theology and chicana feminisms, Asian American theology and ethics, womanist and black feminist theology and ethics, African women's theology and ethics, and postcolonial and two-thirds-world theo-ethical discourse.

In the formation of WoC ethics, mutuality (as opposed to self-sacrifice) serves as a central feature. The ongoing spirit of creation and sharing of resources (including ideas) helps promote the flourishing of women of color. Common to the history of women, women are valued when they sacrifice themselves for "the greater good." Women of color critiques this model of self-sacrifice and in place of this antiwoman model promote commitment to mutuality.

Similarly, suffering is often a common label for the women's movement. But suffering reduces (or stabilizes) women into people hurting or "suffering" for a cause. When women of color are valued as material subjects who embody goodness and

BOX 10.2

Mujerista

Mujerista is a contested term. On one hand, Latina American scholars claim that it was coined by Virginia Vargas, Peruvian women whom Maria Pilar Aquino cites as abandoning the feminist movement. On the other hand, it is suggested that Cuban American and Catholic theologian Ada María Isasí-Díaz conceptualized this term in two main texts: *A Mujerista Theology: A Theology for the Twenty-First Century* and *En La Lucha/In the Struggle: Elaborating a Mujerista Theology*. As a result, many Latin American, Latina, and US Latina women reject this term. Maria Pilar Aquino provides three reasons for such a rejection: this word *mujerista* refers to a specific "sociopolitical meaning in the context of Latin American feminism," *mujerismo* projects an abstract construction for women, and as a theory, mujerista establishes a "false consciousness." Conversely, Ada María Isasí-Díaz provides three reasons for her use of mujerista. First, she defines it as a conceptual framework that provides both an identification method of understanding. Second, she claims that it is a means by which Latinas exercise agency in defining their future. Third, she suggests that mujerista theology enables Latinas to "understand how much they have already bought into the prevailing systems in society—including the religious systems—thus internalizing their own oppression."

A theology of *mujerisma* sought not only to interrogate the experiences of Latin American women but also to take the experiences of Latin American women as primary for theological

BOX 10.2 (continued)

reflection. Influenced by womanist thought, Isasí-Díaz conceptualized mujerista theology as a socioanalytic theo-ethical framework that emphasizes a preferential option for Latina women. Particular to this framework is someone who takes the ongoing struggle for liberation seriously. Mujerista theology is committed to recognizing the need for mujeristas to liberate themselves not only as individuals but also as valued members of the Latino community. Mujeristas work to build bridges among Latina/os. Furthermore, mujeristas do this work of bridging and understand their task to be gathering the hopes and expectations of the people about justice and peace. Mujeristas believe that their call, though not exclusively theirs, is that God chooses to once again lay claim to the divine image and likeness made visible in Latinas. Isasí-Díaz's work in mujerista theology is to orient Latinas to their call/vocation: to gestate new women and new men; a new Latino community that is willing to work for the common good of the people; and to acknowledge that this work requires the commitment to denounce all destructive sense of self-abnegation, which is important for Latinas to do on an ongoing basis.

capability, suffering no longer has the capacity to be an identifier for women. Struggle (as opposed to suffering) is how women of color imagine themselves relative to the structures and institutions against which they are fighting. When suffering is replaced with an ongoing commitment to struggle, resistance (or the politics of resistance) begins to take shape in material ways. Bodies form

BOX 10.3

Postcolonial and Two-Thirds World Theo-ethical Discourse

Leela Gandhi, professor of English, is paving the way for postcolonial ethics. There is no discipline proper of "postcolonial ethics," but there are many ethicists who utilize postcolonial theory in formulating their evaluation of ethics. Postcolonial theories have substantively originated out of the humanities and have proliferated in English. These theories have sought to challenge existing structures and theories that reify and reinscribe colonialist discourse. Knowledge and power reproductions are central to postcolonial theories and are, in many ways, central to ethics, since ethics is about formation. In light of this, ethics and postcolonial thinking have often become synonymous in that both "disciplines" are central to evaluating and negotiating power structures. However, until recently, most postcolonial theories (and ethics for that matter) have emerged from first-world scholars. The two-thirds world received ethics and postcolonial theories about them. Now, the two-thirds world is producing postcolonial theories and ethics that take seriously the need to evaluate power and knowledge productions from the "margins," from the dispossessed, that are becoming increasingly helpful for first-world scholars; an example of this is the Postcolonial Theology Network Group, which has been formative in collaborating across nations and states to make postcolonial theories more visible, especially from scholars who do not have the privilege of the first-world education system and/or access to resources.

and engage in relationships to resist powers and structures that have historically prevented women of color from flourishing.

WoC ethicists, who construct disciplinary goals within the field and are committed to a liberative orientation to justice-making in today's world, began by employing praxis (or a praxis-oriented ethics) over against a theory-only model. They constructed their socioanalytic mediation with praxis in mind, and achieved a type of ethics that is propelled by a commitment to action. In this way, WoC ethics illustrates women of color's responses to both the rhetoric and social circumstances that suppressed the flourishing of the entire human community.

Similar to (white) feminist movements, which valued experience as a source of theorizing, women of color also value experience in the ongoing construction of a praxis-oriented ethics. For women of color, valuing experience as a source means they take the history of their communities and their experiences as something particular to the ways in which they achieve liberation. Likewise, embodiment is another central feature of women of color ethics. The recognition that the body is favorable in light of the pursuit of ethical action helps orient bodies within community, relationally, toward one another and toward justice-oriented actions.

KEY TERM 10.2

Praxis. Popularized by the movement(s) of liberation theologies and the theories of Paulo Freire, *praxis* is a term that indicates an emphasis on practice and action over against theory and concepts. In liberation theologies, there is careful attention paid to God's being disclosed in the "historical 'praxis' of liberation," which is relative to action, over doctrinal teachings.

LIBERATIVE ETHICS IN ACTION 10.1

Liberative Ethics in Action 1: Wangari Maathai and the Issue of Ecological Justice

In the 1970s, Wangari M. Maathai realized that one of the most persistent daily difficulties facing women in Kenya was their access to resources for everyday domestic needs and general economic sustainability. In particular, Maathai noticed that firewood for cooking and obtaining clean water was scarce. Learning from the women about the environmental and social conditions that affected them, Maathai began to educate and advocate for poor, rural Kenyan women, raising consciousness concerning the environmental and humanitarian injustices they faced.

In 1977, Maathai started the Green Belt Movement, working with the government and local communities to improve the environment and empower the people in poor, rural areas. She suggested that planting trees would attend to wood provision for cooking, sustenance for animals, materials for building, nutrient cultivation for the soil, and much more. Each element of this environmental sustainability project would improve the local agriculture and have a significantly positive impact on women's lives. The Green Belt Movement has garnered support and cooperation, resulting in planting more than 47 million trees.

Her method of responding to these realities was multifocal, drawing on concepts of praxis, intersectional analysis, empowerment, and interdependence. She focused attention on the actual experiences of the people while reflecting and planning with them about ways to improve their conditions. Her praxis-oriented approach garnered support from both governmental agencies and local residents. In community, they analyzed connections between the lack of resources, health and economic issues, and environmental sustainability. Theirs was an effort to consider women's issues from several angles. In addition, Maathai used an assets-based approach, assuming that the power of resources *within* the community could, in fact, produce a huge resource of power *for* the community. She helped create people coalition, using skills and resources to improve the livelihood of many members of various communities.

For improving the quality of life and the agricultural conditions across the country, Maathai was awarded the 2004 Nobel Peace Prize. Her work called attention to the connections between poverty, environmental destruction, disempowerment, and government policies. For her, planting trees went hand-in-hand with advocating for democracy, peace, and human rights. Indeed, this project was a catalyst for a broader in-depth social, economic, and political agenda. Planting trees was literal and metaphoric, practical and esoteric, capturing the imagination of everyday people, the Kenyan community, and various funding sources. Maathai's efforts to build sustainability actually generated coalitions, instituted government policies, and renewed cultural appreciation. Through such projects, Maathai helped sensitize people to the matrix of oppression at work within their environment as well as possibilities for social change.

Part of what makes Maathai's activism so praiseworthy is her ongoing acknowledgment of the connections between the lack of environmental sustainability and poverty. Working in response to the immediate

LIBERATIVE ETHICS IN ACTION 10.1 (continued)

conditions and everyday realities of poor, rural women, Maathai developed an ethical framework and activist posture that built on the difficulty many women faced. She illustrated that activism in both attention to and critique of the values and norms that shape society, and she showed the usefulness of praxis-oriented responses to such moral frameworks. Finally, Maatha demonstrated how a multifocal lens opens possibilities for radical change.

LIBERATIVE ETHICS IN ACTION 10.2

Liberative Ethics in Action 2: Delores Huerta and the Issue of Worker Justice and "Feminist" Seeds

Dolores Huerta found her calling as an organizer while providing leadership service at the Stockton Community Service Organization (CSO). During this time, she founded the Agricultural Workers Association, set up voter registration drives, and pressed local governments for barrio improvements. In 1955, through CSO founder Fred Ross Sr., she met CSO executive director César E. Chávez. The two soon discovered that they shared the common vision of organizing farmworkers. In the spring of 1962, Chávez and Huerta resigned from CSO and launched the National Farm Workers Association. While Huerta's organizing skills were essential to the growth of this budding organization, she faced many challenges. In one of her letters to Chávez, she joked: "Being a now (ahem) experienced lobbyist, I am able to speak on a man-to-man basis with other lobbyists."

Huerta and Chavez were infamous for their blowout arguments, an element that was a natural part of their working relationship. To them, this was a healthy and necessary part of the growth process for any collaboration. While Huerta was busy breaking down gender barriers, she was seemingly unaware of the tremendous impact she was having not only on farmworker women but also on young women everywhere. Though she embraced the term *feminist*, Huerta initially dismissed the 1960s women's liberation movement as a "middle-class phenomenon." However, while directing the first national boycott of California table grapes out of New York, she came into contact with Gloria Steinem and the burgeoning feminist movement, who rallied behind the cause. Huerta realized they shared more in common than previously imagined. Having found a supportive voice with another feminist, Dolores consciously began to challenge gender discrimination within the farmworker movement.

At eighty-one, Dolores Huerta continues to work tirelessly, developing leaders and advocating for the working poor, women, and children. There are thousands of working-poor immigrants in the agriculture-rich San Joaquin Valley of California. Because they are unfamiliar with laws or agencies that can protect them or benefits to which they are entitled, they are often preyed upon. Huerta teaches these individuals that they

LIBERATIVE ETHICS IN ACTION 10.2 (continued)

have power and that personal power needs to be coupled with responsibility and cooperation to create the changes needed to improve their lives. Her method of interdependence with a praxis-oriented methodology helps to empower farmworkers. Certainly, her subject position is that of a feminist of color. While not conceptually uncomplicated, feminism is the political identity/category that Huerta embodies.

The courage to claim one's own personal power is tedious and time-consuming work, and rarely practiced today (outside of communities of color). Yet, the work of mutuality, interdependence, and embodiment are central features of Huerta's work, and the results are long lasting. While people are in the process of building organizations, they learn lessons they will never forget, and transformative roots are planted. The fruit is the leadership that is developed and the permanent changes in the community. In other words, this is how "grassroots democracy" or participatory democracy, works.

Fig. 10.1. Grape boycotters picket a Jewel Food Store in 1973.

KEY TERM 10.3

Racism, Sexism, Classism. As social constructions, the categories of race, sex, and class are interlocking categories often used to discriminate women, children, and people of color. Each of these categories is dependent on an overarching ideology—the systematic elevation of whiteness, maleness, heteropatriarchy, and/or wealth. In fact, one might define any of those "isms" as a systematic and/or individualized application of power and belief that one identity (race, sex, class, sexuality, etc.) is superior to others. Often these categories are referenced as interlocking systems of oppression that are used to limit the flourishing of women, men, and children (particularly of color).

Need for Liberation and Central Issues

The question of liberation for women of color is complicated but necessary, requiring a commitment to the politics of resistance to aid in the ongoing unraveling of the complexities in general, and an ongoing commitment to valuing interdependence within community in particular.

Existing in a heteropatriarchal world that is solidified by the ideologies of whiteness (and maleness, particular to patriarchy), women of color have learned to marshal within themselves an orientation to justice that materializes in their moral basis for ethical action. A normative value for ethics that is liberative and particular to women of color transcends strict disciplinary boundaries and instead seeks a liberative orientation toward communities (and/or structures) that provide elements of human flourishing. A WoC liberative

ethical orientation is a fundamental commitment against structures that limit or prevent the flourishing and abundant life of women of color. One particular community investment is the recognition of the history of liberation relative to the ways in which liberation has affected women of color.

Such an example of the commitment to this recognition is WoC responses to the feminist movement, primarily composed of white women. The feminist movements have sought to critique structures that limit women's freedom and flourishing. Yet, Western feminist movements have maintained (for many) a particularly white, heteronormative, middle-class orientation that has not always been inclusive to women of color. While white feminist movements highlighted the inequality and inequity of women relative to white men, women of color continued to seek liberation and continued to struggle and resist social circumstances and freedom movements

KEY TERM 10.4

Interdependence. Interdependence is a term used often in today's feminist philosophy. Notably, Carol Gilligan was an early proponent of the view that interdependence rather than rules created the basis of morality. Gilligan explores this in her work *In a Different Voice.* While this work might be outdated today, it has been a significant part of feminist ethics, ethics of care, and feminist philosophy. While interdependence can refer to one human's relation to another—a relationship, for example, that is interdependent and shares particular features of responsibility— this term can also point to the interdependence of thought and action in that neither thought nor actions are independent of one another in the work of WoC scholarship.

that homogenize womanhood. The depiction of WoC stories, experiences, and struggles, especially through the chicana feminist movement, black feminists, and womanist movements, has worked to de-essentialize and destablize womanhood. This struggle of inclusion has been a radical commitment to dismantling oppressive matrices and building coalitions. Important values within WoC ethics, interdependence and building community through recognizing diverse experiences, have been foundational to resisting white, male-dominated structures and institutions that are not inclusive of women of color or conscious of the values of community within them. Through various resistance efforts (scholarship, teaching, religious leadership, activism), women of color created counterstructures to support an ongoing commitment to human flourishing.

As black feminist bell hooks elaborates in *Talking Back: Thinking Feminist, Thinking Black*, the struggle for liberation is central to feminism, and feminism itself must exist on its own terms and in relationship to the larger struggle of seeking to eradicate all forms of domination. The reality is that heteropatriarchy shares an ideological foundation with the intersecting oppressions of racism, classism, sexism, and so on; and without dismantling these intersections, we cannot see the eradication of oppression. This knowledge should always inform our theory and praxis. It is in this sense that the normative value of radical inclusion creates the framework for liberative thought and practice. Radical inclusion, which is the ongoing attempt to include all women of varying colors, becomes the starting point for WoC ethics and is in fundamental opposition to stabilized categories that are a feature of liberationist ethics or feminist ethics. Radical inclusion creates the conditions for women of color to enflesh a liberative orientation to creative life-giving structures.

As both the first and second waves of the feminist movement stabilized women in an essentialized gender category, they used the language of

KEY TERM 10.5

Oppression. An act done by one human person, an institution, or a group of persons, oppression can be understood as systemic actions, like political oppression, or as actions of inhumanity relative to one's gender, sex, or class status. Several groups (largely consisting of communities of color) have resisted the rise of oppression, both systemic and institutional.

equality and civil rights to achieve homogenized notions of liberation. Women of color faced similar realities in various nationalist and racial empowerment movements, in which the discourse for freedom was androcentric and often sexist. Confronting gender and racial inequities, women of color realized the importance of social justice efforts that responded to a matrix of oppressions. WoC liberative ethics has drawn on this realization and developed a theo-ethical response to the religious discourse that supported such oppressive "liberation" rhetoric.

In short, WoC liberative ethics recognizes the need to illustrate the complex array of injustices that stem from invisibility in normative culture, feminist movements, and many racial/nationalist movements. Moreover, WoC ethicists realize that these attempts toward collective liberation require keen attention to economic disparities and injustices. To be sure, embodying a liberative orientation to creating structures that are life-giving and that promote a radical notion of human flourishing for moral action runs counter to traditional notions of liberation, which seek to give a preferential option to those who are impoverished or "marginalized." WoC liberative ethics certainly privileges women of color as the primary mode for analysis, but it does so by destabilizing both the "center" and "margin," drawing attention to the complex and intersecting forces of oppression that affect all people.

While several WoC scholars are contributing to theological and ethical discourse these days, there are some whose work is either foundational to or exemplary of WoC ethics. For instance, the roots of modern theological womanism grew out of works from Jacquelyn Grant, Delores Williams, and Katie G. Cannon. Grant, a theologian, has argued that James Cone developed a theological position regarding black experiences that does not take into account black women's experiences. In her text *White Women's Christ, Black Women's Jesus: Feminist Christology and Womanist Response*, she asserts that black women's oppression is distinctive from both black men and white women. Poor black women, she claims, simultaneously face racism, sexism, and classism. Williams expands on Grant's work by suggesting womanist theology ought to be grounded in black women's experiences and their own theological reflections on their faith. This approach to theology, suggests Williams, would be the best way to both combat oppression and affirm the moral agency of the black community as a whole. One of Williams's most groundbreaking texts is *Sisters in the Wilderness: The Challenge of Womanist God-Talk*. These womanist pioneers have reshaped conversations in theology and have paved the way for other womanist writers like theologians Kelly Brown Douglas in *Sexuality and the Black Church* and Monica Coleman in *Making a Way Out of No Way: A Womanist Theology* to push theological conversations in several new directions.

For womanist scholar Cannon, the intersecting forces of racism, sexism, and classism prompt critical ethical analysis. In her books *Black Womanist Ethics* and *Katie's Canon: Womanism and the Soul of the Black Community*, she also utilized black women's experiences to illustrate their moral agency and survivalist techniques. For Cannon, it is important that readers understand that black women make their moral and ethical decisions out of an environment of survival, not freedom. Following Cannon's lead, several other womanist ethicists have contributed foundational texts. Marcia Riggs's definition of ethics in *Plenty Good Room: Women Versus Male Power in the Black Church* suggests that doing ethics is a matter of analyzing both experiences and contexts in relation to the Christian tradition. Cheryl Kirk-Duggan adds to Riggs's delineation the idea that womanist ethics has a responsive and evaluative orientation because it destabilizes oppressive regimes. Emilie Townes's *Womanist Ethics, Womanist Hope* and *In a Blaze of Glory: Womanist Spirituality as Social Witness* also establish a community-oriented, women-prompted, social-justice-oriented, praxis-driven ethical framework. Additionally, Traci West's texts *Wounds of the Spirit: Black Women, Violence, and Resistance Ethics* and *Disruptive Christian Ethics: When Racism and Women's Lives Matter* have expanded womanist methodologies in relation to experience to include oral histories, slave narratives, and ethnographies.

Religious scholarship that highlights Latinas' experiences and focuses on Latinas as a primary analytic framework has been primarily conceived within an American Catholic and/or a Latin American Roman Catholic perspective. This work primarily emerged out of a liberation theology framework. Central figures are María Pilar Aquino (Mexican and Roman Catholic) and Ada María Isasí-Díaz (Catholic Cuban American). Within the milieu of Latina feminism, others have emerged: Merecedes Baca, Nancy Bedford, Virgina Vargas, Virginia Azcuy, Loida Martell-Otero. Many of these scholars focus on a theology and ethics of interculturality. The following list is certainly not exhaustive but shows Latinas' commitment to the study of religion. As the feminist movement was in full swing in the late 1970s and early 1980s, feminist scholarship began to surface. The equivalent for Latinas and other women of color in the United States was *This Bridge Called My Back: Radical Writings by Women of Color*. This book continues to serve as a central text for women of color.

Beyond the discipline of religion, there are several Latinas and women of color who are invested in interrogating religion, spiritual activism, and whose work creates a much more robust notion of the critical study of religion. Contributing scholars are Ana Louise Keating, Gloria Anzaldúa, and Cheríe Moraga. As Argentine poet (and an identifiable early feminist), Alfonsina Storni wrote: "*el mundo late*—the world palpitates—and is pregnant with hope, promises, and potentiality for all women." It is in this spirit that Latinas and women of color seek to produce religious and spiritual activist scholarship.

Asian American religious scholarship has largely been pioneered by Kwok Puil-lan (*Hope Abundant: Third World and Indigenous Women's Theology* and *Introducing Asian Feminist Theology*) and Rita Nakashima Brock (*Proverbs of Ashes: Violence, Redemptive Suffering, and the Search for What Saves Us* and *Casting Stones: Prostitution And Liberation In Asia and The United States*). Other Asian American voices who have emerged are Gale Yee (*Poor Banished Children of Eve: Woman as Evil in the Hebrew Bible*), Anne Joh (*Heart of the Cross: A Postcolonial Christology*), and Chung Hyung Kyung (*Struggle to Be the Sun Again: Introducing Asian Women's Theology*). Certainly Kwok Pui-lan and Chung Hyung Kyung have contributed significantly to the field of Asian feminist theology, and Pui-lan has recently incorporated a postcolonial critique to her theology. This is an important move, and theologians, such as Anne Joh, have followed suit in their own theological conceptions. Asian feminists using postcolonial theories within the field of religion have certainly contributed to a much more critical and illustrative concept of Asian feminism.

Possible Future Trends

Historically, WoC groups, though valuing and seeking to practice the particularities of "radical" hospitality, have not been as open as perhaps today's WoC groups. Women of color have struggled to work with one another across differences of race, gender, class, and sexuality. In order to embody a liberative approach to ethics, working intersectionally is important, and when this commitment is absent, struggle becomes apparent and is rooted in the fabric of WoC groupings.

The term *women of color* is illustrative of a political category derived from the necessity of framing an identity relative to the ongoing struggle against structures; it is indicative of a politics of resistance. WoC groups have varied in population or construction. Puerto Rican women have been included in black feminist groups, and chicana feminists have opened themselves to including black women. Doing this has destabilized the existing WoC grouping to include a much more robust notion of women, and complicates the ways in which we understand women (of color).

The process of navigating ethics and human difference involves constant respectful negotiation and a productive approach to conflict, rather than static defining. Important to this task is the ongoing and critical engagement of relationships. WoC groups engage in particular relationships that seek to encourage their human flourishing. This negotiation of human difference relative to human relating, encompassing varying elements of intimacy, is a radically productive approach to conflict and human flourishing that transcends the stasis of definitions.

Slippage between identity categories and political designations (or motivations?) are dangerous and have to be rigorously examined. Breaking out of the essentialized identity categories and embodying identities (which are equally political) that invite a fluidity of categories help women of color engage in the embodiment of a liberative approach to ethics. If WoC groups can negotiate and critically engage the politics of race, class, sex, and gender intersectionally, then these categories can become much fuller (and broader), and in turn embody the potential of becoming a much more robust intersectional movement for women of color, and their liberative ethics.

Stories and individuals are important, but we must know that they do not represent the entire group. In fact, narratives that we continue to share may in fact complicate our current struggle, so we must certainly learn the stories that have preceded us, but we must also (and with a critical eye) engage the present struggle (and its features) in order to truly embody a liberative approach. For example, the project of anthologies was/is a bold and liberative ethical move to bring WoC voices together, in different forms, showing that ethics happens both inside and outside "traditional" academic spaces and frameworks. Yet, while these anthologies bring voices and scholars of color together, these projects also characterize the movement in (perhaps) stabilizing ways. Certainly anthologies are important (and *This Bridge We Call Home* is one such anthology), but we must continue to complicate the anthology projects to become much more radically inclusive.

Working and critically engaged in the scholarship and investigating the intersections of race,

class, sexuality, and post/coloniality, one learns that this type of scholarship exposes the commonalities and differences of each of these social constructions. This is especially true if one looks at the intersections through different racial lenses, sexual practices, and post/colonial experiences. Many new works have been published that push us to see the intersections in new ways. For example, the subtitle of *Strange Affinities* is worth paying attention to: *The Gender and Sexual Politics of Comparative Racialization*. Such a text as this is cutting-edge because its essays explore the production of racialized, gendered, and sexualized difference, and also includes the possibilities for progressive coalitions, or "strange affinities." The text helps one to imagine "alternative identifications," "undisciplined knowledges," and "unincorporated territories, interrupted times."

The authors of this chapter belong to the generation that has challenged and pushed against the boundary of the white canon and white scholarship. As a result, we see a new wave of scholarship on the horizon, and while horizons are not attainable, these authors believe that we can participate in this critically engaging work and achieve a new horizon of liberative scholarship. As such, we believe that this new wave that is reaching forward toward the liberative horizon radically interrogates assumptions about race, gender, sexuality, culture, national citizenship,

---

CASE STUDY 10.2

There are varying types of violence relative to women. Within so-called first-world countries, domestic violence is typical of violence commonly associated with women. However, several other kinds of violence associated with women exist, particularly for women of color. In many countries, women are victims of traditional practices that violate their human rights. The persistence of physically and psychologically harmful customs can be attributed to deeply rooted practices within the tradition and culture of societies. For example, in the two-thirds world, female genital mutilation, son preference, dowry-related violence, and early marriage are examples of violence against women. The statistics for female genital mutilation, according to the World

Health Organization, ranges from 85 to 115 million girls and women who have undergone some form of female genital mutilation and suffer from its adverse health effects. Every year an estimated 2 million young girls undergo this procedure. Most live in Africa and Asia, but an increasing number can be found among immigrant and refugee families in Western Europe and North America, even though the practice has been outlawed in some European countries.

Son preference affects women in many countries, particularly in Asia. Its consequences can range from fetal or female infanticide to neglect of the girl child over her brother in terms of such essentials as nutrition, basic health care, and education. In China and India, some women choose to terminate their pregnancies if they are expecting daughters but carry their pregnancies to term when expecting sons. According to reports from India, genetic testing for sex selection has become a booming business, especially in the country's northern regions. Indian gender-detection clinics drew protests from women's groups after the appearance of advertisements suggesting that it was better to spend $38 now to terminate a female fetus than $3,800 later on her dowry. A study of amniocentesis procedures conducted in a large Bombay hospital found that 95.5 percent of fetuses identified as female were aborted compared with a far smaller percentage of male fetuses.

Other forms of violence relative to women include rape, sexual assault within marriage, sexual harassment, prostitution, and trafficking. Violence within migrant communities commonly consists of pornography. Female migrant workers typically leave their countries for better living conditions and better pay; however, the real benefactors are the host countries and the countries of origin. For countries of origin, money sent home by migrant workers is an important source of hard currency, while host countries are able to find workers for low-paying jobs that might otherwise go unfilled. Meanwhile, migrant workers fare badly, and at times tragically. Many become virtual slaves, subject to abuse and rape by their employers. Even women who are migrating along migrant trails are subject to violence, including rape.

In the Middle East and Persian Gulf region, there are an estimated 1.2 million women, mainly Asians, who are employed as domestic servants. According to the independent human rights group Middle East Watch, female migrant workers in Kuwait often suffer beatings and sexual assaults at the hands of their employers.

The police are often of little help. In many cases, women who report being raped by their employers are sent back to the employer or, in some cases, are assaulted at the police station. Working conditions are often so appalling that employers prevent women from escaping by seizing their passports or identity papers. How does the violence against women's bodies make women invisible in today's word? Is privileging male children violence to women's bodies, or is this type of preference a way of sustaining patriarchy? And if the latter, how is this a violence to women? How might an ethics that privileges women help in reducing violence against women's bodies?

Fig. 10.2. Knives used for female genital mutilation in East Africa.

BOX 10.4

Asian and Asian American Women's Theological Ethics

In the late 1970s and early 1980s, Asian and Asian American women began organizing grassroots networks to publish theological writings and meeting at conferences to discuss the many and varied experiences of their lives through a theological lens. Many women use these meetings and writings to discuss the Bible in relation to their faith. Others use the new intellectual camaraderie to examine shared and unshared social issues affecting their lives in different parts of Asia and as Asian women in America. By adding a transnational focus to the discourse and illustrating their diverse experiences, these women challenged the fixed boundaries of nation and homogeneity of culture often reflected in Asian religious discourses. Asian feminist theology has a primary commitment to the history of struggle within the parameters of migration, nationalism, and religious commitments. To that end, Asian feminist theology initially began as a theological project of learning to be human again and reorienting themselves toward the sun. This is identified as the struggle to be the sun and is, comparatively, a statement of Asian feminists' work to know that they are made in the image of God. This ethical enterprise cuts across the transnational foci of their theologies.

global sovereignty, and global futures. Critically engaged in the politics and struggles, we find that this is brilliant and groundbreaking scholarship. As such, many argue that these new works stretch our static concepts and methods, introduce us all to the new vocabularies of globalized unconscious and fragmentation of sovereignties, and investigate the connection between violence and social formations of difference. New trends are seeking to theorize the nation and the global south in ways much more sophisticated than what our previous generation of brothers and sisters have done.

Study Questions

1. In your own words, how would you define "women of color"? With which framework does your definition seem to connect (identity category vs. political function)? Has this changed after reading this chapter? How might using a different definition make a difference in terms of how you understand issues of oppression and injustice?

2. What basic assumptions or worldviews make WoC ethics distinctive? What sorts of methods have various women of color used to think and act morally?

3. What sorts of tools are needed to engage in praxis (reflection and action)? What, if any, significant barriers are there to implementing WoC ethics? What kinds of activism and political perspectives could help change these barriers?

4. In what ways is WoC ethics similar to other kinds of liberative ethics? In what ways is it different?

5. As you consider oppression and injustice in your own life (including your experiences within your family, community, and religious institutions), how can WoC ethics help? How could you draw on this form of liberative ethics as a source?

Suggested Readings

Aquino, María Pilar. *Our Cry for Life: Feminist Theology from Latin America*. Maryknoll, NY: Orbis, 1993.

Cannon, Katie G. *Black Womanist Ethics*. Atlanta: Scholars, 1988.

Cannon, Katie G., Emilie M. Townes, and Angela D. Sims, eds. *Womanist Theological Ethics: A Reader*. Louisville: Westminster John Knox, 2011.

Chung, Hyun Kyung. *Struggle to Be the Sun Again: Introducing Asian Women's Theology*. Maryknoll, NY: Orbis, 1990.

hooks, bell. *Talking Back: Thinking Feminist, Thinking Black*. Cambridge, MA: South End, 1989.

Isasí-Díaz, Ada María. *En La Lucha/In the Struggle: Elaborating a Mujerista Theology*. Minneapolis: Fortress Press, 1993.

———. *La Lucha Continues: Mujerista Theology*. Maryknoll, NY: Orbis, 2004.

Kwok Pui-Lan. *Introducing Asian Feminist Theology*. Sheffield: Sheffield Academic, 2000.

———. *Postcolonial Imagination and Feminist Theology*. Louisville: Westminster John Knox, 2005.

Lewis, Nantawan B., et al., eds. *Sisters Struggling in the Spirit: A Women of Color Theological Anthology*. Louisville: Women's Ministries Program, Presbyterian Church USA, 1994.

Mananzan, Mary John, et al., eds. *Women Resisting Violence: Spirituality for Life*. Maryknoll, NY: Orbis, 1996.

Mohanty, Chandra Talpade. "Under Western Eyes: Feminist Scholarship and Colonial Discourses." In *Third World Women and the Politics of Feminism*, edited by Chandra Talpade Mohanty, 51–81. Bloomington: Indiana University Press, 1991.

Moraga, Cherríe, and Gloria Anzaldúa, eds. *This Bridge Called My Back: Writings by Radical Women of Color*. New York: Kitchen Table, Women of Color Press, 1983.

Oduyoye, Mercy Amba, ed. *The Will to Arise: Women, Tradition, and the Church in Africa*. Maryknoll, NY: Orbis, 1992.

Russell, Letty M., et al., eds. *Inheriting Our Mothers' Gardens: Feminist Theology in Third World Perspective*. Philadelphia: Westminster, 1988.

Trinh, T. Minh-ha. *Women, Native, Other: Writing Postcoloniality and Feminism*. Bloomington: Indiana University Press, 1989.

Williams, Delores. *Sisters in the Wilderness: The Challenge of Womanist God-Talk*. Maryknoll, NY: Orbis, 1993.

11

Lesbian, Gay, Bisexual, and Transgender Liberative Ethics

Patrick S. Cheng

WHAT IS "RIGHT" OR "good" for lesbians, gay men, bisexual, and transgender ("LGBT" or "queer") people? That is the central question that an LGBT liberative ethics tries to address. This chapter will focus on what LGBT ethicists have said about what is "right" or "good" with respect to LGBT communities. This approach to LGBT ethics is liberative because it focuses on the ethical reflection of LGBT people themselves, as opposed to ethical reflection that is imposed on them by non-LGBT people. In other words, this approach lifts up the

> ### KEY TERM 11.3
>
> *LGBT*. Acronym for lesbian, gay, bisexual, and transgender; umbrella term for individuals who engage in same-sex acts and/or gender-variant behaviors.

voices of the very people who are on the margins of power and privilege with respect to their sexualities and gender identities and expressions.

LGBT people differ from many of the other marginalized communities covered in this textbook because they often experience Christianity and the institutional church as the primary *source* of oppression and suffering. That is, instead of being a source of liberation and freedom (as in the case with many liberative theologies), Christianity and the institutional church are often experienced by LGBT people as being complicit with the very oppression that needs to be overturned and eradicated. For example, Christians are often the most vociferous opponents of LGBT nondiscrimination laws as well as marriage equality laws.

> ### KEY TERM 11.1
>
> *Gay*. A man who is sexually attracted to other men; may also be used sometimes to describe lesbians.

> ### KEY TERM 11.2
>
> *Lesbian*. A woman who is sexually attracted to other women.

KEY TERM 11.4

Queer. Umbrella term for LGBT people; also refers to an ethical norm of transgression and/or deconstructing false binaries such as female and male or homosexual and heterosexual.

KEY TERM 11.5

Transgender. A person who identifies with a gender that differs from that person's assigned sex at birth.

Nevertheless, for nearly half a century—since at least the mid-1950s—LGBT Christian scholars and their allies have argued that Christianity is not intrinsically opposed to same-sex and gender-variant behaviors. Indeed, many of these scholars have articulated theological and ethical positions from the perspective of LGBT people. Accordingly, this chapter will trace the highlights of what these scholars have said about LGBT ethics and will examine the various ethical norms upon which LGBT people have relied to determine what is "right" and "good."

History and Development of LGBT Liberative Ethics

Although same-sex and gender-variant behaviors have existed in societies and cultures around

KEY TERM 11.6

Allies. Individuals who are supportive of LGBT people but who do not identify themselves as LGBT.

the world for thousands of years, it has only been since the mid-1950s that LGBT Christian scholars and their allies have engaged in sustained ethical reflection on such behaviors. During the course of the last half century, such ethicists have articulated at least four strands of LGBT ethics: (1) affirmation ethics, (2) liberation ethics, (3) mutuality ethics, and (4) queer ethics. This section will provide a brief overview of each of these four strands.

The first strand of LGBT ethical reflection, "affirmation ethics," is based on the ethical norm that "gay is good." This strand of ethical reflection is a direct response to the traditional Christian condemnation of same-sex and gender-variant behavior as sinful and deserving of divine punishment. The traditional condemnation of such behavior is based primarily on two sources: the Bible and the natural law. Since the 1950s, LGBT people have engaged in LGBT affirmation ethics by refuting biblical as well as natural law arguments that condemn LGBT people. Specifically, the adherents of affirmation ethics make the argument that a careful reading of the Bible and a careful examination of the natural law should result in the conclusion that same-sex and gender-variant behaviors are morally neutral if not intrinsically good.

The second strand of LGBT ethical reflection, "liberation ethics," is based on the ethical norm that LGBT people must be liberated from political, religious, and other forms of oppression. This strand of ethical reflection arises out of the contextual theologies of the 1960s and 1970s, which include Latin American liberation theology and black liberation theology. A key moment of liberation for the LGBT community in the United States was the Stonewall Riots of June 1969, during which LGBT people fought back against a routine police raid on a New York City bar, the Stonewall Inn, and ignited the contemporary LGBT civil rights movement. Like the ancient Israelites who were led by God out of the slavery of Egypt to the promised land, LGBT people similarly are called

Fig. 11.1. Photo of the Stonewall Inn on Christopher Street in Greenwich Village,
site of the Stonewall Riots of 1969.

by God to throw off the shackles of homophobia and heterosexism.

The third strand of LGBT ethical reflection, "mutuality ethics," is based on the ethical norm of mutuality or right relationship. This strand of ethical reflection is influenced heavily by the feminist theologies of the 1980s and 1990s. Instead of understanding relationships as hierarchical—that is, one person's having power "over" another person—an ethics of mutuality focuses on the need for equal power between the two persons. In rejecting hierarchical power structures such as patriarchy (that is, the worldview that men are intrinsically superior to women), an ethics of mutuality calls LGBT people to exhibit mutuality and justice in all of their relationships, sexual or otherwise.

The fourth strand of LGBT ethical reflection, "queer ethics," is based on the ethical norms of transgression and resistance to binary thinking. This strand of ethical reflection is influenced heavily by the rise of queer theory in the academy during the 1990s and 2000s. Queer theory challenges a binary view of the world with respect to gender identity, biological sex, and sexuality. For example, instead of understanding gender identity as consisting of only two choices (that is, masculine or feminine), queer theory deconstructs that binary and introduces a third concept: "transgender." Similarly, in order to challenge the biological sex binary of male and female, queer theory recognizes a third condition, "intersex" (or "disorders of sexual development"—DSD). Finally, in order to challenge the sexual binary of heterosexuality and homosexuality, queer theory recognizes the third concept of "bisexual." Queer ethics, like queer theory, is also based on the ethical norms of transgressing categories and deconstructing false binaries of gender, sex, and sexuality.

As noted above, human beings have engaged in same-sex acts and gender-variant behaviors from the beginning of recorded time and in cultures around the world. The earliest known depiction of a same-sex couple, from 2400 BCE, depicts two royal manicurists in ancient Egypt who were buried together in the same tomb. The late Yale University historian John Boswell uncovered evidence of Christian liturgical rites for same-sex couples during the Middle Ages and documented such

KEY TERM 11.7

Bisexual. A person who is sexually attracted to both women and men.

KEY TERM 11.8

DSD. Acronym for disorders of sex development, a term frequently used by intersex people to describe themselves.

KEY TERM 11.9

Intersex. A person who has physical characteristics, genital and/or chromosomal, of both the male and female sexes.

KEY TERM 11.10

Polyamory. A person who has more than one sexual relationship at the same time with the consent of all involved.

BOX 11.1

Harvey Milk

Harvey Bernard Milk (1930–1978) was a member of the San Francisco board of supervisors and the first openly gay man to be elected to public office in the United States as a nonincumbent. Milk was born and raised in New York and served in the US Navy. Following his honorable discharge, Milk worked as an insurance actuary before moving to San Francisco and opening a camera store in the Castro neighborhood. Beginning in 1973, Milk took a leadership role in the neighborhood and was known as the "mayor of Castro Street." In 1977, Milk was elected to the San Francisco board of supervisors. As a result of receiving death threats, he tape recorded a message saying that "if a bullet should enter my brain, let that bullet destroy every closet door." On November 10, 1978, Milk and Mayor George Moscone were assassinated by former supervisor Dan White. In 2009, Milk was posthumously awarded the Presidential Medal of Freedom for his contributions to the LGBT rights movement.

rites in his book *Same-Sex Unions in Premodern Europe.* There was even a flourishing culture of same-sex and gender-variant activity in the United States during the 1920s among African Americans during the Harlem Renaissance.

Nevertheless, it was not until the mid-1950s that Christian scholars began to examine and challenge the classical Christian ethical tradition that uniformly condemned same-sex and gender-variant behaviors as sinful and counter to the will of God. This section will trace the genealogy, or historical development, of the four strands of LGBT

Fig. 11.2. Niankhkhnum and Khnumhotep, two royal Egyptian manicurists buried together (c. 2400 BCE), are depicted embracing one another in this scene from their joint mastaba (tomb).

liberative ethics since the 1950s. Although these four strands—affirmation ethics, liberation ethics, mutuality ethics, and queer ethics—emerged in roughly chronological order over the course of the last half century, they are not intended to be mutually exclusive categories or to denote rigid time periods. Rather, these strands should be understood as models for classifying the different types of ethical reflection in which LGBT people engage today.

Affirmation ethics emerged in the mid-1950s, when Christian scholars began to question the traditional view that homosexuality was always sinful and intrinsically evil. In 1955, the Anglican priest Derrick Sherwin Bailey published his groundbreaking work *Homosexuality and the Western Christian Tradition.* Bailey's book argued that the church's antihomosexual views were actually *not* supported by a careful reading of the relevant biblical, historical, and theological texts. Bailey's work helped to lay the groundwork for a new ethical norm that "gay is good." This new affirming perspective was reflected in 1964 by the founding of the Council on Religion and the Homosexual (CRH) in San Francisco. The founding of the CRH was a significant event because, for the first time, it brought together leaders in both the religious and the homosexual communities who sought to find common ground with each other. In 1976 the Roman Catholic priest John J. McNeill published *The Church and the Homosexual*, which included a chapter about moral theology and the "positive contribution of the homosexual community." McNeill, a member of the Jesuit order, was silenced by the Vatican for his book, and he was subsequently expelled from his order in 1987, when he refused to cease his public ministry with LGBT people.

Liberation ethics emerged in the late 1960s and 1970s, when LGBT Christian scholars were influenced by the emergence of Latin American, black, and other liberation theologies. These theologies focused on the exodus narrative and the Israelite journey out of Egypt as metaphors for political and social freedom for oppressed groups. LGBT Christian scholars were also influenced by the birth of the contemporary gay rights movement following the Stonewall Riots of June 1969. These events give rise to a new ethical norm of liberation that focused on freedom from the political and social oppression of gay and lesbian people. For example, in 1974, Sally Gearhart and William R. Johnson edited the anthology *Loving Women, Loving Men: Gay Liberation and the Church.* The anthology included an essay titled "The Good News of Gay Liberation," and it called for gays and lesbians, just like other oppressed minority groups, to revolt against all forms of discrimination, injustice, and violation of dignity.

Mutuality ethics emerged in the 1980s and 1990s, when LGBT Christian scholars were deeply influenced by feminist theologies of mutuality. These theologies of mutuality emphasized the importance of maintaining relationships of equal power between individuals, as opposed to the hierarchical nature of patriarchal relationships. Such theologies gave rise to a new ethical norm of mutuality. A key work in this area was Carter Heyward's 1989 book, *Touching Our Strength: The Erotic as Power and the Love of God*. Heyward, one of the first women to be ordained to the Episcopal priesthood and currently a professor emerita at the Episcopal Divinity School, drew upon Audre Lorde's notion of the erotic as an embodied yearning for mutuality and making deep connections between people. Heyward argued that God is found in the sacred power of the erotic, as well as in mutuality and friendship. For Heyward, God is not above us but rather in between us.

Finally, queer ethics emerged in the 1990s and 2000s. This strand of LGBT liberative ethics was strongly influenced by the rise of queer theory in the academy, which gave rise to a new ethical norm of transgression. One influential book on queer ethics was Michael Warner's 1999 book, *The Trouble with Normal: Sex, Politics, and the Ethics of Queer Life*. In that book, Warner—a professor of English at Rutgers University—defines an ethic of queerness as maintaining dignity in the face of shame. That is, Warner calls on LGBT people affirmatively to embrace "queer" behaviors that would normally invoke sexual stigma or shame. Queer ethics was also influenced by activism in the LGBT community. Starting in the late 1980s, radical queer activist groups such as ACT-UP and Queer Nation challenged societal apathy with respect to LGBT issues (such as HIV/AIDS) by disrupting, or transgressing, the status quo. For example, ACT-UP created a great controversy by disrupting Mass at St. Patrick's Cathedral in New York City in December 1989. Queer ethical reflection by LGBT people continues to this day.

BOX 11.2

Audre Lorde

Audre Lorde (1934–1992) was a lesbian Caribbean American author and activist. She often described herself to her audiences as a "Black, Lesbian, Mother, Warrior, Poet." Born in New York City, Lorde received a master's degree in library science from Columbia University. In the 1960s, Lorde published a number of poems and was involved in the civil rights and antiwar movements. Lorde later challenged white feminists for failing to confront their own racism and failing to acknowledge the experiences of black women. For example, Lorde wrote an open letter that sharply criticized the radical lesbian feminist philosopher Mary Daly but never received a reply. Lorde published many books, including *Zami: A New Spelling of My Name* (1983) and *Sister Outsider: Essays and Speeches* (1984). Lorde died in 1992 after fighting breast cancer and liver cancer for fourteen years. Her memory lives on through many groups, including the Audre Lorde Project, a New York City community-based organization for queer people of color.

Need for Liberation

As noted above, liberative ethics is defined as an ethic written from the perspective of those individuals who are on the margins of power and privilege. Thus LGBT liberative ethics is written from the perspective of LGBT people and *not* heterosexual individuals or cisgender (that is, non-transgender) individuals. Because LGBT liberative ethics focuses on marginalized people, it is by definition committed to overturning structures of oppression that affect such people. Such an ethical approach is also committed to raising certain issues and questions relating to the liberation of such people.

Affirmation ethics, the first strand of LGBT liberative ethics, is committed to liberating LGBT people from oppressive readings of the Bible as well as oppressive uses of the natural law. For example, an affirmation ethics would be opposed to bibliolatry, or a fundamentalist reading of the Bible that refuses to take into account either the social context of the ancient Near East or the social context of today.

For example, an affirmation ethics would reject oppressive readings of the Bible that

Fig. 11.3. AIDS quilt spread out in front of city hall during Taiwan Pride 2005.

condemn LGBT people simply on the basis of biblical proof-texting (for example, the traditional LGBT "clobber texts" of Gen. 19, Lev. 18:22 and 20:13, Rom. 1:26-27, 1 Cor. 6:9, and 1 Tim. 1:10). Although a close examination of such "clobber text" passages has been discussed extensively elsewhere, an affirmation ethics would contend that these passages were not addressing the loving same-sex relationships of today, but rather issues of male rape, sexual exploitation, and maintaining sexual patriarchy (for example, rejecting same-sex acts that blur the distinction between the "masculine" penetrator and the "feminine" penetrated).

An affirmation ethics also would be opposed to an oppressive or dishonest use of the natural law. For example, even though natural law adherents claim that natural law principles are based on observing the created world, these individuals ignore the fact that there are hundreds of species of animals, birds, and insects in the animal kingdom that engage in same-sex and gender-variant behaviors. In sum, an affirmation ethics would conclude that same-sex and gender-variant behaviors do not violate the natural law.

Liberation ethics, the second strand of LGBT liberative ethics, is committed to liberating LGBT people from political and religious oppression. In a number of countries around the world, same-sex acts are punishable by the death penalty. Even in the United States, where same-sex acts are no longer subject to criminal penalties, there is a need for LGBT people to be liberated from oppression. For example, a liberation ethics would be committed to the passage of federal and state laws that prohibit discrimination on the basis of sexual orientation and gender identity in employment, housing, public accommodations, and other matters. An ethics of liberation would also be committed to ensuring that LGBT people have equal access to civil marriage and the numerous rights and privileges—both federal and state—that come with civil marriage.

Mutuality ethics, the third strand of LGBT liberative ethics, is committed to liberating LGBT people from patriarchy, which is an ideology that perpetuates the view that men are intrinsically superior to women. Patriarchy is based on a hierarchical view of power; that is, men are naturally "above" women in the created order. This hierarchical view of gender roles is reinforced by the household codes in the New Testament (for example, Col. 3:18—4:1 and Eph. 5:29—6:1) that analogize the husband-wife relationship to that of a master-slave relationship. As LGBT scholars have noted, homophobia and transphobia are grounded in patriarchy. That is, what is particularly threatening about same-sex and gender-nonconforming behavior is that it reverses or blurs the "natural" order of men over women. Mutuality ethics, by contrast, would reject the entire framework of disparity in power between men and women. It would seek to establish an ethical norm of mutuality or right relationships between women and men—and, in fact, between all relationships.

Queer ethics, the fourth strand of LGBT liberative ethics, is committed to liberating LGBT people from shame as well as from false binary thinking. For example, a queer ethics refuses to accept the toxic shame that traditionally surrounds nonreproductive sex acts. Christian theology has traditionally stigmatized such acts because they are grounded purely in pleasure and are not justified by the "good" of procreation. A queer ethics would challenge this erotophobic view and seek to reclaim the goodness of embodied pleasure in its many forms. A queer ethics is also about challenging false binaries that divide the world into dualistic categories (for example, masculine and feminine, male and female, and homosexual and heterosexual). Such an ethics would open up a third space between such categories and embrace transgender, intersex, and bisexual identities.

In addition to being committed to overturning structures of oppression, an LGBT liberative ethic raises a number of larger issues and questions. Not surprisingly, each of the four strands of the LGBT liberative ethics discussed above focus on slightly different issues.

For example, affirmation ethics raises the question of how to read biblical texts that on their face seem to condemn same-sex and gender-variant behaviors. That is, to what extent should scholarly discoveries about the broader social context of such behaviors in the ancient Near East—and how they differ from our own context today—influence such readings? Such an approach also raises the question of how to apply natural law principles to such behaviors. That is, to what extent should scientific discoveries about the natural world—including the existence of same-sex and gender-variant behavior in the animal

BOX 11.3

Christine Jorgensen

Christine Jorgensen (1926–1989) was a leading spokesperson for the rights of transgender people and the first person to achieve international fame for undergoing sex reassignment surgery. Jorgensen was born in New York City as George William Jorgensen. Jorgensen served in the US Army and later trained to be a medical and dental assistant. In the early 1950s, Jorgensen traveled to Europe to seek sex reassignment surgery. While in Copenhagen, she underwent a series of surgeries and transitioned to being a woman. In December 1952, when she was still in Europe, the *New York Daily News* ran a front-page story about her. She became a celebrity upon her return to the United States, in 1953. In 1970, a film, *The Christine Jorgensen Story*, was made about her life story. She toured college campuses in the 1970s and 1980s to speak about her experiences, and she also worked as an actress, singer, and nightclub performer. Jorgensen died in 1989.

kingdom—influence interpretations of natural law principles?

By contrast, liberation ethics raises the question of what kind of political, religious, and other forms of oppression face the LGBT community and how best to liberate the LGBT community from such oppressions. As noted above, one unique question faced by the LGBT community is the role of Christianity and churches in contributing to such oppression. Unlike many of the other marginalized groups discussed in this book, LGBT people often experience a great deal of discrimination and rejection from the institutional church. What would it mean, therefore, to use liberation ethics to critique particular aspects of the church that are oppressive to LGBT people?

Mutuality ethics raises the question of how to define ideal relationships, sexual or otherwise. What does it mean to live out an ethics of mutuality in the context of same-sex relationships? What would it mean if friendship—and not marriage—were the central relationship for LGBT people? Would that change the way LGBT people relate to each other? Does mutuality always mean monogamy, or can an ethics of mutuality accommodate other forms of relational configurations such as consensual open relationships? What does an ethics of mutuality have to say about safer sex practices and barebacking? What about alternative sexual practices such as bondage, discipline, and sadomasochism (BDSM)?

Finally, a queer ethics raises the question of how to preserve marginal or transgressive norms as a positive value for the LGBT community. To what extent does an ethics of queerness privilege BDSM, kink, or leathersex over "vanilla" sex? To what extent should such a queer ethics seek to preserve marginal sexual practices such as sex clubs and public cruising areas? To what extent should an ethics of queerness—to the extent

KEY TERM 11.11

Barebacking. The practice of two men having unprotected anal sex (that is, without using condoms).

KEY TERM 11.12

BDSM. Acronym for bondage, discipline, and sadomasochism; sexual practices relating to consensual role play involving power and pain.

that it is committed to deconstructing binaries—ensure nondiscrimination with respect to transgender and intersex folk who fall outside of the conventional gender and sex binary system? To what extent should an ethics of queerness challenge the invisibility faced by bisexual people?

Leading Scholars and Figures

Having covered the ways in which the four strands of LGBT liberative ethics seeks to liberate LGBT people from structures of oppression, this chapter now turns to the work of leading scholars in LGBT liberative ethics. There is an increasing number of scholars who are writing in the field of LGBT liberative ethics. This section will first highlight the work of leading scholars in each of the four strands and will then explore possible future trends, with a particular focus on intersectional ethics, which addresses the connections between sexuality and race.

Affirmation Ethics

One leading scholar with respect to LGBT affirmation ethics is William Countryman. Countryman, who is an Episcopal priest and a professor emeritus at the Church Divinity School of the Pacific, is the author of the 1988 book *Dirt, Greed, and Sex: Sexual Ethics in the New Testament and Their Implications for Today*. In that book, Countryman argues that New Testament sexual ethics—including sexual ethics relating to LGBT people—must be understood in the context of the purity laws and property laws of Jesus' day. Countryman concludes that, in light of such purity and property laws, the Bible should *not* be used to condemn LGBT people. For example, Countryman argues that Jesus' extensive intersections with unclean people in the New Testament releases Christians from the traditional purity codes of the Hebrew Bible, including the prohibitions of Leviticus 18:22 and 20:13. However, the one purity ethic that does remain, according to Countryman, is one's purity of heart with respect to hatred.

LIBERATIVE ETHICS IN ACTION 11.1

Liberative Ethics in Action: The Issue of Same-Sex Marriage

As of August 2012, six states (Connecticut, Iowa, Massachusetts, New Hampshire, New York, and Vermont) and the District of Columbia have legalized same-sex marriage. However, these jurisdictions are the exception and not the rule. Numerous states have passed legislation and/or constitutional amendments that expressly prohibit same-sex marriage. Furthermore, Congress has prohibited the United States federal government from recognizing same-sex marriages under the Defense of Marriage Act, which was enacted in 1996. As a result, same-sex couples who are legally married under state law are denied over one thousand rights that are otherwise available to opposite-sex couples under federal law. From the perspective of LGBT liberative ethics, same-sex couples should have the right to marry and to receive the same legal rights as opposite-sex couples. This is especially true with respect to the strands of affirmation ethics, liberation ethics, and mutuality ethics. Although the strand of queer ethics does not oppose same-sex marriage rights for LGBT people per se, it would caution against the unintentional creation of a new "norm" that would further marginalize LGBT people who engage in nonnormative sexual acts or are in nonnormative relationships.

Another leading scholar with respect to LGBT affirmation ethics is the late Gareth Moore. Moore, who was a Roman Catholic priest in the Dominican Order and a lecturer in theology at Oxford, published *A Question of Truth: Christianity and Homosexuality* in 2003. In that book, Moore questions the Roman Catholic Church's traditional reliance on natural law in order to reject same-sex and gender-variant acts. For Moore, the central question with respect to natural law analysis must be, Is it true? Thus he asks whether it is true that same-sex acts are always a moral evil. Are such acts always intrinsically disordered? In the absence of convincing evidence that same-sex and gender-variant acts are always intrinsically disordered (for example, within a loving same-sex relationship), Moore argues that the Roman Catholic Church should not use natural law to condemn LGBT people.

Liberation Ethics

A leading scholar with respect to LGBT liberation ethics is Robert Goss. Goss, an ordained minister with the Metropolitan Community Church and a prolific queer theologian, published *Jesus Acted Up: A Gay and Lesbian Manifesto* in 1993 as a response to the institutional church's shocking apathy and indifference with respect to LGBT people as well as the HIV/AIDS crisis. For Goss, LGBT liberation ethics is found in a *basileia* (that is, kingdom) ethics that ushers in the reign of God. Goss argues that such a *basileia* ethics requires LGBT people to be constantly engaged in the struggle for sexual justice. This includes challenging those ecclesial institutions that, through their teachings, perpetuate homophobia and violence against LGBT people. For Goss, the heart of LGBT liberation is freedom from such oppression.

Another leading scholar with respect to LGBT liberation ethics is the late Robert Williams. Williams was one of the first openly gay priests ordained in the Episcopal Church, and he published *Just As I Am: A Practical Guide to Being Out, Proud, and Christian* in 1992, shortly before he died from complications of HIV/AIDS. In that book, Williams builds on the work of black and feminist liberation theologians in constructing his own LGBT liberation ethics. According to Williams, God is never neutral. Rather, God is always on the side of the oppressed, as demonstrated by the exodus and the deliverance of the Israelites from slavery in Egypt. As a result, God is always on the side of LGBT people and against heterosexual privilege. Furthermore, this means that LGBT people must define their own ethical norms and not be bound by the ethical norms of non-LGBT people.

Mutuality Ethics

A leading scholar with respect to LGBT mutuality ethics is Mary E. Hunt. Hunt, the cofounder and codirector of the Women's Alliance for Theology,

---

CASE STUDY 11.2

St. Cecelia's Church, a Roman Catholic parish located in the South End of Boston, which is a predominantly gay neighborhood, planned to offer a Mass during LGBT Pride month that was advertised as welcoming all persons, regardless of sexual identity or gender identity. The archdiocese of Boston unilaterally canceled the Mass after it received complaints from conservative Roman Catholics who objected to the Mass on the grounds that same-sex and gender-variant behaviors are sinful. How would you respond to the archdiocese's actions from the perspective of each of the four strands of LGBT liberative ethics?

Ethics, and Ritual (WATER), is the author of the 1991 book *Fierce Tenderness: A Feminist Theology of Friendship*. According to Hunt, friendship—and not marriage—should be the ethical norm for all relationships, including LGBT relationships. Hunt builds on feminist notions of right relationship to create an ethic of justice-seeking friendship. By doing so, Hunt decenters marriage as the primary ethical norm for relationships. This opens up the possibility of a much broader variety of relational configurations, including friendships with sexual components. Furthermore, Hunt's ethical norm of justice-seeking friendship applies not only to relationships between human beings but also to relationships with the entire created order.

Another leading scholar with respect to LGBT mutuality ethics is Marvin M. Ellison. Ellison, who is a professor at Bangor Theological Seminary, is the author of the 1996 book *Erotic Justice: A Liberating Ethic of Sexuality*. In that book, Ellison argues for a sexual ethic that refuses to eroticize power relationships of domination and submission (that is, patriarchal relationships). Instead, Ellison argues for a sexual ethic of erotic justice that eroticizes mutual respect and pleasure. For Ellison, such an ethic would transform sexuality into a power that affects our everyday lives as human beings. Ellison also coedited, along with Kelly Brown Douglas, the second edition of the *Sexuality and Sacred: Sources for Theological Reflection* anthology, which was published in 2010 and contains a number of provocative essays about contemporary LGBT sexual ethics. Ellison's newest book on sexual ethics, published in 2012, is *Making Love Just: Sexual Ethics for Perplexing Times*.

Queer Ethics

A leading scholar with respect to LGBT queer ethics is Kathy Rudy. Rudy, a professor of women's studies and ethics at Duke University, is the author of the 1997 book *Sex and the Church:*

Gender, Homosexuality, and the Transformation of Christian Ethics. In that book, Rudy proposes a queer ethical norm of hospitality, which is a reversal of the sin of inhospitality that God condemned by destroying Sodom and Gomorrah. (That is, the men of Sodom exhibited the sin of extreme inhospitality by trying to rape the angelic visitors who were staying as guests at Lot's home.) Under Rudy's ethic of hospitality, sexual acts that would normally be shamed or condemned—such as anonymous or public sex—could be affirmed as long as such acts exhibited hospitality toward the other partner or partners. Similarly, the fact that a sexual act occurs within the context of a marriage or a long-term relationship does not necessarily mean that it is hospitable. According to Rudy, the relational quality of the sexual encounter—as "queer" as it might be—is what matters, not the form.

Another leading scholar with respect to LGBT queer ethics is W. Scott Haldeman. Haldeman, a professor of worship at Chicago Theological Seminary, has written about rethinking fidelity in the context of queer relationships. In his essay "A Queer Fidelity: Reinventing Christian Marriage," which appears in the second edition of *Sexuality and the Sacred*, Haldeman argues for moving away from an ethics of exclusivity and toward an ethics of self-care and truth-telling. For Haldeman, an ethics of self-care and truth-telling would take responsibility for one's own desires and permit safe, consensual, and nonexploitative sexual encounters with third parties outside of marriage, especially if one spouse has more need for physical intimacy than the other.

Other queer ethicists, including Michael Warner—the English professor at Rutgers University—would go much further than both Rudy and Haldeman in terms of constructing an LGBT queer ethics. As noted above, Warner proposes an ethics of maintaining dignity in the face of shame. That is, Warner would embrace behaviors that are normally seen as transgressive and shameful, including nonvanilla sex acts such as BDSM, kink, and fetishes. Not surprisingly, Warner is critical of the single-minded focus by the LGBT community on legalizing same-sex marriage and obtaining marriage equality. For Warner, such a focus is ultimately problematic because it creates a new definition of "normal" that will further stigmatize a large part of the LGBT community that engages in nonnormative sexual acts.

Possible Future Trends

One possible future trend in the area of LGBT liberative ethics is that of intersectional ethics. Intersectional ethics relates to situations in which a person is a member of intersecting oppressed groups (for example, to be both a queer person *and* a person of color). Thelathia Nikki Young, a recent graduate of the doctoral program at the Candler School of Theology at Emory University, has proposed a black queer ethics (BQE) that critiques traditional African American views of family and that also provides a more nuanced view of love and justice. According to Young, the BQE approach would lift up and privilege black queer voices and experiences, as well as bridge the existing gaps between womanist, feminist, and queer ethics.

In recent years, there has been an increase in religious and theological scholarship about intersectional issues involving LGBT people. For example, Roger Sneed, a professor at Furman University, recently published the 2010 book *Representations of Homosexuality: Black Liberation Theology and Cultural Criticism*, which addresses intersectional issues with respect to race, sexuality, and religion within the African American community. Similarly, Patrick S. Cheng, a professor at the Episcopal Divinity School, has published

---

BOX 11.4

Gloria Anzaldúa

Gloria Evangelina Anzaldúa (1942–2004) was an author, activist, and leading independent scholar of chicana and queer studies. Anzaldúa grew up on the Texas-Mexico border, and she coined the term *new mestiza* in her writings to describe a person who uses her multiple identities to challenge a binary, or either-or, view of the world. She also wrote many of her works in "Spanglish," a mixture of several Spanish and English dialects, in order to reflect her borderlands identity and complex linguistic background. Anzaldúa coedited *This Bridge Called My Back: Writings by Radical Women of Color* (1981) with Cherríe Moraga, and she wrote *Borderlands/La Frontera: The New Mestiza* (1987). She also wrote poetry and fiction, and her writings addressed various intersecting issues relating to race, sexuality, and spirituality. Consistent with her writings, Anzaldúa viewed herself as having multiple racial, sexual, and spiritual identities. Anzaldúa, who died in 2004, was posthumously awarded a PhD in literature from the University of California, Santa Cruz.

---

a number of works, including the 2011 essay "'I Am Yellow and Beautiful': Reflections on Queer Asian Spirituality and Gay Male Cyberculture," on intersectional issues with respect to the LGBT Asian American community. The work of Young, Sneed, and Cheng points to a possible future role for intersectional ethics in LGBT liberative ethics.

Finally, another possible future trend in the area of LGBT liberative ethics is that of transgender

BOX 11.5

Kiyoshi Kuromiya

Kiyoshi Kuromiya (1943–2000) was a prominent gay Japanese American civil rights and antiwar activist. Born in an internment camp in Wyoming during World War II, Kuromiya was raised in a Los Angeles suburb and moved to Philadelphia for college. On July 4, 1965, he participated in one of the first public gay rights demonstrations, which took place in front of Independence Hall. Kuromiya was an assistant to Martin Luther King Jr., and he also served as an openly gay delegate to the 1969 Black Panther convention at Temple University. Kuromiya was a founder of the Gay Liberation Front in Philadelphia and was active with ACT-UP Philadelphia. He founded the Critical Path Project, which was one of the earliest sources of treatment information for people living with HIV/AIDS. Kuromiya was an advocate of free speech on the Internet and was a plaintiff in the successful lawsuit against the 1996 Communications Decency Act. He died in 2000 from complications relating to AIDS.

and intersex ethics. In recent years, there has been an increase in transgender and intersex theological reflections by individuals such as Justin Tanis, Virginia Mollenkott, and Susannah Cornwall. However, these reflections have been primarily theological in content. It will be interesting to see what develops in the future with respect to transgender and intersex ethics. One ethical issue for parents and doctors, for example, relates to postponing genital surgery on an intersex child until she or he is old enough to make a choice about such surgery.

In sum, a number of significant works about LGBT liberative ethics have been published since the mid-1950s, when Derrick Sherwin Bailey published his groundbreaking work *Homosexuality and the Western Christian Tradition* in 1955. Since then, a number of different strands relating to LGBT liberative ethics have arisen, including affirmation ethics, liberation ethics, mutuality ethics, and queer ethics. Each of these four strands poses slightly different questions, although all four arise out of the perspective of LGBT people. Some possible future trends in this area include intersectional ethics as well as transgender and intersex ethics.

CASE STUDY 11.3

In November 2011, the Massachusetts state legislature passed a bill that provided civil rights protections to transgender people with respect to employment, housing, education, and credit. It also amended the state's hate crimes laws to include gender identity. During a ten-month period during 2009 and 2010, a transgender advocacy group received nearly three hundred requests for help from transgender people who had experienced harassment or discrimination. As of June 2010, fifteen states and the District of Columbia included protections for gender identity and expression in their state laws. Numerous people testified both for and against the bill. How would you have assessed this legislation from the perspective of each of the four strands of LGBT liberative ethics?

Study Questions

1. Name and describe the four strands of LGBT liberative ethics and one or two scholars in each strand.
2. Which strand or strands of LGBT liberative ethics speak to you the most? The least? Why?
3. Describe some of the oppressive structures the LGBT community faces and how an LGBT liberative ethics addresses such structures.
4. How can allies of the LGBT community benefit from a knowledge of LGBT liberative ethics?
5. Name some possible future trends of LGBT liberative ethics.

Suggested Readings

Boswell, John. *Christianity, Social Tolerance, and Homosexuality: Gay People in Western Europe From the Beginning of the Christian Era to the Fourteenth Century*. Chicago: University of Chicago Press, 1980.

Cheng, Patrick S. *From Sin to Amazing Grace: Discovering the Queer Christ*. New York: Seabury, 2012.

———. *Radical Love: An Introduction to Queer Theology*. New York: Seabury, 2011.

Countryman, L. William. *Dirt, Greed, and Sex: Sexual Ethics in the New Testament and Their Implications for Today*. Rev. ed. Minneapolis: Fortress Press, 2007.

De La Torre, Miguel A. *A Lily Among the Thorns: Imagining a New Christian Sexuality*. San Francisco: Josey-Bass, 2007.

———. *Out of the Shadows into the Light: Christianity and Homosexuality*. St. Louis: Chalice, 2009.

Ellison, Marvin M. *Erotic Justice: A Liberating Ethic of Sexuality*. Louisville: Westminster John Knox, 1996.

———. *Making Love Just: Sexual Ethics for Perplexing Times*. Minneapolis: Fortress Press, 2012.

Ellison, Marvin M., and Kelly Brown Douglas. *Sexuality and the Sacred: Sources for Theological Reflection*. 2nd ed. Louisville: Westminster John Knox, 2010.

Goss, Robert. *Jesus Acted Up: A Gay and Lesbian Manifesto*. San Francisco: HarperSanFrancisco, 1993.

Hunt, Mary E. *Fierce Tenderness: A Feminist Theology of Friendship*. New York: Crossroad, 1994.

Jordan, Mark D. *The Ethics of Sex*. Oxford: Blackwell, 2002.

McNeill, John J. *The Church and the Homosexual*. 4th ed. Boston: Beacon, 1993.

Meem, Deborah T., Michelle A. Gibson, and Jonathan F. Alexander. *Finding Out: An Introduction to LGBT Studies*. Thousand Oaks, CA: SAGE, 2010.

Moore, Gareth. *A Question of Truth: Christianity and Homosexuality*. London: Continuum, 2003.

Nelson, James B., and Sandra P. Longfellow. *Sexuality and the Sacred: Sources for Theological Reflection*. Louisville: Westminster John Knox, 1994.

Rudy, Kathy. *Sex and the Church: Gender, Homosexuality, and the Transformation of Christian Ethics*. Boston: Beacon, 1997.

Sneed, Roger A. *Representations of Homosexuality: Black Liberation Theology and Cultural Criticism*. New York: Palgrave Macmillan, 2010.

Stryker, Susan. *Transgender History*. Berkeley: Seal, 2008.

Tanis, Justin. *Trans-Gendered: Theology, Ministry, and Communities of Faith*. Cleveland: Pilgrim, 2003.

Warner, Michael. *The Trouble with Normal: Sex, Politics, and the Ethics of Queer Life*. Cambridge: Harvard University Press, 1999.

Williams, Robert. *Just as I Am: A Practical Guide to Being Out, Proud and Christian*. New York: HarperPerennial, 1992.

12

Disability Liberative Ethics

Deborah Beth Creamer

THE FOUNDATION FOR DISABILITY ethics from a liberative perspective is the recognition that disability is not simply an experience of loss or of physical, intellectual, or emotional impairment. Rather, disability is a social and political experience at least as much as it is a personal one. To begin with, we observe that barriers of architecture and of attitude are just as significant as, if not more significant than, physical difference: what is "disabling" to someone is more often a flight of stairs, a tasteless joke, a denied job interview, or a violent crime than one's particular physical condition itself. In addition, a liberative perspective proposes that nondisability is not better or more desirable than disability, and, most importantly, that there is nothing wrong with being a person with a disability.

This perspective is somewhat counterintuitive for those who have been immersed in dominant narratives of nondisability and disability, where nondisability is defined as normal and good, and disability is defined as defective and bad. It is perhaps a sign of how entrenched these notions

are that many people struggle to even imagine that disability might itself be valuable or that, if given a choice, one might choose disability over nondisability. Disability advocates remind us here of similar attitudes from other positions of privilege—for example, of men who say that there is nothing wrong with women but that they would not want to be one, or of people who identify as heterosexual who say that there is nothing wrong with GLBTQ identity but yet are glad that their children are not queer. It is perhaps a sign of how new the liberative perspective on disability is that even most allies are unable to imagine disability as adding value to one's life.

KEY TERM 12.1

Stigma. A negative stereotype or devaluing that comes from the perception of difference. Disability carries stigma when it is understood as not just different but also as wrong.

Basic Tenets of Disability Liberative Ethics

Key to a liberative perspective on disability is recognition of the various definitions or models of disability that surround us. Four primary models can be identified, two of which are entrenched in dominant/oppressive narratives of disability and two which offer liberative possibilities. The first of these is known as the *moral model*, where one's ability status is observed to be either good or bad. Disability is understood as a curse or a blessing, and the person with a disability as either a sinner or a saint. Disability becomes weighted with a sense of being a punishment for sin, a test of faith, an opportunity for redemption, or a demonstration of God's power. Examples of this perspective are readily found in ancient times, including the Hebrew Bible and New Testament, but still creep in today when a person with a disability is automatically and stereotypically perceived as inspirational or pitiable, even before we know anything specific about the person other than the fact of his or her physical (or other) impairment. Whenever disability is interpreted with intrinsic moral weight, prior to any other source of information, the moral model of disability is at play.

Second is the *medical model*, where attention is focused strictly on what one can or cannot physically or functionally do. This model is closest to the commonsense idea that a disability is something one has when one's body or mind does not work properly. Labels such as "crippled," "handicapped," and "retarded" all stem from this model. Two interrelated assumptions constitute this model: first, that disability is primarily a medical or biological condition (something that is found in the body), and second, that disability means a difference from the ideal human body. Here, disability status is granted either by a medical professional or by a government agency, but reinforced by broader social understandings of what it means to be normal: if we did not have a shared understanding of "normal," the word "disability" would make no sense. The definition of disability used in the Americans with Disabilities Act comes directly from the medical model.

A liberative perspective appears within the context of the *social model*, also known as the minority or political model. Here we observe that people with disabilities make up a distinct minority group, where members share particular experiences of discrimination and oppression. According to this model, individuals are considered disabled because of their experiences of prejudice and exclusion—the focus is no longer on physical impairment itself, but rather on the

KEY TERM 12.2

Normal. While this term ought to mean something like "common" or "unsurprising" (e.g., it is normal to experience disability), it more often implies a worldview based on an ideal and unachievable sense of what it means to be human, often overlapping with the idea of perfection.

KEY TERM 12.3

Impairment. Typically understood as an abnormality or loss of bodily form or function, but can also represent a different kind of barrier or obstacle such as a social or architectural one. Depending on one's perspective, an impairment could be equivalent to a medical diagnosis, such as paralysis, or it might be an entryway with a staircase but no ramp.

CASE STUDY 12.1

The case of Terri Schiavo gained significant press coverage from the late 1990s until her death in 2005. In 1990, Schiavo experienced a severe cardiac arrest, which led to significant brain damage, such that she was unable to communicate or care for herself. Her situation was frequently referred to as a persistent (and later, a permanent) vegetative state—from a liberative lens, we can observe how this implies particular kinds of values concerning what it means to be a human being (e.g., that a human can think and act, and that anyone who cannot do these things has the same value as a vegetable). After many years of treatment led to no noticeable change in her condition, her husband petitioned the courts in 1998 to have her feeding tube removed, the likely outcome of which would be her death. Her parents were opposed to this action, and extensive legal and political battles ensued, escalating all the way to involvement by Florida governor Jeb Bush and the US Congress. The final court decision supported removal of the feeding tube, and Schiavo died on March 31, 2005.

In the media, this debate was frequently construed as a conflict between conservative values, which argue for the sanctity of human life, and liberal ones, which support the right to make decisions about one's own life (and that since Terri was unable to make this decision for herself, her husband ought to be able to make it for her). A liberative disability perspective highlights how this sort of case involves structural issues that go beyond making sense of an individual life. For example, it questions what sorts of values we put on disability and nondisability experiences, and how these become intertwined with end-of-life decisions. The disability rights group Not Dead Yet is one example of an advocacy organization that engages these issues on a regular basis, highlighting the ways in which societal prejudice against disability is often connected to right-to-die situations. Schiavo's case also highlights ways in which our society tends to avoid issues of disability altogether, as the controversy would likely have been avoided if she had completed a living will or left other directives about her wishes—practices that one might imagine would be common if we understood illness and disability to be a normal part of human life.

Based on a moral or medical understanding of disability, one can imagine making a decision such as whether to remove Terri Schiavo's feeding tube based on whether her husband or her parents had her best interests in mind. How might a liberative perspective on disability influence your approach to this issue?

social experience of being treated as someone who is not only different but also less valuable (e.g., as an employee, a voter, or a friend). This model highlights the fact that individuals are often more handicapped by the physical and attitudinal barriers in society than by their own abilities, particularly as our communities are not organized according to the needs of (or, even the existence of) people with differing abilities. This model also argues that disability itself is socially constructed, more a set of beliefs and practices than anything inherently existing in bodies. Built into this model is a sense that addressing the "problem of disability" means working against unjust

BOX 12.1

People-First Language

People with disabilities have often been referred to primarily, or solely, based on something that looks like a diagnostic label: blind, deaf, crippled, invalid, spastic, retarded. Not only do these terms stick around long after medical understandings change, but they also mask the complexity of both the particular impairment and the full life of the person. For example, referring to someone as "blind" neither gives accurate information about the person's vision (as the majority of people who are legally blind have some degree of sight) but also seems to suggest that "blind" is the most important adjective in describing this person's life. Thus one is seen as a diagnosis or a problem first rather than as a person. As an alternative, people-first language (e.g., person with a disability, person with a visual impairment, person with a cognitive difference) is a conscious act that highlights that the first and most important characteristic is one's humanity, that there is more to life than one's disability status, and that it is a person who experiences (or "has") a disability rather than a disability that controls (or "is") a person. Like other shifts in language, the move toward people-first constructions can sometimes feel like political correctness (saying things a certain way so as not to offend someone) and it does not give attention to other complexities, such as social and structural understandings of disability. Still, people-first language has the ability to disrupt some of our typical interpretations of disability, making space for different interpretations and possibilities.

KEY TERM 12.4

Handicap. Literally meaning "to hinder" or "to place at a disadvantage," this denotes the consequence that results from impairment. From the above example, whether one understands the impairment to be biological or social, the handicap is that a person is unable to enter the building.

social structures, focusing on issues of access and liberation.

Finally, the *limits model* begins to break down some of the false distinctions between nondisability and disability. The Census Bureau estimates that 18 percent of the US population has some level of disability (using a medical-model definition) and that 12 percent have what is considered to be a severe disability. Most people will experience disability at some point in their lives, and almost all of us regularly experience limitations that may benefit from medication (such as headaches), assistive technology (eyeglasses), or architectural adjustments (elevators or curb cuts for suitcases and strollers). The limits model highlights the ways in which disability, broadly understood, is a more normal (common, unsurprising) human experience than nondisability, making us all at most temporarily able-bodied. This model also highlights the ways in which disability exists on a continuum (not as solely distinct categories of ability and disability) and yet that each experience of disability is unique, for example noting that a person who is blind may have more in common with a person who uses eyeglasses than with a person who is cognitively different or uses a wheelchair. In other words, the limits model invites us to rethink "us versus them" understandings of disability and to begin a revaluation of disability more broadly.

BOX 12.2

Disability Pride

In a society where disability is primarily understood as a medical impairment and a moral failing, it seems as if everyone, if given the choice, would prefer to be nondisabled rather than disabled. This makes the idea of disability pride almost incoherent, as we imagine that disability would be something that would bring about regret or that we would want to minimize rather than something that would bring about pride. But within disability-rights advocacy, great attention has been given to notions of disability pride, of not only accepting but also claiming and celebrating one's disability status. In part, this comes from recognition that disability opens us to experiences, perspectives, and insights not available within society at large—in technical terms, an epistemological privilege. But it also comes from a sense of celebration that life with disability can be very good. Disability pride includes taking terms that have the potential to be offensive, such as *crip*, and reclaiming these words in ways that are playful and positive (as in the emerging academic field of crip theory). It also comes in reframing events that used to be focused primarily on fundraising and pity, casting these instead as celebrations. As within other communities, pride also takes the form of honoring the lives of significant people with disabilities, recognizing holidays like the International Day of Persons with Disabilities (December 3), designing slogans and merchandise (such as bumper stickers and T-shirts), and engaging in other forms of public celebration and pride.

History and Development of Disability Liberative Ethics

Liberative understandings of disability are not new, even if they are a fairly recent addition to both scholarship and broader public awareness. People with disabilities in the United States have been organizing for centuries to struggle against their experiences of being isolated, incarcerated, institutionalized, and in other ways treated as less human. Examples of oppression are numerous but include things like prohibitions against marriage, forced removal from one's home and family, mandatory mainstreaming (including prohibitions against the use of sign language or other forms of communication), exclusion from education or employment more broadly, and use as sensationalized objects (often without their own consent) in medical education or as sideshow freaks.

So-called ugly laws forbade people with disabilities from appearing in public, and practices such as forced sterilization received widespread legal support, even from the United States Supreme Court. In the early to mid-1800s, local groups began to rally against these practices, emphasizing the right to education for people with disabilities. By the late 1800s, these local initiatives began to grow into national organizations, such as the National Association of the Deaf, formed in 1880 around the rights of deaf people to organize and to use sign language. By the mid 1900s, numerous other national rights-based organizations emerged, many of which were motivated by the return of disabled soldiers after World War II. Parents of disabled children formed self-help groups that grew into national advocacy organizations, and people with disabilities asserted their right to study, work, and live in communities rather than in custodial institutions.

Inspired by the African American civil rights movement and the women's movement, these various disability communities began to coalesce in the

CASE STUDY 12.2

In 2008, the Special Olympics organization launched a campaign to eliminate the use of the words *retarded* or *retard* in everyday language. The medical profession had already shifted to use of either more general terms like intellectual disability or more specific diagnostic terms like Down syndrome, and advocacy organizations had made similar changes, as in the renaming of the American Association of Mental Retardation into the American Association on Intellectual and Developmental Disabilities. Rosa's Law, signed by President Obama in 2010, will replace the term *mental retardation* with *intellectual disability* in all of federal law. Yet the R-word campaign goes beyond simply suggesting that this term is outdated or inaccurate, and instead argues that it is hate speech, not unlike derogatory terms used against other minority groups.

What makes the R-word offensive, when only a short time ago it was considered to be an appropriate diagnostic term? A liberative perspective is central to understanding this issue, as it begins with the assumption that people with disabilities are not simply medically different but are also an oppressed group within society. This campaign also rests on the commitment that people with disabilities, specifically those with cognitive disabilities, are fully human and deserve to be treated with respect. The campaign begins by observing the ways in which terms like *retard* and *retarded* have been used as insults against nondisabled people, often within the context of bullying, as synonyms for *dumb* or *stupid*. The term not only perpetuates stereotypes of people with disability as being incompetent but is also used to intentionally demean other people. A liberative perspective suggests that this term keeps us from recognizing that people with intellectual disabilities deserve our profound respect, either out of recognition of the social barriers they must engage every day or simply because they, too, are human.

Media personalities and politicians who have used the words *retard* or *retarded* since the launch of the R-word campaign have been subject to public criticism and protest. Often they respond by saying they did not mean to be offensive, or else they evoke their right to free speech. How might a liberative perspective on disability influence how you would respond to such situations?

1960s, giving rise to the modern disability rights movement. Key among these was the Independent Living Movement in Berkeley, which initiated a new level of political involvement, not just seeking individual rights but rather coalescing as a distinct political movement, one focused on the social nature of disability and on shared experiences of social oppression. In the decades since that time, disability rights advocates have scored numerous legal and legislative victories, most notably the passage of the Americans with Disabilities Act of 1990.

While many of these organizations and legal movements have focused primarily on rights, it is important to note that this is not the only motivating factor. Alongside these political movements has been the emergence of a disability culture that challenges traditional notions and assumptions about disability. Disabled artists, writers, performers, and activists celebrate disability as a facet of human diversity. This shift is important, not just arguing that people with disabilities ought to have equal access or the same level of rights as people

Fig. 12.1. President George H. W. Bush signs into law the Americans with Disabilities Act of 1990 on the South Lawn of the White House.

without disabilities but also noting that disability itself is something valuable. Disability, therefore, becomes about more than just equalizing a playing field; it attends to the unique perspective and gift that comes from disability.

From a theological perspective, this begins with the idea that we are all made in the image of God, and that when God looked at creation, God saw it as very good (Genesis 1). Within the Christian narrative, disability theologians highlight the stories where Jesus invited "the crippled, the lame, and the blind" (Luke 14:13) and in other ways demonstrated a preferential option for those who experienced disability (as a medical and a social condition), welcoming them and living in solidarity with them. Even the story of Jesus' resurrection, with his body still containing scars and marks of physical difference and disfiguration, leads scholars like Nancy Eiesland to offer the image of the disabled God, one who shares the experience of pain and rejection and who values embodiment in all its diversity, serving as a profound example of inclusion, love, and acceptance. Such perspectives suggest that disability may be something that can be valued by and within communities, not because of how it is similar to nondisability or because of the demand for rights alone, but because it is a valued experience, bodily and socially, in and of itself.

Fig. 12.2. Vicki Killingsworth, the incoming president of Living Independence for Everyone (LIFE), uses a ramp to enter a FEMA ADA-compliant trailer on exhibit at the Purvis, Mississippi, staging area in 2005. The interior of the trailer has been configured to allow people with physical disabilities to be able to use the trailer.

Need for Liberation

A liberative ethical lens draws primarily on definitions of disability from the social and limits models. As a result, liberation here comes not from trying to change to one's physical condition or impairment but rather by working to change oppressive social structures and practices. While in some ways it may seem that society engages disability better now than it did in the past, contemporary examples of discrimination and oppression are still numerous. For example, the US Census Bureau states that the rate of poverty among people with disabilities is more than three times that of the general population, and that more than half of all people with disabilities between the ages of twenty and sixty-four are unemployed. Crimes against people with disabilities occur one and a half times more often than in the nondisabled population, and women with disabilities are more than twice as likely to experience violent crime than women without disabilities. Domestic partners and caregivers are responsible for a large proportion of both violent and white-collar crimes against people with disabilities, and particularly against people with more severe impairments and those who live in institutions. Statistical reports also show the significant ways in which people with disabilities have limited access to housing, education, transportation, and social and religious communities.

Some people with disabilities face profound architectural barriers—even when buildings are in compliance with the Americans with Disabilities Act (ADA); for example, people who use wheelchairs are often forced to use service elevators that are away from normal public spaces, the same ones that are used to take out the garbage. Even when institutions state that they provide assistive listening devices, people with hearing impairments often find such equipment to be out of date, broken, or lost. People who experience visual impairment or dyslexia are unable to apply for jobs in which they might otherwise be successful simply because application forms are inaccessible to them. Students who request ADA accommodations at their schools find that alternate-format textbooks arrive too late in the term to be useful. The list of practical barriers is endless.

Even when physical spaces are accessible, discrimination and oppression still emerge in other ways due to prejudice and narrow value systems. People with disabilities are often treated as if they were less intelligent simply because they communicate or move in different ways, as observed when nondisabled people use simpler words or a childlike tone of voice when talking to them. If a person with a disability is accompanied by a nondisabled person, it is often the nondisabled person who is engaged, and the person with the disability is ignored altogether. Children are told not to stare at people with disabilities, as if there were something wrong with being interested in physical difference, and yet adults frequently stare at people with disabilities in ways that objectify them as examples of freakery, oddity, or horror. While these may seem like relatively simple and harmless examples of interpersonal discomfort, these all speak to underlying structures that lead to the continued practical discrimination against people who are physically, cognitively, or emotionally different than what is considered normal. These structures have significant practical consequences, whether economic, social, or political, and at their extremes contribute to violence, terror, and death.

BOX 12.3

Ableism

Similar to more familiar words like *sexism* and *racism*, the notion of ableism highlights attitudes, beliefs, and practices that foster discrimination and exclusion of people with disabilities. Ableism rests on particular understandings of what is "normal" or desirable, but often does so in ways that are largely invisible to those who are not aware of liberative understandings of disability. At its core, ableism suggests that it is better to be nondisabled than to be disabled, that people with disabilities are less valuable than people without disabilities, and that discrimination on the basis of disability is, at best, unavoidable and, at worst, not really a problem. Ableist attitudes are often revealed in exclusive language, as when someone describes a "lame" idea (equating lame with pathetic) or talks about being "blind" to the truth (equating blindness with ignorance). Ableism can often be observed in stereotypes perpetuated by the media, such as portraying a person with a disability as either an inspirational hero or a pitiable victim. Ableism is also found in prejudicial and discriminatory behaviors around access to employment, housing, and transportation—for example, by assuming that a particular building does not need to be wheelchair accessible because "nobody like that would come here anyhow." Ableism is linked to the idea of able-bodied privilege, where someone who is (or appears to be) nondisabled has certain structural and interpersonal advantages (for example, in applying for jobs or receiving service in a restaurant) simply by appearing nondisabled.

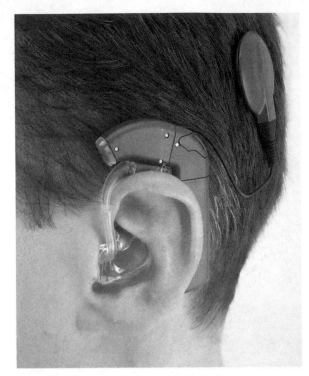

Fig. 12.3. A cochlear implant.

Issues and Questions

It is important to note that the disability community is not all of one perspective when it comes to ethical lenses, or to liberative understandings more generally. Clearly, people with disabilities have lives that are made up of more than just their disability status. They carry a variety of other identity characteristics, including race, ethnicity, gender, sexual identity, and socioeconomic status. They do not have the same embodied experiences or attitudes toward their disabilities as each other, and they have dramatically different life experiences as well. While this is true within all identity groups, it is perhaps more strikingly so within disability, where one might wonder whether there is anything that links a person who uses a wheelchair, a person who is Deaf, a person with chronic pain, and a person on the autism spectrum, other than the artificial category of

disability—not only the embodied experiences, but even the social experiences of discrimination experienced by each of these is radically different. Even the experiences of two wheelchair users may have very few areas of overlap, particularly if one has had the experience since birth (and may thus understand it as natural and intrinsic to who they are) and another gained disability as a result of an accident that was considered to be traumatic. While there are surely advantages in shared alliances and talking about disability as if it were a singular and coherent category, it is essential to remember not only that people with disabilities are already participants in each of the other liberative lenses and identity characteristics described elsewhere in this volume (and that each of those identities and communities also includes people with disabilities), but also that there is no single perspective of disability.

These multiple lenses add depth to the sorts of issues and questions that disability ethics, and disability advocacy more broadly, must struggle with. One key question relates to the issue of experience: does one need to be a person with a disability in order to do work in these areas? And, if so, what kinds of disability experiences count? An important rallying cry of the movement has been "nothing about us without us," a standpoint grounded in the notion that people with disabilities ought to have control of our own bodies, our own agendas, and our own political work. And yet, as scholars in disability studies have noted, the exclusion of nondisabled people is not always helpful, for a number of reasons.

First, this also leads us to overlook people with certain kinds of disabilities, as the demand to "speak for ourselves" tends to ignore those with profound cognitive or interpersonal limitations, leaving these perspectives absent from our work. Second, it tends to ignore the systemic nature of disability oppression, particularly that nondisabled people are often the ones with the power to influence larger structures and that they are often the ones who most need new ways of acting and thinking. And finally, it overlooks the fact that simply being in a nondominant role does not itself give someone a significantly different perspective than those in the dominant role have, and that simply having an experience of disability does not automatically lead to a liberative understanding of disability. For all of these reasons, the issue of experience is still very significant, and contested.

These sorts of diversities of perspective lead to complexity around other issues as well. For example, questions around prenatal decisions and end-of-life care occupy a very significant place within disability ethics and advocacy, and yet perspectives on these questions, and the related moral and ethical concerns that accompany them, vary widely. Even what counts as disability is somewhat contested, as recent questions have arisen over whether obesity, depression, or even infancy (when one is unable to care for oneself independently) can be included in the category of disability.

CASE STUDY 12.3

A cochlear implant is a piece of technology that enables people with severe hearing impairments to have access to sound. It differs from a hearing aid in that parts of it are surgically implanted and, rather than just amplifying sound as other assistive listening devices do, it instead converts sound into electronic impulses and transmits them directly to auditory nerves and the brain. It does not restore hearing, but some users are able to utilize it to recognize and respond to speech and other sounds. It is not effective in all cases and is sometimes described as being painful or disruptive. Like any surgical procedure, there are risks involved, and like any technological equipment, devices may fail or need replacement over time.

When cochlear implants first gained approval from the US Food and Drug Administration, it was assumed by most medical professionals that anyone who could get an implant would want one. After all, isn't it better to be hearing than to be deaf? However, this perspective did not take into account a liberative understanding of disability, and in particular showed a lack of awareness of Deaf culture. Spelled with a small letter d, deaf means the inability to hear. But with a capital letter D, it refers to the belief that being Deaf is much the same as belonging to any cultural group—joined by a common language (e.g., American sign language), a shared history (including stories of institutionalization and oppression), a rich community life, and values that are actively transmitted across generations. Key to Deaf culture is the sense that there is nothing wrong with being Deaf—yes, one cannot hear, but one still can communicate, and there are numerous other advantages and complexities that come with being Deaf that are considered to be valuable, particularly the experience of community life.

A significant controversy emerged between those in favor of cochlear implants and those opposed to them, particularly as this affected children who were having medical decisions made for them by parents or other caretakers. This was explored in the documentary Sound and Fury (2000), which followed an extended family as they wrestled with these issues around two of their children, one who eventually received a cochlear implant and one who did not. Based on a moral or medical understanding of disability, one can imagine making such a decision based primarily on a weighing of the (financial) costs and (medical) risks related to the surgical procedure. How might the social or limits models change how you approach this issue?

BOX 12.4

Americans with Disabilities Act

When the Americans with Disabilities Act (ADA) of 1990 was signed into law, it marked a new era for people with disabilities in the United States. The ADA prohibits certain forms of discrimination, with particular attention to employment, government services, and public accommodations (such as restaurants, hotels, entertainment venues, and stores), and mirrors the Civil Rights Act of 1964 in its prohibition of certain kinds of discrimination on the basis of race, sex, color, religion, or national origin. As amended in 2008, the ADA draws on the medical model to define disability (as "a physical or mental impairment that substantially limits one or more major life activities") but also notes that discrimination can happen whenever someone is perceived as having an impairment, thus overlapping with the social model, which understands disability less as a diagnosis and more as a minority experience. While the ADA has been incredibly important for increasing access for people with disabilities, it is not all-encompassing—for example, some organizations (including certain small businesses, private clubs, and religious institutions) have fought for exemption from the ADA, and not all experiences of impairment or disability are covered under the law. While the ADA addresses issues of access, it does not address underlying prejudices, which still appear in forms ranging from covert discrimination to blatant violence. An example of this can even be seen in the backlash of lawsuits arguing that the ADA causes "undue burden" and that compliance should only be voluntary.

Most of the questions surrounding disability to date have focused on issues of rights, focusing on gaining "equal" access as compared to nondisabled people, to the detriment of other perspectives and questions that are only now emerging. Even the question of progress has become contested, as communities now ask whether it is sufficient to be striving to be the same as nondisabled people or whether a different and more constructive perspective might be possible, particularly one that highlights messiness and diversity rather than the ability to live up to some artificial (and potentially dangerous) norm of the ideal body. While these are philosophical questions at one level, they play out in all sorts of practical ways, whether through engaging questions of mainstreaming versus institutionalization or through considering whether an increasing number of television characters with disabilities (often portrayed by nondisabled actors) is actually beneficial to advocacy concerns or not.

Leading Scholars and Figures

Disability ethics is a relatively new area of study, and exists mostly in the intersection between disability rights (advocacy) and disability studies (scholarship), not as a distinct field of its own. From the side of advocacy, it draws heavily on the legacy of people like Edward Roberts (1939–1995), one of the initial organizers of the Independent Living Movement in Berkeley, or Alan Reich (1930–1995), the founder of the National Organization on Disability, which is the largest US organization focused on the rights of people with disabilities. Paul Longmore (1946–2010) is often identified as central to the emergence of disability studies, with his legacy continued by scholars in a wide range of academic disciplines, which include sociology, anthropology, political science, literature and film studies, philosophy, theology, psychology, architecture and design, and the arts. As is the case in other civil rights movements, there is understood to be a close connection between disability studies as an academic project and disability advocacy as political praxis, and so these areas of advocacy and scholarship frequently overlap, with important scholarly work appearing in editorial columns and blog postings, and with advocacy often beginning in the classroom.

Disability ethics also draws on a broad range of resources that might not self-identify as being intentionally about disability but that are relevant insofar as they highlight various issues of embodiment, shared social oppression, and other related themes. Areas of study that have been drawn on to date have included Sander Gilman's work on disease, David Rothman on asylums, Erving Goffman on stigma, Leslie Fielder on freaks, Susan Sontag on metaphors of illness, Mikhail Bakhtin on the grotesque, Michel Foucault on disease and sexuality, Jacques Derrida on blindness, Judith Butler on gender and sexuality, and Susan Bordo on anorexia. Other conversation partners remain to be identified, some of which will come from historical writings on embodiment and difference and others from contemporary voices around issues of privilege and power, such as we see in gender theory, critical race theory, postcolonial theory, and queer theory.

It is important to note that, while a liberatory understanding of disability ethics is relatively new, this does not mean that traditional ethics has been inattentive to experiences of disability. Examples of attention to disability within the broader field of philosophy can be found from the ancient writings of Plato and Aristotle through to more contemporary work by scholars such as Martha Nussbaum and Eva Kittay. Some of these philosophical works are engaged with great skepticism by many who hold to a liberative understanding of disability, as is seen in reactions to ethicists such as Peter Singer or Stanley Hauerwas, who are challenged for their methodology (typically treating people with disabilities as objects rather than as real people) as well as for their claims (which are often seen as contrary to liberation). Disability has also been the subject of significant attention within the specialty of bioethics, particularly where policies and rights seem to collide. A number of medical schools and research universities now host institutes on disability and bioethics, and discussion of disability has become more substantial within medical, law, ethics, and special-education programs.

Perhaps because of its attention to interdependence and embodied diversity, liberative disability ethics as a whole is less grounded in the work of any particular individual or in a single methodology, but rather is more a viewpoint or set of commitments that refuses to judge disability to be a negative experience. Rather, liberative disability ethics questions our assumptions about disability even as it also questions specific practices or outcomes. As such, the work is open to anyone, from any discipline, as long as they are grounded in the questions and types of awareness and value that come out of the social and limits models of disability.

KEY TERM 12.5

Disabled. The experience of limitation that comes from encountering impairments and handicaps. Note that this can include moral, biological, or social causes and consequences, and can also be understood as an unsurprising characteristic of human life.

Possible Future Trends

The last few years have seen a number of important books within the areas of philosophy and theology (particularly from Hans Reinders, John Gillibrand, and Tom Reynolds) that look at experiences of autism or profound intellectual impairment in order to raise new questions about our assumptions regarding what it means to be human. As this literature develops, the ethical implications are likely to be profound and far reaching, particularly as they suggest that we cannot define what it is to be distinctively human based on one's ability to communicate, to act with autonomy, or to demonstrate rational capabilities. This will have practical consequences related to prenatal decisions and end-of-life issues, and also to questions surrounding the ethical differences between humans and animals. As part of this, rights language may itself begin to dissolve, perhaps to be replaced with notions of relationality or broader senses of justice, and perhaps drawing more intentionally on notions of interdependence and community as found within religious traditions.

From another perspective, the recognition of disability as a relatively normal human experience (as offered by Sharon Betcher and Deborah Creamer) has the potential to recenter disability as a more "universal" or, at least, appropriate ethical starting point than those approaches that do not begin with attention to disability. In addition to making disability a more common topic of engagement, this will also necessarily challenge our commonsense and oppressive notions of what we impose as the good/ideal human body or life. Out of such work, disability may become to be understood to be unavoidable, both as a practical experience and as an ethical lens.

As understandings of disability become more critically nuanced and yet also more commonplace, alliances and collaborative work between disability and other areas of liberation are likely to become more apparent. Some work here is already beginning to emerge, as in Robert McRuer's proposal of crip theory as the intersection of disability and queer studies. Other possible sites of intersection still wait to be explored. For example, neither disability advocacy nor disability studies has paid much attention to people of color, nor have liberative discourses within communities of color attended yet to disability. Not only is such mutual engagement long overdue, but the potential benefit to each discourse (as well as to people of color who experience disability, for example) also seems to make such work exceedingly important.

Finally, as this sort of engagement happens in theological and philosophical arenas more broadly, and continues to move forward in advocacy endeavors, it will be interesting to see whether a specific area of study known as disability ethics itself might begin to emerge more clearly, or whether disability will be highlighted as a central theme within existing lines of work. This question is likely to be complicated by, and perhaps motivated by, the increasing number of people with physical impairments in the United States as a result of the aging "baby boomer" population and as veterans return from war.

LIBERATIVE ETHICS IN ACTION 12.1

Liberative Ethics in Action: The Issue of Genetic Testing

The field of genetics is full of ethical issues and implications, ranging from moral concerns about whether and how scientists ought to try to control the human life to justice concerns over how decisions are made and who has economic access to new medical procedures and technologies. From a disability perspective, bioethical issues surrounding genetic science take on additional complexity, particularly when one does not automatically accept the dominant belief that physical impairment is something that must be eliminated whenever possible.

A particularly contested issue is whether one ought to engage in prenatal testing for Down syndrome or other possible impairments. Disability advocates raise the concern of eugenics, the elimination of those who are perceived to be less valuable (including people with disabilities) as we attempt to create designer babies with what are considered to be ideal characteristics. This, they say, is in the same ethical neighborhood as genocide, the purposeful elimination of a particular culture or category of people. Others argue that it is irresponsible and ethically dangerous to avoid or reject prenatal testing, either because such rejection may lead parents to be unprepared for the physical and cognitive needs of their child or because it allows for the unnecessary suffering of the individual, the parents, extended family, and society at large. At its extreme, this latter perspective has led to legal charges of wrongful birth, where parents sue a doctor for failing to prevent or fully inform them about potential impairments, or of wrongful life, where the individuals themselves sue their parents or doctors for the negligence of allowing them to be born.

Rather than coming down neatly on one side or other of this issue, a liberative perspective on disability demands that we consider these issues in more depth and complexity, looking not only at the individuals who are involved in such situations but also at societal structures at large. For example, a liberative perspective reminds us that some of what is at play here are our understandings and definitions of disability themselves, and suggests that assumptions about disability ought to be articulated and evaluated before any life-changing decisions (such as for or against testing) are made, as it may be prejudice more than science that motivates some of these decisions. Noting that people are often more handicapped by social structures than by their bodies, it proposes that the "cost" or suffering that comes with disability may be more about economic barriers to education and employment than intrinsic suffering itself, and so rather than wrongful birth we might think instead of wrongful environments. This disability perspective reminds us that the desire to eliminate limits is unrealistic, but that it would be similarly irresponsible to ignore our own limits (as parents and providers) as we face issues of reproductive choice. A liberative perspective might not lead to easier decisions, but it honors the complexity of life by helping participants be less driven by fear while simultaneously highlighting broader issues and concerns that might lead toward productive societal change.

Study Questions

1. As you consider disability in your own life (including your experiences with it among your family, friends, and acquaintances), where do you see examples of each of the four models (moral, medical, social, and limits)? Which ones seem primary? Are any missing?

2. In your own words, how would you define disability? Which model (or models) does this definition seem to connect with? Has this changed after reading this chapter? How might trying on a different model or definition of disability make a difference in terms of how you engage people with disabilities and how you understand issues of discrimination and access?

3. As you encounter images of disability in the media (television, movies, music, billboards, etc.), in what ways do you see them drawing on stereotypical portrayals based on moral or medical understandings? How might a liberative perspective change the stories they tell?

4. Which do you see as more the more significant barrier for people with disabilities, architecture (e.g., staircases) or attitudes (e.g., stereotypes)? What kinds of advocacy could help change each of these barriers?

5. In what ways do you see disability ethics as similar to other kinds of liberative ethics? In what ways is it different?

Suggested Readings

Betcher, Sharon V. *Spirit and the Politics of Disablement.* Minneapolis: Fortress Press, 2007.

Creamer, Deborah B. *Disability and Christian Theology: Embodied Limits and Constructive Possibilities.* Oxford: Oxford University Press, 2009.

Davis, Lennard J., ed. *The Disability Studies Reader.* 3rd ed. New York: Routledge, 2010.

Eiesland, Nancy. *The Disabled God: Toward a Liberatory Theology of Disability.* Nashville: Abingdon, 1994.

Pelka, Fred., ed. *The Disability Rights Movement.* Santa Barbara, CA: ABC-CLIO, 1997.

Swinton, John, and Brock, Brian, eds. *Theology, Disability, and the New Genetics: Why Science Needs the Church.* New York: T&T Clark, 2007.

CONCLUSION

Since childhood, we have been taught to see and interpret reality through the eyes of those who create and enforce the rules of society. Not surprisingly, moral analysis has come to be validated as primarily a Eurocentric exercise where excellence and academic rigor is equated with Eurocentric thoughts; thoughts that do not question the power employed in creating the prevailing societal rules. And when such rules cause marginalization, rather than questioning the powers behind the construction of the social order, a move instead is made to simply reform the situation, concentrating on the consequences rather than the cause. Law and order must be maintained at all cost, thus trumping any actions that might be able to bring about a more just society. No matter how dysfunctional the social order may become, no matter how oppressive the economic and political powers may be, reform as opposed to radical change becomes the acceptable course of action.

The ethical paradigms that emanate from the centers of power and privilege that justify the reasons for these rules come to be defined as universal. All too often, when different perspectives are offered, especially those rooted in the social location of the dispossessed and disenfranchised, they are usually relegated to a realm lacking any universal gravitas. In this fashion, the ethics that emerge from the margins of society are more often than not able to be kept marginalized. Nevertheless,

it is this rejected stone that becomes the cornerstone for cutting-edge ethical analysis. The ethical paradigms advocated in this book are liberative; a contextual ethical analysis rooted in the life experience of those who experience oppression, an analysis whose purpose is developing and implementing actions—praxis—which can lead the community (not just the individual) toward a more just social order. This is a subversive ethics because its very nature threatens the accumulated power and privilege of the dominant culture, radically calling for its dismantling.

In this introductory textbook, we have strived to center the margins of ethical thought by providing the reader with the foundational ethical principles and paradigms employed by different communities, communities whose voices are usually ignored and dismissed. And yet, these represent the majority of the world's population. Even in the United States, where tectonic demographic shifts are occurring, those who for centuries have been the majority will, by 2050 (if not before), cease to be able to claim majority status. Nevertheless, in an ironic sleight of hand, it is the majority of the world's population that is minoritized while the so-called minorities, those who are represented in this book, both outside and within the United States, constitute the majority. Hence this is not a book about the ethical perspectives of the minorities; but rather, this is the majority ethical perspective.

These chapters have demonstrated that there exists no value-free ethical perspective. The subjectivity of Eurocentric ethics has academically been interpreted as universally objective because those who teach the discipline retain the power to define a reality that secures and protects their own privilege. But if ethics is the construction of a particular type of culture, then those born to and/or raised from within the Euro-American culture become a product of a society where white supremacy and class privilege have historically been interwoven with how Americans have been conditioned to normalize and legitimize how they see and organize the world around them.

Of course, ethical positions held within the dominant culture are neither uniform nor monolithic; nevertheless, certain common denominators exist, such as a propensity toward hyperindividualism, a call for law and order, an emphasis on charity, an uncritical acceptance of the market economy, an emphasis on orthodoxy, and a prominence for deductive ethical reasoning. The authors of this book resist this ethical worldview held by many within the dominant culture because it fails to consider its own complicity with the social structures that privilege and protect their place within society. The major concern with Eurocentric ethical paradigms is that they usually advocate for and are reinforced by a social location privileged by economic class and whiteness. While such an ethics is congruent with the dominant culture, it is damning for those residing on the margins of society, because of how it reinforces the prevailing social structures responsible for the causes of disenfranchisement. As alluring as Eurocentric types of ethics may appear to be, most remains embedded within social structures that are detrimental to disenfranchised groups. Eurocentric ethics fails us whenever it refuses to consider its complicity with oppressive social structures and in fact becomes a moral justification of maintaining a status quo that privileges one group at the expense of many.

The ultimate failure of the ethics of the dominant culture, which the chapters of this book attempt to correct, is the lack of seriously conducting power analysis and uncritically locating their discourse with and within the prevailing power structures. Such complicity relieves the dominant ethical paradigms of any responsibility to actually establish a justice that can be liberating for marginalized communities. Eurocentric ethics becomes a product of power—power held by those who benefit by making their ethics normative for everyone else. As such, Eurocentric ethics is not an exercise of establishing justice, but rather becomes a justification for activating power. By contrast, all the chapters of this book are primarily concerned with the *doing*, not simply the thinking about justice.

Simply stated, Euro-American ethics will not save disenfranchised and dispossessed communities, which remain invisible and voiceless. For ethics to be liberative, it must move beyond the ethics of the dominant culture, even when such ethics are liberal and progressive. Why? Because most Euro-American-based ethics remains detrimental to the marginalized. Any ethics that fails to address oppressive structures is of little use to disenfranchised communities. For this reason, this introductory textbook represents a fundamental attempt to move beyond the ethical paradigms that have mainly kept marginalized communities in their place. Our hope then is that you—the reader—begin to move away from a prevailing ethical paradigm that communally changes little. We hope you find in this resource the introductory and foundational concepts being employed by many of those who have historically found themselves relegated to the underside of society.

ACKNOWLEDGMENTS

1.2. *U.S. News & World Report* Magazine Photograph Collection, Library of Congress.

2.1. Oxfam East Africa /Creative Commons Attribution 2.0 Generic license.

3.1. US Department of Defense / US National Archives.

3.2. Thomas Schoch / Creative Commons Attribution-Share Alike 3.0 license.

4.1. Ben Schumin / Creative Commons Attribution 2.0 Generic license.

4.2. Miguel A. De La Torre.

5.2. Jonathan McIntosh / Creative Commons Attribution 2.0 Generic license.

6.1. *U.S. News & World Report* Magazine Photograph Collection, Library of Congress.

6.2. US National Archives / public domain.

6.3. US National Archives / public domain.

7.1. US National Archives / public domain.

7.2. David Shankbone / Creative Commons Attribution 2.0 Generic license.

8.1. US National Archives / public domain.

8.2. US National Archives / public domain.

9.1. American Press Association, 1912 / public domain.

9.2. London Student Feminists blogspot / GNU Free Documentation license.

9.3. Capt. John Severns USAF /public domain.

9.4. Harry Wad / Creative Commons Attribution 3.0 license.

10.1. US National Archives / public domain.

10.2. Wikimedia Commons / GNU Free Documentation License.

11.1. Johannes Jordan / Creative Commons Attribution-Share Alike 3.0 license.

11.2. Ahmad Badr / Creative Commons Attribution-Share Alike 3.0 license.

12.2. FEMA (US Government agency) / public domain.

12.3. US National Archives / public domain.

INDEX

ableism. *See* disability

abortion, 74, 106, 129, 165, 171, 174, 176, 180, 184, 203

Abzug, Bella, 190

Academy of Catholic Hispanic Theologians of the United States (ACHTUS), 98

action. *See* praxis

ACT-UP, 212, 220

Addams Hull, Jane, 68–69

Adeyemo, Tukunboh, 33, 43

affirmative action, 102, 106

Africa; Africanization, 32; Afro-pessimism, 35, Botswana, 39; Canaan, 110; church, 206; community of, 3, 48, 95; economic marginalization, 11, 33–36; Egypt, 58, 169, 208, 210–11, 217; environmentalism, 35–37; feminism, 38, 41, 43, 192; gender oppression, 38–39; genital mutilation, 203; government corruption, 35–38, 42; HIV/AIDS, 39–42; identity, 32, 48; independence of, 29, 32; LGBT, 214; Kenya, 40, 43, 195; liberative ethics, 29–45; Liberia, 173; music, 113–14; Namibia, 35; Nigeria, 34, 37, 111; non-blacks, 30, 43; philosophy, 30–34, 43–45; sexism, 30–31, 38–43; South Africa, 31, 33, 35, 38, 44–45, 124; sub-Saharan, 30–31, 35, 40, 42, 59; Tanzania, 48; theology, 32–33; ubuntu, 31, 34, 38, 40, 45; Uganda, 214; wars, 35, 37; Zambia, 42; Zimbabwe, ix, 35–36, 38, 44. *See also* African Americans

African Americans; and Asian American tension, 131; black church, ix, 71–72, 86, 100–101, 116, 120, 122, 200; Black Nationalism, 117–18; black queer, x, 219; Civil Rights Movement, 71–72, 86, 116–18, 165, 172, 212, 227, 233; as chattel, 110, 149; community of, 3, 109–26, 181, 190–91; diasporas, Guyana Haiti and Jamaica, 103–4; economic struggle of, 71–72, 77–78; feminism, 121, 166, 172, 188, 192, 199–201, 217, 219; Harlem Renaissance, 210; hip-hop, 122; identity, 74, 118, 190–91, 212; indigenous faiths, 110–11; intragroup equality, 115, 125; Jamaicans, 103–4; LGBT, 219; liberative ethics, 109–26; mulatez, 94; oppression of, 67–69, 101, 109–15; philosophy, 116, 119, 123; and slavery, 29, 31, 36, 67, 109–15, 121, 166, 173; theology, 115–25, 128, 208, 211, 217; womanists, 4, 38, 115, 121–22, 124, 126, 182, 191–93, 199–200, 205–6, 212, 219. *See also* Africa

Agricultural Workers Association, 196

Ahn Byung-Mu, 57

Albrecht, Gloria, 74, 86

Alessandrini, Jorge, 19

Alfred, Taiaiake, 157, 160–61

alienation, 2, 67, 133

Allen, Paula Gunn, 155, 161

Allende, Salvador, 19–20

al-Qaeda, 132

Amaladoss, Michael, 62, 65

American Academy of Religion, ix, 92, 98, 184

American Association on Intellectual and Developmental Disabilities, 228